THE

POETRY AND HISTORY

OF

WYOMING:

CONTAINING

CAMPBELL'S GERTRUDE,

AND THE

HISTORY OF WYOMING FROM ITS DISCOVERY

TO THE

BEGINNING OF THE PRESENT CENTURY

BY WILLIAM L. STONE.

AUTHOR OF THE LIFE OF BRANT, LIFE AND TIMES OF RED JACKET, ETC.

THIRD EDITION,

WITH AN INDEX.

WILKES-BARRE:

C. E. BUTLER, BOOKSELLER.

1873.

PREFACE.

The "Happy Valley" to which the illustrious author of Rasselas introduces his reader in the opening of that charming fiction, was not much more secluded from the world than is the Valley of Wyoming. Situated in the interior of the country, remote from the great thorough-fares of travel, either for business, or in the idle chase of pleasure, and walled on every hand by mountains lofty and wild, and over which long and rugged roads must be travelled to reach it, Wyoming is rarely visited, except from stern necessity. And yet the imagination of Johnson has not pictured so lovely a spot in the vale of Amhara as Wyoming.

Much has been said and sung of the beauty of Wyoming; yet but comparatively little is actually known to the public of its history. That a horrible massacre was once perpetrated there, and that the fearful tragedy has been commemorated in the undying numbers of Campbell, every body knows. But beyond this, it is believed that even what is called the reading public is but inadequately informed; and there are thousands, doubtless, who would be surprised on being told that, independently of the event from which the poet has woven his thrilling tale of Gertrude, Wyoming has been the theatre of more historical action, and is invested with more historical interest, than any other inland district of the United States of equal extent. The revolutionary occurrence, supplying the Muse's theme in the beautiful tale just referred to, forms but a single incident in a course of fifty years of various and arduous conflict between belligerent parties of the same race and nation, each contending for the exclusive possession of that fair valley, and for the expulsion of the rival claimants. Added to which is its antecedent Indian history, extending back more than fifty years prior to the intrusion of the white man, and perhaps a hundred. The dusky Indians were engaged in bloody strife with each other there, hand to hand and foot to foot. All that is fierce and brutal, selfish and unrelenting, bitter and vindictive, in the passions of men embroiled in civil strife, has been displayed there. All that is lofty in patriotism,—all that is generous, noble, and self-devoted in the cause of country and liberty, has been proudly called into action there. All that is true, confiding, self-denying, constant, heroic, virtuous, and enduring, in woman, has been sweetly illustrated there.

Nevertheless the remark may be repeated that but comparatively little of the actual history of this secluded district, —a history marked by peculiar interest, and a district upon which nature has bestowed beauty, with a lavish hand,—is known to the general reader. True, indeed, Wyoming is mentioned in almost every book of American history written since the Revolution, as the scene of *the* massacre; but for the most part, *that* is the only occurrence spoken of; the only fact that has been rescued from the rich mine of its historic lore. The reader of poetry has probably dreamed of Wyoming as an Elysian field, among the groves of which the fair Gertrude was wont to stray while listening to the music of the birds and gathering wild-flowers; and the superficial reader of every thing has regarded it as a place existing somewhere, in which the Indians once tomahawked a number of people.

And yet Wyoming has had its own historian. More than twenty years ago a gentleman resident there, Mr. Isaac Chapman, undertook the preparation of a history, but he died before his work was completed. His manuscripts, however, were edited and published some years after his death; but the work was very incomplete. The preliminary Indian history was merely glanced at, while that of the revolutionary war was hurried over in the most imperfect and unsatisfactory manner possible. It was not written in a popular style, nor published in an attractive form. The author, moreover, in regard to the protracted controversy between the Connecticut settlers and the Pennsylvanians, was governed by strong partialities in favor of the former. Proud's History of Pennsylvania comes down no later than 1770; and from this it could scarcely be gathered that there was any such spot as Wyoming known. Gordon's late History only comes down to the Declaration of American Independence. He has, indeed, devoted some twenty or thirty pages to the early stages of the civil contest in Wyoming, but he writes as though he had been a paid counsellor of the old Ogden Land Company, which so long and vainly strove to dispossess the Connecticut settlers. An impartial history, therefore, was a desideratum, and such I have attempted to supply, written in the style of popular narrative, confined to facts without speculation, and divested entirely of documentary citations.

My own attention was directed to Wyoming as a field of historical investigation only about three years ago, when engaged in preparing for the press the Border Wars of the Revolution, as connected with the Life of the Mohawk chieftain, Brant. It became necessary, in executing the plan of that work, to examine the history of Wyoming, so far at least as it had been connected,—most erroneously,—with the name of that distinguished warrior of the woods; and I soon discovered so much of interest in the tales and traditions of the valley—its history, written and unwritten,—independently of the war of the revolution,—that I resolved upon the institution of farther investigations at some more convenient season.

Keeping this object uppermost in my mind, I made a visit of relaxation and pleasure to Wyoming in the summer of 1839, the result of which, through the kind assistance of my friend Charles Miner, and also of his nephew, Doctor Miner, was a collection of authentic materials sufficient for a small volume appertaining to the history of that valley alone.

The name of Mr. Miner will frequently appear in the notes and references of the present volume. He is an able man, a native of Norwich, Connecticut, and emigrated to the Valley of Wyoming in the year 1799,—being then nineteen years of age. He first engaged in school teaching. Having a brother, a year or two older than himself, who was a practical printer, he invited him to join him in his sylvan retreat, and establish a newspaper. The brother did so; and the twain conjointly established the "Luzerne Federalist." This paper was subsequently superseded by "The Gleaner," but under the same editorial conduct,—that of Charles Miner. It was through the columns of the Gleaner that Mr. Miner, for a long series of months, instructed and amused the American people by those celebrated essays of morals and wit, of fact and fancy, and delicate humor, purporting to come "From the Desk of Poor Robert the Scribe," and which were very generally republished in the newspapers. The Gleaner and its editor became so popular, that the latter was invited to Philadelphia, as associate editor of the "Political and Commercial Register," so long and favorably known under the conduct of the late Major Jackson.

Not liking the metropolis as well as he did the country, Mr. Miner soon retired to the pleasant town of Westchester, eighteen miles from Philadelphia, where, in connexion with his brother Asher, who had also removed from Wilkesbarre, he established the Village Record,—a paper which became as popular for its good taste, and the delicacy of its humor, as the Gleaner had been aforetime. Poor Robert here wrote again under the signature of "John Harwood." While a resident of Westchester, Mr. Miner was twice successively elected to Congress, in a double district, as a colleague of the present Senator Buchanan.

While in Congress Mr. Miner showed himself not only a useful, but an able member. In the subject of slavery he took a deep interest, laboring diligently in behalf of those rational measures for its melioration which were doing great good before a different feeling was infused into the minds of many benevolent men, and a different impulse imparted to their action on this subject. There is another act for which Mr. Miner deserves all praise. It was he who awakened the attention of the country to the silk-growing business. He drew and introduced the first resolution upon the subject, and wrote the able report which was introduced by the late General Stephen Van Rensselaer, as chairman of the committee on agriculture, to whom that resolution had been referred.

It is now about eight years since Mr. Miner relinquished business in Westchester, and, with his brother, returned to Wyoming, where both have every promise of spending the evening of their days most happily.

But to return from this digression: A farther illustration of the history of Wyoming having been determined on, the next question presented was the manner in which it should be brought out. The idea occurred to me, when about to commence the composition of the historical portion of the present volume, six weeks ago, to prefix to the *history*, the *poetry* of Campbell,—thus comprising, in a single portable volume, the POETRY and HISTORY of WYOMING. This suggestion was approved by Messrs. Wiley and Putnam, who are to be the publishers; and in addition to all, Mr. WASHINGTON IRVING has kindly furnished a biographical sketch of the author of Gertrude.

W. L. S.

New-York, Dec. 25th, 1840.

PREFACE TO THE SECOND EDITION.

The author of this little volume — or rather of that portion of it which is offered to the public as original — was induced to believe that neither the poem and notes of Campbell, nor the brief and imperfect notices to be found in works of general history, were capable of affording that information respecting the murderous assault upon Wyoming, with which readers would rest satisfied; that the melancholy story possessed interest enough to demand a more complete and faithful narrative. Favoring circumstances had enabled him to collect the materials for this purpose; and he thought them worthy of being presented to the American people.

The result proved that his opinion was not fallacious. The first edition was speedily taken up, and the continued inquiry for the work has made it his duty to publish a second. The publication of the volume has been the means of bringing to his knowledge additional facts of value, and some few corrections, all of which have been incorporated in this new, enlarged and revised edition.

W. L. S.

NEW-YORK, OCTOBER, 1843.

A

BIOGRAPHICAL SKETCH

OF

THOMAS CAMPBELL,

BY

WASHINGTON IRVING.

It has long been admitted as a lamentable truth, that authors seldom receive impartial justice from the world, while living. The graves seem to be the ordeal to which in a manner their names must be subjected, and from whence, if worthy of immortality, they rise with pure and imperishable lustre. Here many, who through the caprice of fashion, the influence of rank and fortune, or the panegyrics of friends, have enjoyed an undeserved notoriety, descend into oblivion, and it may literally be said "they rest from their labors, and their works do follow them." Here likewise many an ill-starred author, after struggling with penury and neglect, and starving through a world he has enriched by his talents, sinks to rest, and becomes an object of universal admiration and regret. The sneers of the cynical, the detractions of the envious, the scoffings of the ignorant, are silenced at the hallowed precincts of the tomb; and the world awakens to a sense of his value, when he is removed beyond its patronage for ever. Monuments are erected to his memory, books are written in his praise, and mankind will devour with avidity the biography of a man, whose life was passed unheeded before their eyes. He is like some canonized saint, at whose shrine treasures are lavished and clouds of incense offered up, though while living the slow hand of charity withheld the pittance that would have relieved his necessities.

But this tardiness in awarding merit its due, this preference continually shown to departed authors, over living ones of perhaps superior excellence, may be ascribed to more charitable motives than those of envy and ill-nature. Of the former we judge almost exclusively by their works. We form our opinion of the whole flow of their minds and the tenor of their dispositions from the volumes they have left behind; without considering that these are like so many masterly portraits, presenting their genius in its most auspicious moments, and noblest attitudes, when its powers were collected by solitude and reflection, assisted by study, stimulated by ambiton and elevated by inspiration. We witness nothing of the mental exhaustion and languor which follow these gushes of genius. We behold the stream only in the spring-tide of its current, and conclude that it has always been equally profound in its depth, pure in its wave, and majestic in its course.

Living authors, on the contrary, are continually in public view, and exposed to the full glare of scrutinizing familiarity. Though we may occasionally wonder at their eagle soarings, yet we soon behold them descend to our own level, and often sink below it. Their habits of seclusion make them less easy and engaging in society than the mere man of fashion, whose only study is to please. Their ignorance of the common topics of the day, and of matters of business, frequently makes them inferior in conversation to men of ordinary capacities, while the constitutional delicacy of their minds and irritability of their feelings, make them prone to more than ordinary caprices. At one time solitary and unsocial, at another listless and petulant, often trifling among the frivolous, and not unfrequently the dullest among the dull. All these circumstances tend to diminish our respect and admiration of their mental excellence, and show clearly, that authors, like actors, to be impartially critized, should never be known behind the scenes.

Such are a few of the causes that operate in Europe to defraud an author of the candid judgment of his countrymen, but their influence does not extend to this side of the Atlantic. We are placed, in some degree, in the situation of posterity. The vast ocean that rolls between us, like a space of time, removes us beyond the sphere of personal favor, personal prejudice, or personal familiarity. An European work, therefore, appears before us depending simply on its intrinsic merits. We have no private friendship nor party purpose to serve by magnifying the author's merits, and in sober sadness the humble state of our national literature places us far below any feeling of national rivalship.

But while our local situation thus enables us to exercise the enviable impartiality of posterity, it is evident we must share likewise in one of its disadvantages. We are in as complete ignorance respecting the biography of most living authors of celebrity, as though they had existed ages before our time, and indeed are better informed concerning the character and lives of authors who have long since passed away, than of those who are actually adding to the stores of European literature. Few think of writing the anecdotes of a distinguished character while living. His intimates, who of course are most capable, are prevented by their very intimacy, little thinking that those domestic habits and peculiarities, which an every day's acquaintance has made so trite and familiar to themselves, can be objects of curiosity to all the world besides. Thus then we who are too distant to gather those particulars concerning foreign authors, that are circulated from mouth to mouth in their native countries, must content ourselves to remain in almost utter ignorance; unless perchance some friendly magazine now and then gives us a meagre and apocryphal account of them, which rather provokes than satisfies our curiosity. A proof of these assertions will be furnished in the following sketch, which, unsatisfactory as it is, contains all the information we can collect, concerning a British poet of rare and exquisite endowments.

Thomas Campbell was born at Glasgow on the 27th September, 1777. He was the youngest son of Mr. Alexander Campbell, a merchant of that city, highly spoken of for his amiable manners and unblemished integrity; who united the scholar and the man of business, and amidst the engrossing cares and sordid pursuits of business, cherished an enthusiastic love of literature.

It may not be uninteresting to the American reader to know that Mr. Campbell, the poet, had near connexions in this country. His father passed several years of his youth at Falmouth, in Virginia, but returned to Europe before the revolutionary war. His uncle, who had accompanied his father across the Atlantic, remained in Virginia, where his family uniformly maintained a highly respectable station in society. One of his sons was district attorney under the administration of Washington, and was celebrated for his demeanor. He died in 1795. Robert Campbell, a brother of the poet, settled in Virginia, where he married a daughter of the celebrated Patrick Henry. He died about 1807.

The genius of Mr. Campbell showed itself almost in his infancy. At the age of seven he displayed a vivacity of imagination and a vigor of mind surprising in such early youth. He now commenced the study of Latin under the care of the Rev. David Alison, a teacher of distinguished reputation. A strong inclination for poetry was already discernible in him, and it was not more than two years after this, that, as we are told, "he began to try his wings." None of the first flutterings of his muse, however, have been preserved, but they had their effect in rendering him an object of favor and attention, aided no doubt by his personal beauty, his generous sensibility, and the gentleness and modesty of his deportment. At twelve he entered the university of Glasgow, and in the following year gained a bursary on Bishop Leighton's foundation, for a translation of one of the comedies of Aristophanes, which he executed in verse. This triumph was the more honorable from being gained after a hard contest over a rival candidate of nearly twice his age, who was considered one of the best scholars in the university. His second prize-exercise was the translation of a tragedy of Æschylus, likewise in verse, which he gained without opposition, as none of the students would enter the lists with him. He continued seven years in the university, during which time his talents and application were testified by yearly academical prizes. He was particularly successful in his translations from the Greek, in which language he took great delight; and on receiving his last prize for one of these performances, the Greek professor publicly pronounced it the best that had ever been produced in the university.

He made equal proficiency in other branches of study especially in Moral Philosophy; he attended likewise the academical course of Law and Physic, but pursued none of these studies with a view to a profession. On the contrary, the literary passion, we are told, was already so strong with him, that he could not endure the idea of devoting himself to any of the dull and sordid pursuits of busy life. His father influenced by his own love of literature, indulged those wayward fancies in his son, building fond hopes on his early display of talent. At one time, it is true, a part of the family expressed a wish that he should be fitted for the Church, but this was overruled by the rest, and he was left without further opposition to the impulses of his genius, and the seductions of the muse.

After leaving the university he passed some time among the mountains of Argyleshire, at the seat of Colonel Napier, a descendant of Napier Baron Merchester, the celebrated inventor of logarithims. It is suggested that he may have imbibed from this gentleman his taste and knowledge of the military arts, traces of which are to be seen throughout his poems. From Argyleshire he went to Edinburgh, where the reputation he had acquired at the university gained him a favorable reception into the literary and scientific circles of that intellectual city. Among others he was particularly noticed by professors Stewart and Playfair. To the ardor and elevation of mind awakened by such associates may we ascribe, in a great measure, the philosophical spirit and moral sublimity displayed in his first production, "The Pleasures of Hope," written during his residence in Edinburgh, when he was but twenty years of age.

Inexperienced in authorship, and doubtful of success, he disposed of the copy-right of his poem for an inconsiderable sum. It was received by the public with acclamation, and ran through two editions in the course of a few months, when his bookseller permitted him to publish a splendid edition for himself, by which means he was enabled in some measure, to participate in the golden harvest of his talent. His great reward, however, was the bright and enduring reputation which he instantly acquired, as one of the legitimate line of British poets.

The passion for German literature which prevailed at this time in Great Britian, awakened a desire in Mr. Campbell to study it at the fountain head. This, added to a curiosity to visit foreign parts, induced him to embark for Germany in the year 1800. He had originally fixed upon the college of Jena for his first place of residence, but on arriving at Hamburgh he found, by the public prints, that a victory had been gained by the French near Ulm, and that Munich and the heart of Bavaria were the theatre of an interesting war. "One moment's sensation," he observes in a letter to a relation in this country, "the single hope of seeing human nature exhibited in its most dreadful attitude, overturned my past decisions. I got down to the seat of war some weeks before the summer armistice of 1800, and indulged in what you will call the criminal curiosity of witnessing blood and desolation. Never shall time efface from my memory the recollection of that hour of astonishment and suspended breath, when I stood with the good monks of St. Jacob, to overlook a charge of Klenaw's cavalry upon the French under Grennier, encamped below us. We saw the fire given and returned, and heard distinctly the sound of the French *pas de charge*, collecting the lines to attack in close column. After three hours' awaiting the issue of a severe action, a park of artillery was opened just beneath the walls of the monastery, and several wagoners that were stationed to convey the wounded in spring wagons, were killed in our sight. My love of novelty now gave way to personal fears I took a carriage in company with an Austrian surgeon back to Landshut," &c. This awful spectacle he has described with all the poet's fire, in his Battle of Hohenlinden ; a poem which perhaps contains more grandeur and martial sublimity, than is to be found any where else in the same compass of English poetry.

From Landshut Mr. Campbell proceeded to Ratisbon, where he was at the time it was taken possession of by the French and expected as an Englishman to be made prisoner, but he observes "Moreau's army was under such excellent discipline, and the behavior both of officers and men so civil, that I soon mixed among them without hesitation, and formed many agreeable acquaintances at the messes of their brigade stationed in town, to which their *chef de brigade* often invited me. This worthy man, Colonel Le Fort, whose kindness I shall ever remember with gratitude, gave me a protection to pass through the whole army of Moreau."

After this he visited different parts of Germany, in the course of which he paid one of the casual taxes on travelling, being plundered among the Tyrolese mountains, by a scoundrel Croat, of his clothes, his books, and thirty ducats in gold. About midwinter he returned to Hamburgh, where he remained four months, in the expectation of accompanying a young gentleman of Edinburgh in a tour to Constantinople. His unceasing thirst for knowledge, and his habits of industrious application, prevented these months from passing heavily or unprofitably. "My time at Hamburgh," he observes, in one of his letters, "was chiefly employed in reading German, and, I am almost ashamed to confess it, for twelve successive weeks in the study of Kant's Philosophy, I had heard so much of it in Germany, its language was so new to me, and the possibility of its application to so many purposes in the different theories of science and belles-lettres was so constantly maintained, that I began to suspect Kant might be another Bacon, and blamed myself for not perceiving his merit. Distrusting my own imperfect acquaintance with the German, I took a Disciple of Kant's for a guide through his philosophy, but found, even with all this *fair play*, nothing to reward my labor. His metaphysics are mere innovations upon the received meaning of words, and the coinage of new ones convey no more instruction than the distinctions of Dun Scotus and Thomas Aquinas. In belles-lettres, the German language opens a richer field than in their philosophy. I cannot conceive a more perfect poet than their favorite Wieland."

While in Germany an edition of his Pleasures of Hope was proposed for publication in Vienna, but was forbidden by the court, in consequence of those passages which relate to Kosciusko, and the partition of Poland. Being disappointed in his projected visit to Constantinople, he returned to England in 1801, after nearly a year's absence, which had been passed much to his satisfaction and improvement, and had stored his mind with grand and awful images. "I remember," says he, "how little I valued the art of painting before I got into the heart of such impressive scenes; but in Germany, I would have given anything to have possessed an art capable of conveying ideas inaccessible to speech and writing. Some particular scenes were indeed rather overcharged with that degree of the terrific which oversteps the sublime, and I own my flesh yet creeps at the recollection of *spring wagons and hospitals*—but the sight of Ingolstadt in ruins, or Hohenlinden covered with fire, seven miles in circumference, were spectacles never to be forgotten."

On returning to England, he visited London for the first time, where, though unprovided with a single letter of introduction, the celebrity of his writings procured him the immediate notice and attentions of the best society. The following brief sketch which he gives of a literary club in London, will be gratifying to those who have felt an interest in the anecdotes of Addison and his knot of *beaux esprits* at Button's coffee house, and Johnson and his learned fraternity at the Turk's head.—"Mackintosh, the Vindiciæ Gallicæ was particularly attentive to me, and took me with him to his convivial parties at the King of Clubs, a place dedicated to the meetings of the reigning wits of London, and, in fact, a lineal descendant of the Johnson, Burke, and Goldsmith society, constituted for literary conversations. The dining table of these knights of literature was an arena of very keen conversational rivalship, maintained, to be sure, with perfect good nature, but in which the gladiators contended as hardly as ever the French and Austrians in the scenes I had just witnessed. Much, however, as the wit and erudition of these men pleases an auditor of the first or second visit, this trial of minds becomes at last fatiguing, because it is unnatural and unsatisfactory. Every one of these brilliants goes their to shine; for conversational powers are so much the rage in London, that no reputation is higher than his who exhibits them. Where every one tries to instruct, there is in fact but little instruction: wit, paradox, eccentricity, even absurdity, if delivered rapidly and facetiously, takes priority in these societies of sound reasonings and delicate taste. I have watched sometimes the devious tide of conversation, guided by accidental associations, turning from topic to topic and satisfactory upon none. What has one learned? has been my general question. The mind, it is true, is electrified and quickened, and the spirits finely exhilarated, but one grand fault pervades the whole institution; their inquiries are desultory, and all improvements to be reaped must be accidental."

The friendship of Mrs. Siddons was another acquisition, of which Mr. Campbell spoke with great pleasure; and what rendered it more gratifying was its being unsought for. It was the means of introducing him to much excellent society in London. "The character of that great woman," he observes, "is but little understood, and more misrepresented than any living character I know, by those who envy her reputation, or by those of the aristocracy, whom her irresistible dignity obliges to pay their homage at a respectable distance. The reserve of her demeanor is banished toward those who show neither meanness in flattering her, nor forwardness in approaching her too familiarly. The friends of her fireside are only such as she *talks to and talks of* with affection and respect.

The recent visit of Mr. Campbell to the continent had increased rather than gratified his desire to travel. He now contemplated another tour, for the purpose of improving himself in the knowledge of foreign languages and foreign manners in the course of which he intended to visit Italy and pass some time at Rome. From this plan he was diverted, most probably by an attachment he formed to a Miss Sinclair, a distant relation, whom he married in 1803. This change in his situation naturally put an end to all his wandering propensities, and he established himself at Sydenham in Kent, near London, where he devoted himself to literature. Not long afterward he received a solid and flattering token of the royal approbation of his poem of the Pleasures of Hope in a pension of 200*l*. What made this mark of royal favor the more gratifying was, that it was granted for no political services rendered or expected. Mr. Campbell was not of the court party, but of the constitutional whigs. He has uniformly, both before and since, been independent in his opinions and writings; a sincere and enthusiastic lover of liberty, and advocate for popular rights.

Though withdrawn from the busy world in his retirement at Sydenham, yet the genius of Mr. Campbell, like a true brilliant, occasionally flashed upon the public eye in a number of exquisite little poems, which appeared occasionally in the periodical works of the day. Among these were Hohenlinden and Lochiel, exquisite gems, sufficient of themselves to establish his title to the sacred name of poet: and the Mariners of England and the Battle of the Baltic, two of the noblest national songs ever written, fraught with sublime imagery and lofty sentiments, and delivered in a gallant swelling vein, that lifts the soul into heroics.

In the beginning of 1809, he gave to the public his Gertrude of Wyoming, connected with the fortunes of one of our little patriarchal villages on the banks of the Susquehannah, laid desolate by the Indians during our revolutionary war. There is no great scope in the story of this poem, nor any very skilful development of the plan, but it contains passages of exquisite grace, and tenderness, and others of spirit and grandeur; and the character of Outalissi is a classic delineation of one of our native savages :—

A stoic of the woods, a man without a tear.

What gave this poem especial interest in our eyes at the time of its appearance, and awakened a strong feeling of good will toward the author, was, that it related to our own country, and was calculated to give a classic charm to some of our own home scenery. The following remarks were elicited from us at the time, though the subsequent lapse of thirty years has improved the cogency of many of them.

"We have so long been accustomed to experience little else than contumely, misrepresentation, and very witless ridicule from the British press; and we have had such repeated proof of the extreme ignorance and absurd errors that prevail in Great Britain respecting our country and its inhabitants, that we confess, we were both surprised and gratified to meet with a poet, sufficiently unprejudiced to conceive an idea of moral excellence and natural beauty on this side of the Atlantic. Indeed even this simple show of liberality has drawn on the poet the censures and revilings of a host of narrow-minded writers, with whom liberality to this country is a crime. We are sorry to see such pitiful manifestations of hostility toward us. Indeed we must say, that we consider the constant acrimony and traduction indulged by the British press, toward this country, to be as opposite to the interest as it is derogatory to the candor and magnanimity of the nation. It is operating to widen the difference between two nations, which, if left to the impulse of their own feelings, would naturally grow together, and among the sad changes of this disastrous world, be mutual supports and comforts to each other.

"Whatever may be the occasional collisions of etiquette and interest which will inevitably take place between two great commercial nations, whose property and people are spread far and wide on the face of the ocean; whatever may be the clamorous expressions of hostility vented at such times by our unreflecting populace, or rather uttered in their name by a host of hireling scribblers, who pretend to speak the sentiments of the people; it is certain, that the well educated and well informed class of our citizens entertain a deep rooted good-will, and a rational esteem for Great Britian. It is almost impossible it should be otherwise. Independent of those hereditary affections, which spring up spontaneously for the nation from whence we have descended, the single circumstance of imbibing our ideas from the same authors, has a powerful effect in causing an attachment.

"The writers of Great Britain are the adopted citizens of our country, and, though they have no legislative voice, exercise a powerful influence over our opinions and affections. In these works we have British valor, British magnanimity, British might, and British wisdom continually before our eyes, portrayed in the most captivating colors, and are thus brought up, in constant contemplation of all that is amiable and illustrious in the British character. To these works likewise we resort, in every varying mood of mind, or vicissitude of fortune. They are our delight in the hour of relaxation; the solemn monitors and instructors of our closet; our comforters under the gloom of despondency. In the season of early life, in the strength of manhood, and still in the weakness and apathy of age, it is to them we are indebted for our hours of refined and unalloyed enjoyment. When we turn our eyes to England, therefore, from whence this bounteous tide of literature pours in upon us, it is with such feelings as the Egyptian, when he looks toward the sacred source of that stream, which, rising in a far distant country, flows down upon his own barren soil, diffusing riches, beauty, and fertility.

"Surely it cannot be the interest of Great Britian to trifle with such feelings. Surely the good-will, thus cherished among the best hearts of a country, rapidly increasing in power and importance, is of too much consequence to be scornfully neglected or surlily dashed away. It most certainly therefore would be both politic and honorable, for those enlightened British writers, who sway the sceptre of criticism, to expose these constant misrepresentations and discountenance these galling and unworthy insults of the pen, whose effect is to mislead and to irritate, without serving one valuable purpose. They engender gross prejudices in great Britian, inimical to a proper national understanding, while with us they wither all those feelings of kindness and consanguinity, that were shooting forth, like so many tendrils, to attach us to our parent country.

" While therefore we regard the poem of Mr Campbell with complacency, as evincing an opposite spirit to this, of which we have just complained, there are other reasons likewise, which interest us in its favor. Among the lesser evils, incident to the infant state of our country, we have to lament its almost total deficiency in those local associations produced by history and moral fiction. These may appear trivial to the common mass of readers; but the mind of taste and sensibility will at once acknowledge it, as constituting a great source of national pride, and love of country. There is an inexpressible charm imparted to every place, that has been celebrated by the historian, or immortalized by the poet; a charm that dignifies it in the eyes of the stranger, and endears it to the heart of the native inhabitant. Of this romantic attraction we are almost entirely destitute. While every insignificant hill and turbid stream in classic Europe has been hallowed by the visitations of the muse, and contemplated with fond enthusiasm; our lofty mountains and stupendous cataracts excite no poetical feelings, and our majestic rivers roll their waters unheeded, because unsung.

" Thus circumstanced, the sweet strains of Mr. Campbell's muse break upon us as gladly as would the pastoral pipe of the sheperd, amid the savage solitude of one of our trackless wildernesses. We are delighted to witness the air of captivating romance, and rural beauty our native fields and wild woods can assume under the plastic pencil of a master; and while wandering with the poet among the shady groves of Wyoming, or along the banks of the Susquehanna, almost fancy ourselves transported to the side of some classic stream, in the "hollow breast of Appenine." This may assist to convince many, who were before slow to believe, that our own country is capable of inspiring the highest poetic feelings and furnishing abundance of poetic imagery, though destitute of the hackneyed materials of poetry; though its groves are not vocal with the song of the nightingale; though no naiads have ever sported in its streams, nor satyrs and driads gambolled among its forests. Wherever nature displays herself in simple beauty or wild magnificence, and wherever the human mind appears in new and striking situations, neither the poet nor the philosopher can want subjects worthy of his genius."

As we before remarked, the lapse of thirty years has materially impaired the cogency of the forgoing remarks. The acrimony and traduction of the British press produced the effect apprehended, and contributed to hasten a war between the two nations. That war, however, made us completely a nation, and destroyed our mental dependence on England forever. A literature of our own has subsequently sprung up, and is daily increasing with wonderful fecundity; promising to counteract the undue influence of British literature, and to furnish us with productions in all departments of taste and knowledge, illustrative of our country, its history and its people, and in harmony with our condition and the nature of our institutions.

We have but a word or two to add concerning Mr. Campbell. In 1810 he published "O'Connor's Child, or Love lies Bleeding," an uncommonly spirited and affecting little tale. Since then he has given at intervals a variety of minor poems to the public, all possessing the same beauty of thought and delicacy of finish that distinguished his early productions. If some disappointment has been experienced by his admirers, that he has not effected any of those grand achievements in poetry which had been anticipated from his juvenile performances, they should congratulate themselves that he has never sunk from the pure and elevated height to which he so suddenly attained. Many years since, we hailed the productions of his muse as "beaming forth like the pure lights of heaven, among the meteor exhalations and paler fires with which our literary atmosphere abounds;" since that time many of those meteors and paler fires that dazzled and bewildered the public eye, have fallen to the earth and passed away, and still we find his poems like the stars, shining on, with undiminished lustre.

GERTRUDE OF WYOMING.

PART I.

ADVERTISEMENT.

Most of the popular histories of England, as well as of the American war, give an authentic account of the desolation of Wyoming, in Pennsylvania, which took place in 1778, by an incursion of the Indians. The scenery and incidents of the following Poem are connected with that event. The testimonies of historians and travellers concur in describing the infant colony as one of the happiest spots of human existence, for the hospitable and innocent manners of the inhabitants, the beauty of the country, and the luxuriant fertility of the soil and climate. In an evil hour, the junction of European with Indian arms converted this terrestrial paradise into a frightful waste. Mr. Isaac Weld informs us that the ruins of many of the villages, perforated with balls, and bearing marks of conflagration, were still preserved by the recent inhabitants, when he travelled through America, in 1796.

GERTRUDE OF WYOMING.

PART I.

I.

On Susquehannah's side, fair Wyoming!
Although the wild-flower on thy ruin'd wall,
And roofless homes, a sad remembrance bring
Of what thy gentle people did befall,
Yet thou wert once the loveliest land of all
That see the Atlantic wave their morn restore.
Sweet land! may I thy lost delights recall,
And paint thy Gertrude in her bowers of yore,
Whose beauty was the love of Pennsylvania s
shore!

II.

Delightful Wyoming! beneath thy skies,
The happy shepherd swains had nought to do
But feed their flocks on green declivities,
Or skim perchance thy lake with light canoe,
From morn till evening's sweeter pastime grew,
With timbrel, when beneath the forests brown,
Thy lovely maidens would the dance renew;

And aye those sunny mountains half-way down
Would echo flagelet from some romantic town.

III.

Then, where of Indian hills the daylight takes
His leave, how might you the flamingo see
Disporting like a meteor on the lakes—
And playful squirrel on his nut-grown tree:
And every sound of life was full of glee,
From merry mock-bird's song, or hum of men ;
While hearkening, fearing nought their revelry,
The wild deer arched his neck from glades, and then
Unhunted, sought his woods and wilderness again.

IV.

And scarce had Wyoming of war or crime
Heard, but in Transatlantic story rung,
For here the exile met from every clime,
And spoke in friendship every distant tongue:
Men from the blood of warring Europe sprung,
Were but divided by the running brook ;
And happy where no Rhenish trumpet sung,
On plains no seiging mine's volcano shook,
The blue-eyed German changed his sword to pruning-hook.

V.

Nor far some Andalusian saraband
Would sound to many a native roundelay—

But who is he that yet a dearer land
Remembers, over hills and far away?
Green Albin!* what though he no more survey
Thy ships at anchor on the quiet shore,
Thy pellochs† rolling from the mountain bay,
Thy lone sepulchral cairn upon the moor,
And distant isles that hear the loud Corbrechta
roar!‡

VI.

Alas! poor Caledonia's mountaineer,
That want's stern edict e'er, and feudal grief,
Had forced him from a home he loved so dear!
Yet found he here a home, and glad relief,
And plied the beverage from his own fair sheaf,
That fired his Highland blood with mickle glee:
And England sent her men, of men the chief,
Who taught those sires of Empire yet to be,
To plant the tree of life,—to plant fair Freedom's
tree!

VII.

Here were not mingled in the city's pomp
To life's extremes the grandeur and the gloom;
Judgment awoke not here her dismal tromp,
Nor seal'd in blood a fellow-creature's doom,

* Scotland.
† The Gaelic appellation for the porpoise.
‡ The great whirlpool of the Western Hebrides.

Nor mourn'd the captive in a living tomb.
One venerable man, beloved of all,
Sufficed, where innocence was yet in bloom,
To sway the strife that seldom might befall:
And Albert was their judge in patriarchal hall.

VIII.

How reverend was the look, serenely aged,
He bore, this gentle Pennsylvanian sire,
Where all but kindly fervours were assuaged,
Undimm'd by weakness' shade, or turbid ire!
And though, amidst the calm of thought entire,
Some high and haughty features might betray
A soul impetuous once, 'twas earthly fire
That fled composure's intellectual ray,
As Ætna's fires, grow dim before the rising day.

IX.

I boast no song in magic wonders rife,
But yet, oh Nature! is there nought to prize,
Familiar in thy bosom scenes of life?
And dwells in daylight truth's salubrious skies
No form with which the soul may sympathise?
Young, innocent, on whose sweet forehead mild
The parted ringlet shone in simplest guise,
An inmate in the home of Albert smiled,
Or blessed his noon-day walk—she was his only
child.

X.

The rose of England bloomed on Gertrude's cheek—
What though these shades had seen her birth, her sire
A Briton's independence taught to seek
Far western worlds ; and there his household fire
The light of social love did long inspire,
And many a halcyon day he lived to see
Unbroken but by one misfortune dire,
When fate had 'reft his mutual heart—but she
Was gone—and Gertrude climb'd a widow'd father's knee.

XI.

A loved bequest,—and I may half impart,
To them that feel the strong paternal tie,
How like a new existence to his heart
That living flower uprose beneath his eye,
Dear as she was from cherub infancy,
From hours when she would round his garden play,
To time when as the ripening years went by,
Her lovely mind could culture well repay,
And more engaging grew, from pleasing day to day.

XII.

I may not paint those thousand infant charms ;
(Unconscious fascination, undesigned !)

The orison repeated in his arms,
For God to bless her sire and all mankind ;
The book, the bosom on his knee reclined,
Or how sweet fairy-lore he heard her con,
(The playmate ere the teacher of her mind :)
All uncompanion'd else her heart had gone
Till now, in Gertrude's eyes, their ninth blue summer shone.

XIII.

And summer was the tide, and sweet the hour,
When sire and daughter saw, with fleet descent,
An Indian from his bark approach their bower,
Of buskin'd limb, and swarthy lineament ;
The red wild feathers on his brow were blent,
And bracelets bound the arm that help'd to light
A boy, who seem'd, as he beside him went,
Of Christian vesture, and complexion bright,
Led by his dusky guide, like morning brought by night.

XIV.

Yet pensive seem'd the boy for one so young—
The dimple from his polish'd cheek had fled ;
When, leaning on his forest-bow unstrung,
Th' Oneida warrior to the planter said,
And laid his hand upon the stripling's head,
"Peace be to thee ! my words this belt approve ;
The paths of peace my steps have hither led :

This little nursling, take him to thy love,
And shield the bird unfledged, since gone the parent dove.

XV.

"Christian! I am the foeman of thy foe;
Our wampum league thy brethren did embrace:
Upon the Michigan, three moons ago,
We launch'd our pirogues for the bison chase,
And with the Hurons planted for a space,
With true and faithful hands, the olive stalk;
But snakes are in the bosoms of their race,
And though they held with us a friendly talk,
The hollow peace-tree fell beneath their tomakawk!

XVI.

"It was encamping on the lake's far port,
A cry of Areouski* broke our sleep,
Where storm'd an ambush'd foe thy nation's fort,
And rapid, rapid whoops came o'er the deep;
But long thy country's war-sign on the steep
Appear'd through ghastly intervals of light,
And deathfully their thunder seem'd to sweep,
Till utter darkness swallow'd up the sight,
As if a shower of blood had quench'd the fiery fight!

* The Indian God of War.

XVII.

" It slept—it rose again—on high their tower
Sprang upward like a torch to light the skies,
Then down again it rain'd an ember shower,
And louder lamentations heard we rise ;
As when the evil Manitou,* that dries
Th' Ohio woods, consumes them in his ire,
In vain the desolated panther flies,
And howls amidst his wilderness of fire :
Alas ! too late, we reach'd and smote those Hurons dire !

XVIII.

" But as the fox beneath the nobler hound,
So died their warriors by our battle brand :
And from the tree we, with her child, unbound
A lonely mother of the Christian land :—
Her lord—the captain of the British band—
Amidst the slaughter of his soldiers lay.
Scarce knew the widow our delivering hand ;
Upon her child she sobb'd, and swoon'd away,
Or shriek'd unto the God to whom the Christians pray.

XIX.

" Our virgins fed her with their kindly bowls
Of fever-balm and sweet sagamité :
But she was journeying to the land of souls,
And lifted up her dying head to pray

* Manitou, Spirit or Deity.

That we should bid an ancient friend convey
Her orphan to his home of England's shore ;—
And take, she said, this token far away,
To one that will remember us of yore,
When he beholds the ring that Waldegrave's Julia wore.

XX.

" And I, the eagle of my tribe,* have rush'd
With this lorn dove."—A sage's self-command
Had quell'd the tears from Albert's heart that gush'd
But yet his cheek—his agitated hand—
That shower'd upon the stranger of the land
No common boon, in grief but ill-beguiled
A soul that was not wont to be unmann'd ;
" And stay," he cried, " dear pilgrim of the wild,
Preserver of my old, my boon companion's child !—

XXI.

" Child of a race whose name my bosom warms,
On earth's remotest bounds how welcome here !
Whose mother oft, a child, has fill'd these arms,
Young as thyself, and innocently dear,

* The Indians are distinguished, both personally and by tribes, by the names of particular animals, whose qualities they affect to resemble, either for cunning, strength, swiftness, or other qualities :—as the eagle, the serpent, the fox, or bear.

Whose grandsire was my early life's compeer.
Ah, happiest home of England's happy clime!
How beautiful e'en now thy scenes appear,
As in the noon and sunshine of my prime!
How gone like yesterday these thrice ten years of
time!

XXII.

"And, Julia! when thou wert like Gertrude
now,
Can I forget thee, favorite child of yore?
Or thought I, in thy father's house, when thou
Wert lightest hearted on his festive floor,
And first of all his hospitable door
To meet and kiss me at my journey's end?
But where was I when Waldegrave was no more?
And thou did'st pale thy gentle head extend
In woes, that e'en the tribe of deserts was thy
friend!"

XXIII.

He said—and strain'd unto his heart the boy:—
Far differently the mute Oneida took
His calumet of peace, and cup of joy;*
As monumental bronze unchanged his look;
A soul that pity touch'd but never shook;

* *Calumet of Peace.*—The calumet is the Indian name for the ornamental pipe of friendship, which they smoke as a pledge of amity.

Trained from his tree-rock'd cradle* to his bier
The fierce extremes of good and ill to brook,
Impassive—fearing but the shame of fear—
A stoic of the woods—a man without a tear.

XXIV.

Yet deem not goodness on the savage stock
Of Outalissi's heart disdain'd to grow;
As lives the oak unwither'd on the rock,
By storms above, and barrenness below;
He scorn'd his own, who felt another's wo;
And ere the wolf-skin on his back he flung,
Or laced his moccasins, in act to go,
A song of parting to the boy he sung,
Who slept on Albert's couch, nor heard his friendly tongue.

XXV.

"Sleep, wearied one! and in the dreaming land
Shouldst thou to-morrow with thy mother meet,
Oh! tell her spirit that the white man's hand
Hath pluck'd the thorns of sorrow from thy feet;
While I in lonely wilderness shall greet
Thy little footprints—or by traces know
The fountain, where at noon I thought it sweet

* *Tree-rock'd cradle.*—The Indian mothers suspend their children in their cradles from the boughs of trees, and let them be rocked by the wind.

To feed thee with the quarry of my bow,
And pour'd the lotus-horn,* or slew the mountain roe.

XXVI.

"Adieu! sweet scion of the rising sun!
But should affliction's storms thy blossom mock,
Then come again—my own adopted one,
And I will graft thee on a noble stock:
The crocodile, the condor of the rock,
Shall be the pastime of thy sylvan wars;
And I will teach thee, in the battle's shock,
To pay with Huron blood thy father's scars,
And gratulate his soul rejoicing in the stars!"

XXVII.

So finish'd he the rhyme (howe'er uncouth)
That true to nature's fervid feelings ran,
(And song is but the eloquence of truth:)
Then forth uprose that lone wayfaring man;
But dauntless he, nor chart, nor journey's plan
In woods required, whose trained eye was keen
As eagle of the wilderness to scan
His path, by mountain, swamp, or deep ravine,
Or ken far friendly huts on good savannas green.

* From a flower shaped like a horn, which Chateaubriand presumes to be of the lotus kind, the Indians in their travels though the desert often find a draught of dew purer than any other water.

XXVIII.

Old Albert saw him from the valley's side—
His pirogue launch'd—his pilgrimage begun—
Far, like the red-bird's wing he seem'd to glide;
Then dived, and vanished in the woodlands dun.
Oft, to that spot by tender memory won,
Would Albert climb the promontory's height,
If but a dim sail glimmer'd in the sun;
But never more, to bless his longing sight,
Was Outalissi hail'd, with bark and plumage bright.

GERTRUDE OF WYOMING.

PART II.

GERTRUDE OF WYOMING.

PART II.

I.

A VALLEY from the river-shore withdrawn
Was Albert's home, two quiet woods between,
Whose lofty verdure overlook'd his lawn ;
And waters to their resting-place serene
Came freshening, and reflecting all the scene,
(A mirror in the depth of flowery shelves ;)
So sweet a spot of earth, you might (I ween)
Have guess'd some congregation of the elves,
To sport by summer moons, had shaped it for
    themselves.

II.

Yet wanted not the eye far scope to muse,
Nor vistas open'd by the wandering stream ;
Both where at evening Allegany views,
Through ridges burning in her western beam,
Lake after lake interminably gleam :
And past those settler's haunts the eye might roam
Where earth's unliving silence all would seem ;

Save where on rocks the beaver built his dome,
Or buffalo remote low'd far from human home.

III.

But silent not that adverse eastern path,
Which saw Aurora's hills th' horizon crown;
There was the river heard, in bed of wrath,
(A precipice of foam from mountains brown,)
Like tumults heard from some far distant town;
But softening in approach he left his gloom,
And murmur'd pleasantly, and laid him down
To kiss those easy curving banks of bloom,
That lent the windward air an exquisite perfume.

IV.

It seem'd as if those scenes sweet influence had
On Gertrude's soul, and kindness like their own
Inspired those eyes affectionate and glad,
That seem'd to love whate'er they looked upon;
Whether with Hebe's mirth her features shone,
Or if a shade more pleasing them o'ercast,
(As if for heavenly musing meant alone,)
Yet so becomingly th' expression past,
That each succeeding look was lovelier than the
last.

V.

Nor, guess I, was that Pennsylvanian home,
With all its picturesque and balmy grace,

And fields that were a luxury to roam,
Lost on the soul that look'd from such a face!
Enthusiast of the woods! when years apace
Had bound thy lovely waist with woman's zone,
The sunrise path, at morn, I see thee trace
To hills with high magnolia overgrown,
And joy to breathe the groves, romantic and alone.

VI.

The sunrise drew her thoughts to Europe forth,
That thus apostrophized its viewless scene:
"Land of my father's love, my mother's birth!
The home of kindred I have never seen!
We know not other—oceans are between:
Yet say! far friendly hearts, from whence we came,
Of us does oft remembrance intervene?
My mother, sure—my sire—a thought may claim;
But Gertrude is to you an unregarded name.

VII.

"And yet, loved England! when thy name I trace
In many a pilgrim's tale and poet's song,
How can I choose but wish for one embrace
Of them, the dear unknown, to whom belong
My mother's looks,—perhaps her likeness strong?
Oh, parent! with what reverential awe,
From features of thine own related throng,
An image of thy face my soul could draw!
And see thee once again whom I too shortly saw!"

VIII.

Yet deem not Gertrude sigh'd for foreign joy ;
To soothe a father's couch, her only care,
And keep his reverend head from all annoy :
For this, methinks her homeward steps repair,
Soon as the morning wreath had bound her hair ;
While yet the wild deer trod in spangling dew,
While boatmen caroll'd to the fresh-blown air,
And woods a horizontal shadow threw,
An early fox appeared in momentary view.

IX.

Apart there was a deep untrodden grot,
Where oft the reading hours sweet Gertrude wore ;
Tradition had not named its lonely spot ;
But here (methinks) might India's sons explore
Their father's dust, * or lift perchance of yore,
Their voice to the great Spirit :—rocks sublime
To human art a sportive semblance bore,
And yellow lichens color'd all the clime,
Like moonlight battlements, and towers decay'd
by time.

X.

But high in amphitheatre above,
Gay tinted woods their massy foliage threw :

* It is a custom of the Indian tribes to visit the tombs of their ancestors in the cultivated parts of America, who have been buried for upwards of a century.

Breathed but an air of heaven, and all the grove
As if instinct with living spirit grew,
Rolling its verdant gulfs of every hue;
And now suspended was the pleasing din,
Now from a murmur faint it swell'd anew,
Like the first note of organ heard within
Cathedral aisles,—ere yet its symphony begin.

XI.

It was in this lone valley she would charm
The lingering noon, where flowers a couch had strewn;
Her cheek reclining, and her snowy arm
On hillock by the palm-tree half o'ergrown:
And aye that volume on her lap is thrown,
Which every heart of human mould endears;
With Shakspeare's self she speaks and smiles alone,
And no intruding visitation fears,
To shame the unconscious laugh, or stop her sweetest tears.

XII.

And nought within the grove was seen or heard
But stock-doves plaining through its gloom profound,
Or winglet of the fairy humming-bird,
Like atoms of the rainbow fluttering round;
When, lo! there enter'd to its inmost ground

A youth, the stranger of a distant land;
He was, to weet, for eastern mountains bound;
But late th' equator suns his cheek had tann'd,
And California's gales his roving bosom fann'd.

XIII.

A steed, whose rein hung loosely o'er his arm,
He led dismounted; ere his leisure pace,
Amid the brown leaves, could her ear alarm,
Close he had come, and worshipp'd for a space
Those downcast features:—she her lovely face
Uplift on one, whose lineaments and frame
Wore youth and manhood's intermingled grace;
Iberian seem'd his boot—his robe the same,
And well the Spanish plume his lofty looks became.

XIV.

For Albert's home he sought—her finger fair
Has pointed where the father's mansion stood.
Returning from the copse, he soon was there:
And soon has Gertrude hied from dark greenwood;
Nor joyless, by the converse, understood
Between the man of age and pilgrim young,
That gay congeniality of mood,
And early liking from acquaintance sprung;
Full fluently conversed their guest in England's tongue.

XV.

And well could he his pilgrimage of taste
Unfold,—and much they loved his fervid strain,
While he each fair variety retraced
Of climes, and manners, o'er the eastern main.
Now happy Switzer's hills,—romantic Spain,—
Gay lilied fields of France,—or more refined,
The soft Ausonia's monumental reign;
Nor less each rural image he designed
Than all the city's pomp and home of human kind.

XVI.

Anon some wilder portraiture he draws;
Of Nature's savage glories he would speak,—
The loneliness of earth that overawes,—
Where, resting by some tomb of old cacique,
The lama-driver on Peruvia's peak
Nor living voice nor motion marks around;
But storks that to the boundless forest shriek,
Or wild-cane arch high flung o'er gulf profound,*
That fluctuates when the storms of El Dorado
sound.

XVII.

Pleased with his guest, the good man still would
ply
Each earnest question, and his converse court;

* The bridges over narrow streams in many parts of Spanish America are said to be built of cane, which, however strong to support the passen-

But Gertrude, as she eyed him, knew not why
A strange and troubling wonder stopt her short.
"In England thou hast been,—and, by report,
An orphan's name (quoth Albert) may'st have
known.
Sad tale!—when latest fell our frontier fort,—
One innocent—one soldier's child—alone
Was spared, and brought to me, who loved him
as my own.—

XVIII.

"Young Henry Waldegrave! three delightful years
These very walls his infant sports did see:
But most I loved him when his parting tears
Alternately bedew'd my child and me:
His sorest parting, Gertrude, was from thee;
Nor half its grief his little heart could hold;
By kindred he was sent for o'er the sea;
They tore him from us when but twelve years old,
And scarcely for his loss have I been yet consoled!"

XIX.

His face the wanderer hid—but could not hide
A tear, a smile, upon his cheek that dwell;—
"And speak! mysterious stranger!" (Gertrude
cried)

ger, are yet waved in the agitation of the storm, and frequently add to the effect of a mountainous and picturesque scenery.

"It is!—it is!—I knew—I knew him well!
'Tis Waldegrave's self, of Waldegrave come to tell!"
A burst of joy the father's lips declare,
But Gertrude speechless on his bosom fell;
At once his open arms embraced the pair—
Was never group more blest, in this wide world of care.

XX.

"And will ye pardon, then, (replied the youth)
Your Waldegrave's feigned name, and false attire?
I durst not in the neighborhood, in truth,
The very fortunes of your house inquire,
Lest one that knew me might some tidings dire
Impart, and I my weakness all betray;
For had I lost my Gertrude and my sire,
I meant but o'er your tombs to weep a day,
Unknown I meant to weep, unknown to pass away.

XXI.

"But here ye live,—ye bloom,—in each dear face
The changing hand of time I may not blame;
For there, it hath but shed more reverend grace,
And here, of beauty perfected the frame:
And well I know your hearts are still the same—
They could not change—ye look the very way
As when an orphan first to you I came.

And have ye heard of my poor guide, I pray?
Nay, wherefore weep ye, friends, on such a joyous day?"

XXII.

"And art thou here? or is it but a dream?
And wilt thou, Waldegrave, wilt thou, leave us
more?"—
"No, never! thou that yet dost lovelier seem
Than aught on earth—than e'en thyself of yore—
I will not part thee from thy father's shore;
But we will cherish him with mutual arms,
And hand in hand again the path explore,
Which every ray of young remembrance warms,
While thou shalt be my own, with all thy truth
and charms!"

XXIII.

At morn, as if beneath a galaxy
Of over-arching groves in blossoms white,
Where all was odorous scent and harmony,
And gladness to the heart, nerve, ear, and sight:
There, if, oh gentle Love! I read aright
The utterance that seal'd thy sacred bond,
'Twas listening to these accents of delight,
She hid upon his breast those eyes, beyond
Expression's power to paint, all languishingly
fond.

XXIV.

"Flower of my life, so lovely, and so lone!
Whom I would rather in this desert meet,
Scorning, and scorn'd by fortune's power, than own
Her pomp and splendors lavish'd at my feet!
Turn not from me thy breath, more exquisite
Than odors cast on heaven's own shrine, to please—
Give me thy love, than luxury more sweet,
And more than all the wealth that loads the breeze,
When Coromandel's ships return from Indian seas."

XXV.

Then would that home admit them—happier far
Than grandeur's most magnificent saloon,
While here and there, a solitary star
Flushed in the darkening firmament of June,
And silence brought the soul-felt hour, full soon,
Ineffable, which I may not portray;
For never did the hymenean moon
A paradise of hearts more sacred sway,
In all that slept beneath her soft voluptuous ray.

GERTRUDE OF WYOMING.

PART III.

GERTRUDE OF WYOMING.

PART III.

I.

O Love! in such a wilderness as this,
Where transport and security entwine,
Here is the empire of thy perfect bliss,
And here thou art a god indeed divine.
Here shall no forms abridge, no hours confine
The views, the walks, that boundless joy inspire!
Roll on, ye days of raptured influence, shine!
Nor, blind with ecstasy's celestial fire,
Shall love behold the spark of earth-born time
    expire.

II.

Three little moons, how short! amidst the grove
And pastoral savannas they consume,
While she, beside her buskin'd youth to rove,
Delights, in fancifully wild costume,
Her lovely brow to shade with Indian plume;
And forth in hunter-seeming vest they fare;
But not to chase the deer in forest gloom;

'Tis but the breath of heaven—the blessed air—
And interchange of hearts, unknown, unseen to
share.

III.

What though the sportive dog oft round them
note,
Or fawn, or wild bird bursting on the wing;
Yet who, in love's own presence, would devote
To death those gentle throats that wake the spring,
Or writhing from the brook its victim bring?
No!—nor let fear one little warbler rouse;
But fed by Gertrude's hand, still let them sing,
Acquaintance of her path, amidst the boughs,
That shade e'en now her love, and witness'd first
her vows.

IV.

Now labyrinths, which but themselves can pierce,
Methinks, conduct them to some pleasant ground,
Where welcome hills shut out the universe,
And pines their lawny walk encompass round;
There, if a pause delicious converse found,
'Twas but when o'er each heart th' idea stole,
(Perchance awhile in joy's oblivion drown'd,)
That come what may, while life's glad pulses
roll,
Indissolubly thus should soul be knit to soul.

V.

And in the visions of romantic youth,
What years of endless bliss are yet to flow?
But, mortal pleasure, what art thou in truth?
The torrent's smoothness, ere it dash below!
And must I change my song? and must I show,
Sweet Wyoming! the day when thou wert doom'd,
Guiltless, to mourn thy loveliest bowers laid low?
When where of yesterday a garden bloom'd,
Death overspread his pall, and blackening ashes
gloom'd?

VI.

Sad was the year, by proud oppression driven,
When Transatlantic Liberty arose,
Not in the sunshine and the smile of heaven,
But wrapt in whirlwinds and begirt with woes,
Amidst the strife of fratricidal foes;
Her birth-star was the light of burning plains;*
Her baptism is the weight of blood that flows
From kindred hearts—the blood of British veins—
And famine tracks her steps, and pestilential pains.

VII.

Yet, ere the storm of death had raged remote,
Or siege unseen in heaven reflects its beams,
Who now each dreadful circumstance shall note,

* Alluding to the miseries that attended the American civil war.

That fills pale Gertrude's thoughts, and nightly
dreams ?
Dismal to her the forge of battle gleams
Portentous light ! and music's voice is dumb ;
Save where the fife its shrill reveillé screams,
Or midnight streets re-echo to the drum,
That speaks of maddening strife, and bloodstain'd
fields to come.

VIII.

It was in truth a momentary pang ;
Yet how comprising myriad shapes of wo !
First when in Gertrude's ear the summons rang,
A husband to the battle doom'd to go !
" Nay, meet not thou (she cries) thy kindred foe,
But peaceful let us seek fair England's strand ;"
" Ah, Gertrude ! thy beloved heart, I know,
Would feel like mine the stigmatizing brand,
Could I forsake the cause of Freedom's holy band.

IX.

" But shame—but flight—a recreant's name to
prove,
To hide in exile ignominious fears—
Say, e'en if this I brook'd,—the public love
Thy father's bosom to his home endears :
And how could I his few remaining years,
My Gertrude, sever from so dear a child ?"
So, day by day, her boding heart he cheers ;

At last that heart to hope is half beguiled,
And, pale through tears suppress'd, the mournful
beauty smiled.

X.

Night came,—and in their lighted bower, full
late
The joy of converse had endured—when hark!
Abrupt and loud a summons shook their gate;
And heedless of the dog's obstreperous bark,
A form had rush'd amidst them from the dark,
And spread his arms,—and fell upon the floor:
Of aged strength his limbs retain'd the mark;
But desolate he look'd, and famish'd poor,
As ever shipwreck'd wretch lone left on desert
shore.

XI.

Uprisen, each wondering brow is knit and arch'd:
A spirit from the dead they deem him first:
To speak he tries; but quivering, pale, and parch'd,
From lips, as by some powerless dream accursed,
Emotions unintelligible burst;
And long his filmed eye is red and dim;
At length the pity-proffered cup his thirst
Had half assuaged, and nerved his shuddering
limb,
When Albert's hand he grasp'd;—but Albert
knew not him—

XII.

"And hast thou then forgot," (he cried forlorn,
And eyed the group with half-indignant air,)
"Oh! hast thou, Christian chief, forgot the morn
When I with thee the cup of peace did share?
Then stately was this head, and dark this hair,
That now is white as Appalachia's snow;
But if the weight of fifteen years' despair,
And age hath bow'd me, and the torturing foe,
Bring me my boy—and he will his deliverer
know!"

XIII.

It was not long, with eyes and heart of flame,
Ere Henry to his loved Oneida flew:
"Bless thee, my guide!"—but backward, as he
came,
The chief his old bewildered head withdrew,
And grasped his arm, and look'd and look'd him
through.
'Twas strange—nor could the group a smile con-
trol—
The long and doubtful scrutiny to view:—
At last delight o'er all his features stole,
"It is—my own," he cried, and clasp'd him to
his soul.

XIV.

"Yes! thou recall'st my pride of years, for then
The bowstring of my spirit was not slack,
When, spite of woods, and floods, and ambush'd men,
I bore thee like the quiver on my back,
Fleet as the whirlwind hurries on the rack;
Nor foeman then, nor cougar's crouch I fear'd,*
For I was strong as mountain cataract:
And dost thou not remember how we cheer'd,
Upon the last hill-top, when white men's huts appear'd?

XV.

"Then welcome be my death song and my death,
Since I have seen thee, and again embraced,"—
And longer had he spent his toil-worn breath,
But with affectionate and eager haste,
Was every arm outstretch'd around their guest,
To welcome and to bless his aged head.
Soon was the hospitable banquet placed:
And Gertrude's lovely hands a balsam shed
On wounds with fever'd joy that more profusely bled.

XVI.

"But this is not a time,"—he started up,
And smote his breast with wo-denouncing hand—

* Cougar, the American tiger.

"This is no time to fill the joyous cup;
The Mammoth comes,—the foe,—the Monster Brandt,*—
With all his howling desolating band;—
These eyes have seen their blade and burning pine
Awake at once, and silence, half your land.
Red is the cup they drink; but not with wine:
Awake, and watch to-night, or see no morning shine!

XVII.

"Scorning to wield the hatchet for his bribe,
'Gainst Brandt himself I went to battle forth:
Accursed Brandt! he left of all my tribe
Nor man, nor child, nor thing of living birth:
No! not the dog, that watch'd my household hearth,
Escaped that night of blood, upon our plains!
All perished!—I alone am left on earth!
To whom nor relative nor blood remains,
No!—not a kindred drop that runs in human veins!

XVIII.

"But go!—and rouse your warriors;—for, if right
These old bewilder'd eyes could guess, by signs

* Brandt was the leader of those Mohawks, and other savages, who laid waste this part of Pennsylvania. Vide the note at the end of this poem.

Of striped and starred banners, on yon height
Of eastern cedars, o'r the creek of pines—
Some fort embattled by your country shines:
Deep roars th' innavigable gulf below
Its squared rock, and palisaded lines.
Go! seek the light its warlike beacons show;
Whilst I in ambush wait, for vengeance and the foe!"

XIX.

Scarce had he utter'd when heaven's verge extreme
Reverberates the bomb's descending star,—
And sounds that mingled laugh,—and shout,—and scream,—
To freeze the blood, in one discordant jar,
Rung to the pealing thunderbolts of war.
Whoop after whoop with rack the ear assail'd!
As if unearthly fiends had burst their bar;
While rapidly the marksman's shot prevail'd:—
And aye, as if for death, some lonely trumpet wail'd.

XX.

Then looked they to the hills, where fire o'erhung
The bandit groups, in one Vesuvian glare;
Or swept, far seen, the tower, whose clock unrung,
Told legible that midnight of despair.
She faints,—she falters not,—th' heroic fair,—

As he the sword and plume in haste array'd.
One short embrace—he clasp'd his dearest care—
But hark! what nearer war-drum shakes the glade?
Joy, joy! Columbia's friends are tramping through the shade!

XXI.

Then came of every race the mingled swarm,
Far rung the groves and gleam'd the midnight grass,
With flambeau, javelin, and naked arm;
As warriors wheel'd their culverins of brass,
Sprung from the woods, a bold athletic mass,
Whom virtue fires, and liberty combines:
And first the wild Moravian yagers pass—
His plumed host the dark Iberian joins—
And Scotia's sword beneath the Highland thistle shines.

XXII.

And in, the buskin'd hunters of the deer,
To Albert's home, with shout and cymbal throng:
Roused by their warlike pomp, and mirth, and cheer,
Old Outalissa woke his battle-song,
And, beating with his war-club cadence strong,
Tells how his deep-stung indignation smarts,
Of them that wrapt his house in flames, ere long

To whet a dagger on their stony hearts,
And smile avenged ere yet his eagle spirit parts.

XXIII.

Calm, opposite the Christian father rose,
Pale on his venerable brow its rays
Of martyr light the conflagration throws ;
One hand upon his lovely child he lays,
And one th' uncover'd crowd to silence sways ;
While though the battle flash is faster driven,—
Unawed, with eye unstartled by the blaze,
He for his bleeding country prays to Heaven—
Prays that the men of blood themselves may be
forgiven.

XXIV.

Short time is now for gratulating speech :
And yet, beloved Gertrude, ere begun
Thy country's flight, yon distant towers to reach,
Look'd not on thee the rudest partisan
With brow relax'd to love ? And murmurs ran,
As round and round their willing ranks they
drew,
From beauty's sight to shield the hostile van.
Grateful, on them a placid look she threw,
Nor wept, but as she bade her mother's grave
adieu !

XXV.

Past was the flight, and welcome seem'd the tower,
That like a giant standard-bearer frown'd
Defiance on the roving Indian power.
Beneath each bold and promontory mound
With embrasure emboss'd and armour crown'd,
An arrowy frieze, and wedged ravelin,
Wove like a diadem its tracery round
The lofty summit of that mountain green ;
Here stood secure the group, and eyed a distant
scene,—

XXVI.

A scene of death ! where fires beneath the sun,
And blended arms, and white pavilions glow ;
And for the business of destruction done
Its requiem the war-horn seem'd to blow :
There, sad spectatress of her country's wo !
The lovely Gertrude, safe from present harm,
Had laid her cheek, and clasp'd her hands of
snow
On Waldegrave's shoulder, half within his arm
Enclosed, that felt her heart, and hush'd its wild
alarm !

XXVII.

But short that contemplation—sad and short
The pause to bid each much loved scene adieu !

Beneath the very shadow of the fort,
Where friendly swords were drawn, and banners
flew,
Ah! who could deem that foot of Indian crew
Was near?—yet there, with lust of murderous
deeds,
Gleam'd like a basilisk, from woods in view,
The ambush'd foeman's eye—his volley speeds,
And Albert—Albert—falls! the dear old father
bleeds!

XXVIII.

And tranced in giddy horror Gertrude swoon'd;
Yet, while she clasps him lifeless to her zone,
Say, burst they, borrow'd from her father's wound,
These drops?—Oh, God! the life-blood is her
own!
And falt'ring, on her Waldegrave's bosom thrown,
"Weep not, O love!"—she cries, "to see me
bleed—
Thee, Gertrude's sad survivor, thee alone
Heaven's peace commiserate; for scarce I heed
These wounds;—yet thee to leave is death, is
death indeed!

XXIX.

"Clasp me a little longer on the brink
Of fate! while I can feel thy dear caress:

And when this heart hath ceased to beat—oh
think,
And let it mitigate thy wo's excess,
That thou hast been to me all tenderness,
And friend to more than human friendship just.
Oh! by that retrospect of happiness,
And by the hopes of an immortal trust,
God shall assuage thy pangs when I am laid in
dust!

XXX.

"Go, Henry, go not back, when I depart;
The scene thy bursting tears too deep will move,
Where my dear father took thee to his heart,
And Gertrude thought it ecstasy to rove
With thee, as with an angel, through the grove
Of peace, imagining her lot was cast
In heaven; for ours was not like earthly love.
And must this parting be our very last?
No! I shall love thee still, when death itself is past.

XXXI.

"Half could I bear, methinks, to leave this earth,
And thee, more loved than aught beneath the sun,
If I had lived to smile but on the birth
Of one dear pledge;—but shall there then be
none,
In future times—no gentle little one,

To clasp thy neck, and look, resembling me?
Yet seems it, e'en while life's last pulses run,
A sweetness in the cup of death to be,
Lord of my bosom's love! to die beholding thee!"

XXXII.

Hush'd were his Gertrude's lips! but still their bland
And beautiful expression seem'd to melt
With love that could not die! and still his hand
She presses to the heart no more that felt.
Ah, heart! where once each fond affection dwelt,
And features yet that spoke a soul more fair.
Mute, gazing, agonizing, as he knelt,—
Of them that stood encircling his despair,
He heard some friendly words;—but knew not what they were.

XXXIII.

For now, to mourn their judge and child, arrives
A faithful band. With solemn rites between,
'Twas sung, how they were lovely in their lives,
And in their deaths had not divided been.
Touch'd by the music, and the melting scene,
Was scarce one tearless eye amidst the crowd:—
Stern warriors, resting on their swords, were seen
To veil their eyes, as pass'd each much-loved shroud—
While woman's softer soul in wo dissolved aloud.

XXXIV.

Then mournfully the parting bugle bid
Its farewell, o'er the grave of worth and truth ;
Prone to the dust, afflicted Waldegrave hid
His face on earth ;—him watch'd, in gloomy ruth,
His woodland guide: but words had none to
soothe
The grief that knew not consolation's name:
Casting his Indian mantle o'er the youth,
He watch'd beneath its folds, each burst that came
Convulsive, ague-like, across his shuddering frame!

XXXV.

" And I could weep ;"—th' Oneida chief
His descant wildly thus begun:
" But that I may not stain with grief
The death-song of my father's son,
Or bow this head in wo:
For by my wrongs, and by my wrath !
To-morrow Areouski's breath,
(That fires yon heaven with storms of death,)
Shall light us to the foe ;
And we shall share, my Christian boy !
The foeman's blood, the avenger's joy !

XXXVI.

" But thee, my flower, whose breath was given
By milder genii o'er the deep,

The spirits of the white man's heaven
Forbid not thee to weep :—
Nor will the Christian host,
Nor will thy father's spirit grieve,
To see thee on the battle's eve,
Lamenting, take a mournful leave
Of her who loved thee most :
She was the rainbow to thy sight!
Thy sun—thy heaven—of lost delight!

XXXVII.

" To-morrow let us do or die!
But when the bolt of death is hurl'd,
Ah! whither then with thee to fly,
Shall Outalissi roam the world?
Seek we thy once-loved home?
The hand is gone that cropt its flowers:
Unheard their clock repeats its hours!
Cold is the hearth within their bowers!
And should we hither roam,
Its echoes, and its empty tread,
Would sound like voices from the dead!

XXXVIII.

" Or shall we cross yon mountains blue,
Whose streams my kindred nation quaff'd,
And by my side, in battle true,
A thousand warriors drew the shaft?

Ah! there in desolation cold,
The desert serpent dwells alone,
Where grass o'ergrows each mouldering bone,
And stones themselves to ruin grown,
Like me, are death-like old.
Then seek we not their camp,—for there
The silence dwells of my despair!

XXXIX.

"But hark, the trump!—to-morrow thou
In glory's fires shalt dry thy tears:
E'en from the land of shadows now
My father's awful ghost appears,
Amidst the clouds that round us roll!
He bids my soul for battle thirst—
He bids me dry the last—the first—
The only tears that ever burst
From Outalissi's soul;
Because I may not stain with grief
The death-song of an Indian chief!"

WYOMING,

AND

ITS HISTORY.

"MUCH YET REMAINS UNSUNG."

BY WILLIAM L. STONE.

NEW-YORK:
MARK H. NEWMAN.
1844.

WYOMING.

WYOMING.

CHAPTER I.

Preliminary remarks—Travelling—its facilities—Route to the Valley of Wyoming from New-York.—Muskonetcong Mountain,—Delaware Water-Gap,—Stroudsburg,—Kakatchlanamin Hills or Blue Mountains,—the Wind-Gap,—Pokono Mountains.

THE passion for travelling, so often and so habitually spoken of as a characteristic of the English people, seems to have been transmitted, with many other of their national peculiarities, to their American descendants; stimulated, moreover, to increased activity, by the vast extent, the enlarged community of interests and feelings, and the unequalled facilities for conveyance, which are united in our country. The magnificent steamboats and multitudinous rail-roads which this tendency of the American people, and the necessities of their unbounded commercial enterprise, have called into existence, afford sufficient evidence, in their number and extent, of the great amount of travel at all times in progress; but to obtain a full conception of the locomotive propensity by which the citizens are animated, it is necessary to be a passenger, during either of the summer months, on board one or another of the gigantic steamboats that ply along the principal throughfares of inland navigation—such, for instance, as the Hudson, the Delaware, or the Mississippi. If the boat of which the adventurous observer, entrusts his person should happen to be one of a line engaging at the moment in competition with a rival, and therefore presenting the temptation of a charge reduced almost to nothing, his understanding in the eagerness for travel which animates all classes sexes, and occupations, will be all the more enlarged and enlightened.

A natural consequence of this universal appetite is the zeal with which new scenes and localities are sought out, as the objects of touring industry—a zeal displayed in astonishing activity by the rich and novelty-loving travellers of England, and only in a less degree by their fellow-explorers of America. Of late years we have seen the former pushing their researches into the remotest quarters of the globe—the trackless deserts of Africa, the wild steppes and mountains of Central Asia, the sterile plains of Russia, the dark forests of Norway, the savage prairies of our Western Continent, and the far distant isles of the Pacific; and the latter, in the same spirit though with means more limited and time less entirely at their command, pushing their summer expeditions to the British Provinces and the great lakes of the North-west—not to mention the frequency with which Americans are seen or heard of among the splendid capitals of Europe, or the relics of the wonderful past in Africa and Asia.

Touching these last, no man of intelligence or of enlarged understanding will think for a moment of censuring the spirit in which journies to behold them are undertaken, probably, in the great majority of instances ; the spirit, doubtless, of liberal curiosity and a desire for knowledge. Nevertheless, it is worthy of remark that, familiar as the principal resorts of home tourists may be to thousands upon thousands of Americans—perfectly at home as they may find themselves in Washington, New-York, Philadelphia, Boston, Quebec and Montreal, and generally well informed as to the main features of the country in its different regions—there are yet very many places worthy to be visited, either on account of natural attractions, or events of which they have been the scene, or perhaps of both these causes in combination ; places rarely included within the range of annual excursions, yet rich in scenery or in recollections, worthy to be noted by the curious inquirer, and to be enjoyed by him who seeks in travel refreshment for his mind and gratification for his refined and cultivated tastes.

Such is the valley of Wyoming—exquisitely beautiful in scenery, and invested by the history of the past and the genius of poesy with attractions not less strong or enduring. Such it was found to be, greatly to his own enjoyment, by the author of this unpretending volume, in an excursion performed during the summer of 1839 ; and in the hope of inducing others to procure for themselves pleasures like those which he enjoyed, he has ventured to draw up from his notes a brief description of the scenes and objects by which he was deeply interested, and which, in his humble judgment, fairly entitle the lovely and far-famed Valley of Wyoming to a place in the "itineraries" of the United States, not less distinguished than many other localities have long possessed, whose claims, though more generally recognized, are neither more valid nor more numerous.

Another consideration has had much to do with the production of this volume—one which the author has some diffidence in stating, as its avowal may subject him, though erroneously, to the charge of literary presumption. The reader has seen in the preceding pages, that the name of Wyoming has been illustrated and adorned by the genius of a great poet, and in his lay of perfect music embalmed for everlasting fame. In extent, wherever the English language is read or spoken—in time, so long as that language shall exist, either as living or dead—the Wyoming of Campbell is and will be a creation lovely to the heart and imagination of mankind. But the poet has given to the world a creation that is only imaginary. His Wyoming is not the Wyoming of prosaic reality, nor is the tale to which he has married it in accordance with the facts of history. Of course no reproach is meant for him in making this declaration. His choice of materials and the use he made of them were governed by the purposes and necessities of his own art—not by those of the historian; and as the requirements of his own art would have been perfectly well satisfied by a total invention of incidents, so there was no obligation upon him to use any thing more than such a partial foundation of reality as would be sufficient for the ends he had in view.

But though no exception be taken to the poet for the fanciful colouring he has given to events so full of interest, it is perhaps not unwarrantable to presume that thousands of his admiring readers would desire to know the real features of that picture which, with his embellishments, appears so lovely. Such desire would almost unavoidably spring up from the natural propensity of men to seek after truth; and it would be stimulated, doubtless, by curiosity to compare the real with the imagined.

In this belief the author has found *encourage-*

ment to prepare his little volume for the public; while *motive* was furnished by the injustice done, however innocently, in the poem, to a personage of no mean celebrity, in whose character and life the author has long felt a deep interest. It will be understood, probably, that reference is made to the famous Mohawk chieftain Brant—designated in the poem, with equal wrong to his morals and his patronymic, "the monster Brandt." Coextensive with the knowledge of the poem is the wrong done to his memory by ascribing to him cruelties in which he had no share, and at the perpetration of which he was not even present; and although to the later editions of his poem Campbell has appended a note, acknowledging his error in this respect, the Thayendanegea of history is still "the monster Brandt" to thousands who derive all their knowledge of him from the deathless "Gertrude of Wyoming."

A desire to contribute something toward the rescue of the Indian warrior's fame, was prominent among the considerations that led to the production of the present work; while, independently of the interest with which the valley of Wyoming has been invested by Campbell, it is believed that the actual history of that beautiful region, limited though it be in its geographical dimensions, is sufficiently rich in incident to warrant at least a passing notice from the music of history. In the preparation of these pages, for the sake of convenience, the popular style of the tourist has occasionally been adopted.

Wyoming is a section of the valley of the Susquehanna river, situated due west of the city of New-York, distant, in a direct line, about one hundred miles. The usual route is across New-Jersey to Easton, and the Delaware river, and thence by the Wilkesbarré turnpike, through the "Wind-Gap" of the Blue Mountains, and across the wild and far-famed Pokono. A less direct but more romantic route was chosen by the writer, for the purpose of visiting the stupendous scenery of the Delaware "Water-Gap."

From New-York to Morristown by rail-road, passing through Newark, Orange, Millville and Chatham. The country is agreeably diversified with highland and plain—orchards and cultivated fields—verdant groves crowning the hills, or stretching down their sides to the Passaic river and its tributaries; their superb vegetation running down the dales, where the rich elms and willows bend their branches over the streams and fountains, affording landscape-glimpses of surpassing beauty. On the side of one of these hills, of moderate elevation, sheltered from the northwest, and looking into the valley of the sinuous Passaic, stands the modest country retreat of the Hon.

James Kent, formerly Chief Justice, and afterward Chancellor of the State of New-York. The country thence to the base of Schooley's Mountain —anciently called the Muskonetcong—rapidly assumes a rougher aspect. The hills often aspire to a more respectable size, and with the increasing altitude the farms appear less productive. Still, there are meadows and pastures "full of fresh verdure," while there is beauty to be descried in many a "winding vale" below. A brisk stream laves the eastern base of the Muskonetcong, flowing to the south, and affording abundant water-power for mills and manufactories. The ascent of the mountain is by a winding road sufficiently steep to remind one of Beattie's pathetic exclamation:—

"How hard it is to climb!"

and affording a broad and beautifully varigated landscape, as the traveller occasionally stops to breathe and look behind. The height of the mountain is probably eight hundred or a thousand feet —not above the level of the sea, but from the steppe on which it stands. At the point where it is crossed by the turnpike, the top of the mountain presents the surface of a plain, of perhaps a mile and a half in breadth. It is sufficiently rocky to require strength and patience in its cultivation, and in its primitive condition its aspect must have been most forbidding. Nevertheless the energies of man have triumphed over its original sterility, and worse looking farms may often be seen in a less rugged country.

This elevated spot has enjoyed some celebrity for more than half a century, as a watering-place, from the circumstance that a mineral spring flows from its rocks, the waters of which are esteemed excellent for bathing. There are two public houses, of ancient and respectable aspect, for the accommodation of boarders—those who desire to apply the waters of the fountain, and those who visit this place for the benefit of the elastic and invigorating mountain air. The first of the two large houses approached from the east, is *Belmont Hall*, generally patronised by the New-Yorkers. The house is embosomed in a noble grove of oaks, affording a broad and grateful shade. The other hotel is called the *Heath House*. It stands upon a delightful site, and also, like its rival, wears an aspect of patrician comfort. This house is the favorite resort of the Philadelphians. From both, and indeed from the whole mountain table, the prospect, on every hand, but especially toward the west, affords a broad and magnificent picture—extending over many a deep green valley and laughing hill, even to the Blue Mountains beyond the Delaware.

The mineral spring gushes from a rock—or rather oozes, for it has not power to gush—in a wild glen three-quarters of a mile below, toward the west. It is a lonely, romantic place, and a small bathing-house shelters the spring. The waters are slightly tinctured with iron, and are sufficiently insipid to the taste of those who have just been quaffing from the sparkling fountains of Saratoga.

The descent is along the ravine already mentioned, which is deep and shadowy, and at times, as wild as nature can make it. Emerging from the glen, the charming valley of the Muskonetcong river welcomes the traveller with a scene of placid beauty. Here, crossing the stream, the route that had been chosen diverges toward the north, through the pleasant village of Hackettstown. This section of New-Jersey is not only beautiful to the eye, but evidently fertile. As the tourist leaves the valley, climbing another range of hills, overlooking other magnificent pictures, and again descending to the bed of another clear mountain stream, the varying prospects, the free air and the bright sun, with here and there a flitting mass of cloud darkening for a moment a wood-girt hill, afford a succession of objects for delighted contemplation.

In ascending from one of these valleys, between Hackettstown and Vienna, the road crosses the Morris Canal, leading from Easton to Jersey City, opposite to New-York. It is an important work for New-York, opening, as it does, a direct passage by water to the coal mines of the Lehigh in Pennsylvania.

At the distance of some eight or ten miles from the valley of the Muskonetcong, after crossing the Pequest river, and ascending a hill which aspires to the character of a mountain, a landscape opens to the north, of singular grandeur and magnificence. The Delaware Water-Gap must be more than twenty miles distant, yet the eye, overlooking many a beautiful hill and romantic valley in the foreground, at once catches the bold outline of the cleft mountains in the distance, strongly relieved against the hoary crests of the mountains yet more remote. On the left, from the same elevation, as the eye stretches over the hills beyond the Delaware, the noble range of the Blue Mountains rises in glorious prospect.

At the next resting place, which is the town of Hope, the notice of the stranger is attracted by the peculiar construction of the inn, an ancient stone edifice, unusually large for such a purpose, and having a wide hall across either end, with a flight of steps ascending to the second story in each. It was once a Moravian Church—the United Brethren having originally planted that town, as a missionary post—and hence its name. The feet of Ziesberger and Zinzendorf, of Buettner and Rauch, have trodden that soil, and perhaps this band of self-denying apostles themselves have partaken of the sacramental cup within the very walls now affording shelter and refreshment to any that may choose to call. This, too, was within the missionary region traversed by holy Brainerd, whose principal station, while engaged as a missionary among the Indians, was at the "Forks of the Delaware," as the junction of the Delaware and Lehigh was called.* And where, now, are the dusky congregations of the Aborigines to whom they preached the everlasting Gospel? Echo answers—"*Where?*" The most war-like and noble of the New-Jersey Indians, chiefly Delawares, but some of whom were of the Five Nations, were planted in this section of New-Jersey when the white men came. Nor was the most sagacious among them without gloomy forebodings of what was to be their fate, after the pale faces should obtain a permanent foothold. A sachem of one of these Jersey clans, being observed to look with solemn attention upon the great comet which ap-

*"Whom the gods love die young," says the heathen proverb. It was so with David Brainerd, a wonderful man, who finished his work at the early age of thirty and went to his rest. His frame was slender, and having worn out his feeble constitution by excessive labor, he returned to Northampton,—to the family of the illustrious Edwards, his friend and patron—for the purpose, as he hoped, of recruiting his health,—but in reality to die. "I have often walked in the little foot-path which goes around his quiet resting-place, and even those who have dropped a tear over Martyn's grave in Persia, also drop a tear here. And here at the "Forkes" still wave the tall sycamore trees under which that self-denying man taught the tawny sons of the forest as they came around him as a father, and loved him as they loved their own souls."—*Rev. John Todd*, 1839.

peared in October, 1680, was asked what he thought was the meaning of that prodigious and wonderful object. He answered gravely—"*It signifies that we Indians shall melt away, like the snow in spring, and this country be inhabited by another people.*" The forest king was a prophet as well as a hunter.

Five miles from Hope is Autun's ferry, over which travellers are conveyed by a flat boat; and from hence it is yet seven miles to the Water-Gap, over a rugged road, but through scenery beautifully wild and romantic. The course of the road is generally upon the elevated margin of the river, bright glimpses of which often appear through the trees, like tiny lakes of liquid silver, below. At length the traveller enters the gorge of the mountains—the road winding along their base, beneath their frowning peaks—narrow, and often upon the very verge of a gulf, rendered more appalling by the dimness of the light, and his ignorance of its depth.

Geologists suppose the deep, winding chasm through this stupendous range of mountains, to have been wrought by some mighty convulsion of nature, by which the rocks were cloven, and a passage formed for the river, the waters of which must have previously flowed through some other channel. The distance from the southern entrance of the pass to the hotel, which stands upon a subdued jutting promontory, toward its northern termination, is only two miles, but at least an hour is generally employed in overcoming it, and at night the time seems two. The tourist, however, cannot enjoy to the full the grandeur of the scene, and the feelings of elevated though chastened delight incident to its contemplation, without studying it by night, as well as by day. Sensations of solemn grandeur are awakened by threading a chasm profound and solitary like this, in the gloom of night, studying the sharp outlines of the mountains against the sky, and occasionally catching a glimpse of a precipice beetling over the gulf, by the aid of a casual mass of light thrown against it by the fitful moon, and rendering the shadows below denser and more palpable.

Less thrilling, though not less sublime, and more beautiful, is the view of this wild Alpine landscape in the early morning of a bright day. The masses of naked rocks, on the eastern side of the river toward the southern gorge, rising to an elevation of eight hundred or a thousand feet, in some places as upright and smooth as though a creation of art, and at others spiked, ragged and frowning, are comparatively undistinguishable while obscured by the raven wing of night. But their dusky sublimity is greatly enhanced when revealed to the eye in their unclouded majesty and grandeur by the light of day. In the gray of the morning, before yet the sun has gilded their tops, standing upon the jutting point already mentioned as the site of the hotel, almost the entire section comprising this remarkable passage is distinctly in view,—gloomy from the yet unretreating shade,—and disclosing the abrupt sinuosities of the river, together with all the irregularities of rock and mountain incident to such a formation ;—the mountains, for the most part, clothed with wood to their summits, and the whole scene as wild and fresh as though just from the hand of nature. Low in the gulf, at the base of the mountains, a cloud of milk-white vapor sleeps upon the bosom of the river. In the course of half an hour, with a change of temperature in the superincumbent atmosphere, the vapor begins to ascend, and a gentle current of air wafts it, as by the sweet soft breathing of morn herself, without breaking the cloud, to the western side of the river. There, for a while, it hangs in angel whiteness, like a zone of silver belting the mountain. Below, along the whole course of the gulf, the sides of the mountains are yet clad in solemn and shadowy drapery, while in bright and glorious contrast, the sun having at length begun climbing the sky in good earnest, their proud crests are now glittering with golden radiance.

By climbing a mountain behind the hotel to the northwest, and looking into the chasm toward the south, a fine view of the zig-zag course of the river is afforded, down to the second turn, where its deep narrow volume is apparently brought to an end by the intervention of the buttress of rock on the Jersey shore, already adverted to. But the best position for surveying the whole pass, and enjoying its sublimity to entire satisfaction, is from a small boat paddled along leisurely upon the river through the gulf. The maps furnish no just idea of the channel of the river through the gap—the actual course resembling the sharp curvatures of an angry serpent before he is coiled, or rather, perhaps, this section of the river would be best delineated by a line like a letter S. The general height of the mountain barriers is about sixteen hundred feet. They are all very precipitous ; and while sailing along their bases in a skiff, their dreadful summits, some of them, seem actually to hang beetling over the head. This is especially the case with the Jersey mountains—the surfaces of which, next the river, as already stated, are of bare rock, lying in regular blocks, in long ranges, as even as though hewn, and laid in stratifications, like stupendous masonry—" the masonry of God !"

Not far from the hotel, among the mountains above, is a small lake, which has been dammed at the foot, and converted into a trout-pond. By opening a sluice-gate, an artificial cataract can at any time be formed by the waters of the lake, which come rushing down a precipitous rock two or three hundred feet into the embrace of the river, as though leaping for joy at their liberation. The scene of the Water-Gap, as a whole, and as a point of attraction for the lovers of nature in her wildness and grandeur, by far transcends the highlands of Hudson's river, or even the yet more admired region of the Horicon.*

Unless the tourist descends by the course of the river, twenty miles, to Easton, the route from the Water-Gap to Wyoming is by Stroudsburg, flanking the Kittaninny † Hills, being the northern spur of the Blue Mountains; thence southwest, traveling along their western side to intersect the Easton and Wilkesbarré turnpike, at a notch through that section of these mountains, called the Wind-Gap. The course is north, two and a half miles along the Delaware, to the estuary of a considerable and rapid stream, called Broadhead's Creek, by the moderns, from the name of one of the first white settlers of the country. The Indian name, far more euphonical, is Analomink. Thence west to Stroudsburg. This is a pleasantly situated village, the planting of which was commenced by a gentleman named Stroud, before the war of the American revolution. It stands upon a sweet plain,

* A doubtful Indian name of Lake George.

† Kittaninny is the modern orthography. The ancient was "the Kakatchlanamin Hills." But the name is spelt in almost as many different ways as there are books and manuscripts in which the range is mentioned.

having a mountain for an everlasting prospect on the south, between which and the village flows the Pokono Creek, descending from the mountain range of that name, and uniting with the Analomink in its neighborhood. Stroudsburg is the shire town of Monroe County. The settlements at this place, during the French war of 1755—1763, formed the northern frontier of Pennsylvania, and were within the territory of the Minisink Indians, or Monseys, as they were sometimes called. The chain of military posts erected by the colony of Pennsylvania, extending from the Delaware to the Potomac, was commenced at this point; and the celebrated chief of the Lenelenoppes, or Delaware Indians, Teedyuscung, was occasionally a resident here. This chieftain was an able man, who played a distinguished but subtle part during the border troubles of the French war, particularly toward the close of his life. He was charged with treachery toward the English, and perhaps justly; and yet candor demands the acknowledgment, that he did not take up the hatchet against them without something more than a plausible reason; while by so doing, he was the means of restoring to his people something of the dignity characteristic of his race, but which had almost disappeared under the oppression of the Six Nations. He was professedly a convert to the Moravian Missionaries. His wife was sincerely such, and became a steadfast and exemplary member of the Christian Church. But according to the journals of the missionaries themselves, as collated by Loskiel, his conduct in subsequent years reflected but little credit upon the faith of his new spiritual advisers.* Whether injustice may not have been done him in this respect also, is a question upon which much light will be thrown in a subsequent chapter. He came to a melancholy end: but it is not necessary to anticipate the progress of events, soon to be unfolded for consideration in their regular order.

The country immediately west of the Blue Mountains, at least as far in either direction as it could be viewed from the ancient tavern in the vicinity of the Gap of Æolus, is exceedingly wild and forbidding. A deep and gloomy ravine,

"Tangled with fern and intricate with thorn,"

interposes between the base of the mountain and the partially cultivated land beyond, and the moun-

* "Among those baptised in 1750 was one Tadeuskund, called Honest John by the English. His baptism was delayed some time, because of his wavering disposition. But having once been present at a baptism, he said to one of the brethren:—"I am distressed that the time is not yet come that I shall be baptised and cleansed in the blood of Christ." Being asked how he felt during the baptism, he replied:—'I cannot describe it; but I wept and trembled.' He then spoke with the Missionaries in a very unreserved manner, saying that he had been a very bad man all his life, that he had no power to resist evil, and that he had never before been so desirous to be delivered from sin, and to be made partaker of our Lord's grace, and added—'O that I were baptised and cleansed in his blood!' He evinced this fervor ever after, and was named Gideon."—*Loskiel.*

tain itself is darkly wooded, on that side, to its crest. During the first ten miles of the distance toward Wyoming the country is exceedingly hilly, and for the most part but indifferently cultivated —albeit an occasional farm presents an exception. Several of the hills are steep, and high, and broad. In the direction of Pokono Mountain the country becomes more wild and rugged—affording, of course, at every turn, and from the top of every hill, extensive prospects, and ever-changing landscapes, diversified with woodlands, cornfields, farmhouses, rocks and glens.

When the summit of Pokono is attained, the traveller is upon the top of that wild and desolate table of Pennsylvania, extending for upward of a hundred miles, between and parallel with the Delaware and Susquehanna rivers, and from twenty to thirty-five miles in breadth. Behind him is a noble landscape of wooded hills and cultivated valleys, bounded eastward and south by the Blue Mountains, which form a branching range of the Alleghanies. The Wind-Gap is distinctly and beautifully in sight. But facing westwardly, and glancing toward the north, and the south, the prospect is as dreary as naked rocks, and shrub oaks, and stunted pines and a death-like solitude can make it. The general surface is rough and broken, hills rising, and valleys sinking, by fifties, if not by hundreds, over the whole broad mountain surface. In many places, for miles, there is no human habitation in view, and no one bright or cheerful spot upon which the eye can repose. The gloom, if not the grandeur, of a large portion of this inhospitable region, is increased by the circumstance that it is almost a continuous morass, across which the turnpike is formed by a causeway of logs, insufficiently covered with earth, and bearing the appropriate name of a corduroy road.*

The next stopping place is in the valley of the Tobyhanna, a black looking tributary of the Lehigh—eight miles. Now and then, sometimes at the distance of one mile, and again at the distance of three or four, is passed a miserable human dwelling: but the country presents the same sullen, rude, uncultivable character. From the Tobyhanna to Stoddardsville, on the dreary banks of the Lehigh itself, is another eight miles of most enormous length. There are ravines, and more gentle valleys, but they are not fertile. There are hills, but they are sterile and forbidding—rough with brambles, or destitute of all comely vegetation. The waters of the Lehigh, oozing from fens and marshes, are dark and angry as the Styx. The axes of the lumbermen, and the fires repeatedly kindled to sweep over the mountains by the ruth-

* This route was first cut through by General Sullivan, for the passage of his army, in the celebrated campaign against the country of the Six Nations in 1779

less hunters, have long since destroyed the native forest-pines; and in their stead the whole country has been covered with dwarfs—oak and pine—among which, standing here and there in blackened solitude, may be seen the scathed trunk of a yet unfallen primitive. In the contemplation of such an impracticable mass of matter as this extended mountain range presents, one cannot but apply the language of Dr. Johnson relative to some portions of the highlands of Scotland, who characterizes it as matter which has apparently been the fortuitous production of the fighting elements; matter, incapable of power and usefulness, dismissed by nature from her care, or quickened only by one sullen power of useless vegetation.

CHAPTER II.

Wilkesbarré—The Landscape—Indian names of Wyoming—The Delawares and their origin—Ancient remains—The Shawanese sent to Wyoming—Relations between the Delawares and Six Nations—Indian Council at Philadelphia, in 1742—Canassateego—his speech—The Delawares driven to Wyoming—Tradition of the Delawares respecting their submission to the Six Nations—Refutation by General Harrison.

THE first glance into the far-famed Valley of Wyoming, travelling westwardly, is from the brow of the Pokono mountain range, below which it lies at the depth of a thousand feet, distinctly defined by the double barrier of nearly parallel mountains, between which it is embosomed. There is a beetling precipice upon the verge of the eastern barrier, called "Prospect Rock," from the top of which nearly the entire valley can be surveyed at a single view, forming one of the richest and most beautiful landscapes upon which the eye of man ever rested. Through the centre of the valley flows the Susquehanna, the winding course of which can be traced the whole distance. Several green islands slumber sweetly in its embrace, while the sight revels amidst the garniture of fields and woodlands, and to complete the picture, low in the distance may be dimly seen the borough of Wilkesbarré*; especially the spires of its churches.

The hotel at which the traveller rests in Wilkesbarré is upon the margin of the river, the waters of which are remarkably transparent and pure, excepting in the seasons of the spring and autumnal floods. But a few rods above a noble bridge spans the river, leading from Wilkesbarré to the opposite town of Kingston. From the observatory of the hotel a full view of the whole valley is obtained—or rather, in a clear atmosphere, the steep wild mountains, by which the valley is completely shut in, rise on every hand with a distinctness which accurately defines its dimensions,—while the valley itself, especially on the western, or opposite side of the river, presents a view of several small towns, or scattered villages, planted along, but back from the river, at the distance of a few miles apart,—the whole intervening and contiguous territory being divided into farms and gardens, with fruit and ornamental trees. Comfortable farm-houses are thickly studded over the valley; among which are not a few more ambitious dwellings, denoting by their air, and the disposition of their grounds, both wealth and taste. Midway through the valley winds the river, its banks adorned with grace-

*This compound was formed, and bestowed upon this borough as its name, in honor of *John Wilkes* and *Colonel Barre*—names famous in the annals of British politics at the time when it was planted by the whites.

ful and luxuriant foliage, and disclosing at every turn some bright spot of beauty. On the eastern side, in the rear of the borough, and for a few miles north, the dead level of the valley is rendered still more picturesque, by being broken into swelling elevations and lesser valleys, adorned in spots with groves and clumps of trees, with the ivy and other creeping parasites, as upon the river brink, clinging to their branches and adding beauty to the graceful foliage. The village or borough of Wilkesbarré, so far as the major part of the buildings are to be taken into the account, is less beautiful than it might be. Nevertheless there are a goodly number of well built and genteel houses, to which, and the pleasant gardens attached, the pretty couplet of the poet might be applied :—

> Tall trees o'ershade them, creepers fondly grace
> Lattice and porch, and sweetest flowers embrace.

The people are for the most part the sons and daughters of New-England, and have brought with them into this secluded region the simple manners and habits, and the piety of their fathers.

This valley of Wyoming is rich in its historical associations, even of days long preceding the events of the American revolution, which were the occasion of its consecration in the deathless song prefixed to the present narrative. The length of the valley, from the Lackawannock Gap, where the

Susquehanna plunges into it through a narrow defile of high rocky mountains at the north, to a like narrow pass called the Nanticoke Gap, at the south, is nearly twenty miles—averaging about three miles in width. As already mentioned, it is walled in by ranges of steep mountains of about one thousand feet in height upon the eastern side, and eight hundred feet upon the western. These mountains are very irregular in their formation, having elevated points, and deep ravines, or openings, which are called gaps. They are in general yet as wild as when discovered, and are clothed with pines, dwarf oaks and laurels, interspersed with other descriptions of woods—deciduous and evergreen.

Like many other places of which the red man has been dispossessed, and which may previously have belonged to different clans or tribes of the same race, this valley has been known by a variety of names. By the Lenelenoppes, or Delawares, its original proprietors, so far as its history is known, the valley was called *Maugh-wau-wa-me*, or *The Large Meadows*. The Five Nations, who conquered it from the Delawares, called it *S'gah-on-to-wa-no*, or *The Large Flats*. The early German missionaries, Moravians, catching the sound as nearly as they could, wrote the name *M'-cheweuwami*. Other corruptions and pronunciations succeeded, among which were *Wyomic*, *Wa-*

jomick, *Wyomink*, and lastly *Wyoming*, which will not soon be changed.*

The territory forming the states of Pennsylvania, New-Jersey, Delaware, and part of Maryland, was principally in the occupancy of the Lenelenoppes, consisting of many distinct tribes and sub-divisions, at the time of the settlement of the country by the Europeans. The name *Delaware* was given them by the English, after the name they had bestowed upon the river along which their larger towns were situated, in honor of Lord *De la Warr*.† There were indeed clans or military colonies of the Aquanuschioni, or "United People;" the Maquas or Mengwes of the Dutch, and the Iroquois of the French, but chiefly known in American history as the Five, and afterward the Six Nations, already among them, within the territory now forming both New-Jersey and Pennsylvania. But these were not large, and the Lenelenoppes, or *Original People*, as the name denotes, composed the great majority.‡

* I have two manuscript letters of Sir William Johnson, dated March 23, and 25, 1763, in both of which he writes "Skahandowana, or Wyoming." The Moravian journals forming the basis of Loskiel's history, uniformly gave the name "Wajomick."

† The Indian name of the Delaware was Maku-isk-kiskan.

‡ The Lenelenoppes, at that time, consisted of the Assumpinks, Rankokas, (Lamikas, or Chickaquaas,) Andastakas, Neshaminies, Shackmaxons, Mantas, Minisinks, and Mandes; and within what is now New-Jersey, the Narraticongs, Capitinasses, Gacheos, Munseys, and Pomptons.—*Vide Proud's Pennsylvania.*

It is said by those who are skilled in Indian researches, that the Lenelenoppes, although claiming thus to be the original people, were not the first occupants of the country in the possession of which they were found; but that they came hither from toward the setting sun,—that *terra incognita* "the great west." According to their own traditions, when on their way thence they found strong nations, having regular military defences, in the country of the Mississippi, whom they conquered. Pursuing their course toward the east, they took possession of the sea coast from the Hudson river to the Potomac, including the country of the Delaware and Susquehanna rivers, to their sources. In the allotment of their newly acquired territory, one of their tribes, the Munseys or Minisinks, planted themselves in the region between the Kittatinnunk,* or Blue Mountains, and the Susquehanna. One large division of their tribe kindled their council fire at Minisink, and another in the valley of Wyoming,—formerly occupied by the Susquehannocks,—once a powerful nation which had been exterminated by the Aquanuschioni. Whether there be any just foundation for the legends of the Delawares, as to their battles and conquests over a people so far in advance of themselves in the art of war as to have reared strong and extensive

* Another variation in the orthography of these mountains.

military works, or not, it is nevertheless certain, from the character and extent of the tumuli existing in the valley of Wyoming when taken possession of by the pale faces, and from the fact that large oaks were growing upon some of the mounds, that the country, centuries before, had been in the possession of a race of men far in advance of the Delawares in the arts of civilization and war.

There was a time when the Shawanese Indians, who had been driven from their own country, in what is now Georgia and Florida, by a nation or nations more powerful than themselves, occupied, by permission, a portion of territory at the forks of the Delaware ; but finding them to be troublesome neighbors, the Delawares, then in their greatest numbers residing farther down the river, compelled them to remove,—assigning to their use the valley of Wyoming, (whence the Munseys had returned back to the Delaware,) and a portion of the territory farther down the Susquehanna, at Shamokin. Thither the Shawanese removed—planting themselves anew at both points. They were indeed as Bancroft describes them, "a restless nation of wanderers," and for years subsequent to the commencement of the English colonies in America, their separate clans were straggling in the woods and simultaneously kindling their fires upon the waters of the Mobile, the Santee, the Schenandoah, the Ohio, Delaware and Susquehanna. In Wyoming they built their town upon the west side of the river, below the present town of Kingston, upon what are to this day called the Shawanese Flatts.*

It is difficult to determine the question as to the exact relations subsisting between the Delawares and the Five Nations, at the period under consideration. The latter, it is well known, had carried their arms south to the Tennessee, and claimed the jurisdiction of the entire country from the Sorel, in Canada, south of the Great Lakes, to the junction of the Ohio with the Mississippi, and to the Atlantic coast, from the Santee to the estuary of the Hudson, by the right of conquest. Over the Delawares they claimed, and, at times, exercised, sovereign power, in the most dictatorial and arbitrary manner, although the venerable and excellent Heckewelder, ever the champion of the Delawares, labors hard to show that the latter were never conquered by them. Brant, the celebrated Mohawk chieftain, than whose authority there is

* It was comparatively but a small clan of the Shawanese which came to the Delaware, numbering no more at the first, according to Bancroft, who cited the Logan Mss. for his authority, than sixty or eighty families Their number however, was subsequently increased, so that about the year 1732, they counted between three and four hundred warriors within the territory of Pennsylvania. It is most likely that in leaving the south the larger portion of the nation diverged to the west, on their way from he south, settling at Shawnee-town—on the Ohio,—being afterwards joined by their brethren in the Delaware country. They were certainly a people of so much consideration as to be addressed as "BROTHERS" by the Aquanuschioni.

none better upon such a subject, in a letter to the Rev. Dr. Miller of Princeton, never yet published, claimed but a *quasi* sovereignty for the Aquanuschioni over the Delawares. But there was a transaction in 1742, which shows that the latter were at that time in a situation of the most abject subordination to the Six Nations;* and Proud says this confederacy "had held sovereignty over all the Indians, both in Pennsylvania and the neighboring provinces, for a long series of years."† Though apparently a digression, the transaction referred to is nevertheless intimately connected with the history of Wyoming, and a rapid review of the incident cannot be out of place.

In the summer of 1742, an Indian council was convened in Philadelphia, upon the invitation of Lieutenant Governor George Thomas, at that time administering the government of the Proprietaries, as William Penn and his successors were styled. The council was numerously attended, large delegations being present from each of the Six Nations, excepting the Senecas. Of these there were but three chiefs at the council,—that nation having been prevented sending a stronger deputation by

* Early in the eighteenth century the Five Nations were increased to Six, by the addition of the Tuscaroras, from North Carolina. The Five Nations adopted and transplanted them on account of a similarity in their language to their own, inducing the belief that they were originally of the same stock.

† Proud's Pennsylvania, vol. ii. p. 293.

reason of a famine in their country, "so great that a father had been compelled to sacrifice a part of his family, even his own children, for the support and preservation of himself and the other part."* There seem likewise to have been no Mohawks present.† But the Delawares, several tribes of them, were represented. The chief object for the convocation of this council was "to kindle a new fire," and "strengthen the chain of friendship" with the Indians, in anticipation of a war with France. Other subjects were brought before the council for consideration. Among them, the Governor produced a quantity of goods,—being, as he remarked in his speech, a balance due the Indians for a section of the valley of the Susquehanna, "on both sides of the river," which had been purchased of the Six Nations six years before. Canassatee-go, a celebrated Onondaga chief, who was the principal speaker on the part of the Indians during the protracted sittings of the council, recognized the sale of the land. But in the course of their discussions, he took occasion to rebuke the whites for trespassing upon the unceded lands northward of the Kittochtinny Hills, and also upon the Juni-

* Opening speech of Governor Thomas to the Six Nations. Vide Colden's Canada, Appendix, p. 59.

† To illustrate, in part, the changes which Indian names undergo, in the process of writing them by different hands, it may be noted that at this council, Onondagas was spelt *Onontogos;* Cayugas, *Caiyoquos;* Oneidas, *Anoyints;* Senecas, *Jenontowanos;* Tuscaroras, *Tuscaroros.*

ata. "That country," said Canassateego, "belongs to us, in right of conquest; we having bought it with our blood, and taken it from our enemies in fair war."*

This, however, was not the principal transaction establishing the fact that the Six Nations were in the exercise of absolute power over the Delawares. On the fourth day of the council, the acting Governor called the attention of the Six Nations to the conduct of "a branch of their cousins, the Delawares," in regard to a section of territory, at the Forks of the river, which the Proprietaries had purchased of them fifty-five years before, but from which the Indians had refused to remove. The consequence had been a series of unpleasant disturbances between the white settlers and the redmen; and as the latter were ever prompt in calling upon the Proprietaries to remove white intruders from their lands, the acting Governor now in turn called upon the Six Nations to remove those Indians from the lands at the Forks, which had been purchased and paid for in good faith such a long while ago.

* In regard to this complaint of the encroachments of the white settlers upon their lands, it appears that it had been preferred before. Gov. Thomas, in reply, stated that the Proprietaries had endeavored to prevent those intrusions, and had sent magistrates expressly to remove the intruders. To which Canasseteego rejoined—"They did not do their duty; so far from removing the people, they leagued with the trespassers, and made surveys for themselves!" Thus has it been with the poor Indians always.

After three days' consideration, the Indians came again into council, when Canasseteego opened the proceedings by saying that they had carefully examined the case, and "had seen with their own eyes," that their cousins had been "a very unruly people,"and were "altogether in the wrong." They had therefore determined to remove them. Then turning to the Delawares, and holding a belt of wampum in his hand, he spoke to them as follows:

"COUSINS! Let this belt of wampum serve to chastise you! You ought to be taken by the hair of the head and shaken severely, till you recover your senses and become sober. You don't know what ground you stand on, nor what you are doing. Our brother ONAS'S* cause is very just and plain, and his intentions are to preserve friendship. On the other hand, your cause is bad; your heart far from being upright; and you are maliciously bent to break the chain of friendship with our brother Onas, and his people. We have seen with our eyes a deed signed by nine of your ancestors above fifty years ago, for this very land, and a release signed, not many years since, by some of yourselves and chiefs now living, to the number of fifteen or upward. But how came you

* *Onas*, in the Indian tongue, signifies *Pen*, and was the name by which they always addressed the Governors of Pennsylvania, in honor of its founder.

to take upon you to sell land at all? We conquered you; we made women of you; you know you are women, and can no more sell land than women. Nor is it fit you should have the power of selling lands, since you would abuse it. This land that you claim has gone through your bellies; you have been furnished with clothes, meat and drink, by the goods paid you for it; and now you want it again, like little children—as you are! But what makes you sell land in the dark? Did you ever tell us that you had sold this land? Did we ever receive any part, even the value of a pipe-shank, from you for it? You have told us a blind story,* that you sent a messenger to us to inform us of the sale; but he never came among us, nor did we ever hear any thing about it. This is acting in the dark, and very different from the conduct our Six Nations observe in the sales of land. On such occasions they give public notice, and invite all the Indians of their United Nations, and give them all a share of the presents they receive for their lands. This is the behavior of the wise United Nations. But we find you are none of our blood: you act a dishonest part, not only in this, but in other matters: your ears are ever open to slanderous reports about your brethren: you receive them with as much greediness as lewd women receive

* Referring, probably, to explanations the Delawares had attempted to give in their private consultations.

the embraces of bad men. And for these reasons, we charge you to remove instantly. We don't give you the liberty to think about it. You are women. Take the advice of a wise man, and remove immediately. You may return to the other side of the Delaware, where you came from. But we do not know whether, considering how you have demeaned yourselves, you will be permitted to live there; or whether you have not swallowed that land down your throats, as well as the land on this side. We therefore assign you two places to go to—either to Wyoming, or Shamokin. You may go to either of these places, and then we shall have you more under our eye, and shall see how you behave. Don't deliberate, but remove away, and take this belt of wampum."

This speech having been translated into English, and also into the Delaware tongue, Canassateego took another string of wampum, and proceeded:—

"Cousins! After our just reproof and absolute order to depart from the land, you are now to take notice of what we have further to say to you. This string of wampum serves to forbid you, your children and grand-children, to the latest posterity, forever, meddling with land affairs. Neither you, nor any that shall descend from you, are ever hereafter to presume to sell any land: for which purpose you are to preserve this string in memory of what your uncles have this day given you in charge. We have some other business to transact with our brethren, and therefore depart the council, and consider what has been said to you."*

There was no diplomatic mincing of words in the speech of the Onondaga chieftain. He spoke not only with the bluntness of unsophisticated honesty, but with the air of one having authority, nor dared the Delawares to disobey his peremptory command. They immediately left the council, and soon afterward removed from the disputed territory—some few of them to Shamokin,†

* Canassateego was famous as an orator and counsellor among the Onondagas, and his counsels and memory were cherished by the people of the Six Nations, for a long number of years. Dr. Franklin has somewhere related an amusing anecdote of him, the point of which lies in the circumstance of his visiting Albany once, to sell his furs, and going to church with Hans Jansen, the merchant to whom he expected to sell them. Canassateego took it into his head, during the service, that the minister was preaching about him and his furs. And he was confirmed in this opinion after church, from the fact that Jansen offered him six pence per pound less than he had done before the service. Everybody else, moreover, to whom he afterward offered to sell his furs, would only give him three and sixpence per pound after church, in stead of four shillings per pound, as had been offered before. The old chief therefore concluded that the minister had been preaching down the price of his beaver-skins, and he had no good opinion of the "black coats" afterward. It is stated by some authorities, that he was acompanied by two hundred and thirty warriors on his visit to Philadelphia to attend the council spoken of in the text.

† Shamokin was an Indian town at the junction of the east and west branches of the Susquehanna, sixty miles below Wyoming. It was a sort of military colony of the Six Nations, and the residence of the celebrated Cayuga chief Shickcalamy, or Shikellimus, the father of the yet more celebrated Logan, the chief who has been immortalized by Mr. Jeffersen in his Notes on Virginia. Shamokin stood upon the site of the present town of Northumberland, where Dr. Priestley spent the latter days of his life, and died. Logan was named after James Logan, the companion of Penn—a learned man—for a long time secretary of the colony, and greatly beloved by the Indians.

but the greater portion to Wyoming. The whole tenor of the speech, moreover, goes to establish the fact that the Delawares were the dependants—indeed the abject subjects—of the Aquanuschioni, or Mengwe, as the Six Nations have been frequently called by modern writers. But the questions how, and at what time, the Lenelenoppes were brought into such a humiliating condition, cannot be answered with precision. The Delawares themselves allege that they were *beguiled* into a surrender of their national and political manhood, and Mr. Heckewelder has attempted to sustain the pretension. According to their tradition, the Mengwe and Lenelenoppes had long been at war, and the advantages were with the latter, until for their own common safety the league of the Five Nations was formed. Strengthened by this union, the fortunes of war began to turn in their favor—especially as they were soon afterward supplied with fire-arms by the Dutch, who were now engaged in colonizing the country of the Hudson river. By the aid of fire-arms the Mengwe were enabled for a time to contend both with the Lenelenoppes and their new enemies on the north—the French; but finding themselves at length severely pressed, they hit upon the stratagem by which their older enemy was caught with guile, and disarmed by reason of his own magnanimity. Among the Indians it is held to be cowardly for a warrior to sue for peace. Having taken up the hatchet, he must retain it, however weary of the contest, until his enemy is humbled, or peace restored by some fortuitous means other than a direct application for a truce by himself. It is not so, however, with their women, who frequently become mediators, else their wars would be interminable. They often throw themselves as it were between contending tribes, and plead for peace with great pathos and effect; for notwithstanding the common opinion to the contrary, there is no people on earth among whom woman exercises greater influence than she does upon the aboriginals of America. "Not a warrior," they would say, on such occasions, "but laments the loss of a son, a brother, or a friend. And mothers, who have borne with cheerfulness the pangs of child-birth, and the anxiety that waits upon the infancy and ripening maturity of their sons, behold their promised blessings laid low upon the war-path, or perishing at the stake in unutterable torments." "In the depth of their grief, they curse their wretched existence, and shudder at the idea of child-bearing. They were wont, therefore, to conjure their warriors, on account of their suffering wives, their helpless children, their homes and their friends, to interchange forgiveness, to throw down their hatchets, and, smoking together the pipe of peace, embrace as friends those whom they had regarded only as enemies."* Appeals like these would naturally find a response, even from the most savage heart; and the Delawares allege that the Six Nations, availing themselves of this humane characteristic of the Indian race, by artful appeals to their humanity and benevolence, persuaded them, as the only means of saving the redmen from utter extinction by reason of their own frequent and bloody wars, to assume the character of WOMEN, in order that they might be qualified to act as general mediators. In reply to their objections, it was urged upon them by their dissembling foes that although it would indeed be derogatory for a small and feeble nation to assume the feminine character, a great and strong nation, of approved valor, like the Delawares, could not only take that step with impunity, but win immortal renown for their magnanimity. In an evil hour, and in a moment of blind confidence, the Delawares yielded to the importunity of the Mengwe, and formally assumed the petticoat. The ceremony, as the Delawares affirm, was performed at Albany, or rather Fort Orange, about the year 1617, in the presence of the Dutch garrison—whom they charge as having aided the Mengwe in their artful scheme to subdue without conquering them. The arrogance of the Six Nations, and the rights which they assumed over them of protection and com-

* Heckewelder, and Gordon's History of Pennsylvania.

mand, soon taught the Delawares the extent of the treachery that had been practised against them. But it was then too late.*

Such is the clumsy manner in which the Delawares endeavor to account for the degraded relation in which they so long stood in respect to the Six Nations. But "*Credat Judæus Apella.*" The story of the Six Nations has always been consistent upon the subject, viz.; that the Delawares were conquered by their arms, and were compelled "to this humiliating concession, as the only means of averting impending destruction." General William Henry Harrison, after a brief rehearsal of the tradition, and the efforts of Mr. Heckewelder to establish its truth, thus summarily and effectually disposes of the question :—"But

* Loskiel's valuable history of the Moravian missions among the American Indians, preserves an account of the negotiations between the Iroquois and the Delawares resulting in the arrangement, in detail—giving the preliminary message from the former at length. The Delawares say that immediately after they had submitted to be called *women*, that they might, as peace-makers, prevent the entire destruction of the Indian race, the Iroquois appointed a great feast, at which a solemn speech was delivered in the course of the attending ceremonies, containing three principal points. The first was a declaration that the Delawares were women, in the following words: — "We dress you in a woman's long habit, reaching down to your feet, and adorn you with ear-rings;" meaning that they should no more take up arms. The second point was thus expressed:— "We hang a calabash, filled with oil and medicines, upon your arm. With the oil you shall cleanse the ears of the other nations, that they may attend to good, and not to bad words; and with the medicines you shall heal those who are walking in foolish ways, that they may return to their senses, and incline their hearts to peace." The third point was a laconic exhortation to the pursuits of agriculture, thus:—"We deliver into your hands a plant of Indian corn and a hoe."

even if Mr. Heckewelder had succeeded in making his readers believe that the Delawares, when they submitted to the degradation proposed to them by their enemies, were influenced, not by fear, but by the benevolent desire to put a stop to the calamities of war, he has established for them the reputation of being the most egregious dupes and fools that the world has ever seen. This is not often the case with Indian sachems. They are rarely cowards, but still more rarely are they deficient in sagacity or discernment to detect any attempt to impose upon them. I sincerely wish I could unite with the worthy German, in removing this stigma upon the Delawares. A long and intimate knowledge of them in peace and war, as enemies and friends, has left upon my mind the most favorable impressions of their character for bravery, generosity, and fidelity to their engagements."*

* Discourse of Gen. William Henry Harrison, on the Aborigines of the Valley of the Ohio.

CHAPTER III.

Arrival of the Delawares at Wyoming—The Nanticokes—The Moravian Missions—Count Zinzendorf—The Assassins and the Rattle-snake—French and Indian relations—The Grass-hopper War—Shawanese flee from Wyoming to the Ohio—Teedyuscung chosen chief of the Delawares—Removes to Wyoming—Massacre at Gnadenhutten—Shawanese and Delawares join the French—Interposition of the Quakers for the restoration of peace—Indian Council at Easton—Speech of Teedyuscung—Story of Weekquehela—Treaty of peace with Teedyuscung—The embassies of Christian Frederick Post—Efforts of Sir William Johnson—Equivocal conduct of the Six Nations—Mistake of the French—General Peace with the Indians.

THE removal of the Delawares from the Forks to Wyoming was as speedy as the order to that end had been peremptory. It has been stated in a preceding page, that some years before the Wyoming Valley had been allotted, by the Delawares, to a strong clan of the Shawanese.* These latter had planted themselves upon the flats on the west bank of the river; and on their arrival at the same place, the Delawares selected, as the site of the town they were to build, the beautiful plain on the

* In his account of Zinzendorfs visit to "Wajomick" Loskiel states that "the Shawanese had been invited thither by the Iroquois, with a view to protect the silver mines said to be in the neighborhood, from the White people." No other author has noted this tradition, nor have the silver mines yet been discovered.

eastern side, nearly or quite opposite to the Shawanese town, a short distance only below the present borough of Wilkesbarré. Here was built the town of Maugh-wau-wa-me; the original of Wyoming. Meantime the Nanticoke Indians had removed from the eastern shore of Maryland to the lower part of the Wyoming Valley, which yet retains their name. "Nanticoke Falls" is a rapid on the Susquehanna, almost precipitous at one place, where the river forces its passage through a narrow gorge of the mountains, and escapes from the beautiful valley in which it had been lingering for upward of twenty miles, into a region wild with rock and glen. The Shawanese made no opposition to the arrival of their new neighbors. Indeed both clans were but tenants at will to the Six Nations, and for a season they lived upon terms sufficiently amicable.

It was during the same year that the soil of Wyoming was first trodden by the feet of a missionary of the Christian religion. The Moravians, or "United Brethren," had commenced their missions in the new world several years before,—in Georgia as early as 1734. Their benevolent labors were extended to Pennsylvania and New-York six years afterward. In 1742, their great founder and apostle, Count Zinzendorf, visited America, to look after their infant missions. He arrived at Bethlehem, near the Forks of the Delaware, in the following year. Affecting representations of the deplorable moral condition of the Indians had reached the count before he left Germany, and his attention was early directed to their situation, and their wants, while visiting the missionary stations along the Delaware. He made several journies among the Indians deeper in the interior, and succeeded without difficulty in establishing a friendly intercourse with various tribes. In one of these journies he plunged through the wilderness into the valley of Wyoming, for the purpose of establishing a missionary post in the town of the Shawanese. It was here, during the autumn of that year, that one of those beautiful and touching incidents occurred, which add a charm to the annals of the missionary enterprise.

The count had expected to be accompanied by an interpreter, celebrated in all the Indian negotiations for many years of that age, named Conrad Weiser, whose popularity was equally great among the Indians of all nations by whom he was known. But Weiser was unable to go. Inflexible in his purpose, however, the count determined to encounter the hazards of the journey, with no other companions than a missionary, named Mack, and his wife. On their arrival in the valley, they pitched their tents on the bank of the river, a short distance below the town of the Shawanese ; at that period the most distrustful and savage of the Pennsylvania Indians. A council was called to hear their errand of mercy, but the Indians were not exactly satisfied as to the real object of such an unexpected visit. They knew the rapacity of the white people for their lands; and they thought it far more probable that the strangers were bent upon surveying the quality of these, than that they were encountering so many hardships and dangers, without fee or reward, merely for the future well being of their souls. Brooding darkly upon the subject, their suspicions increased, until they resolved upon the assassination of the count; for which purpose executioners were detailed, who were instructed to carry their purpose into effect with all possible secrecy, lest the transaction, coming to the ears of the English, should involve them in a yet graver difficulty.

The count was alone in his tent, reclining upon a bundle of dry weeds, designed for his bed, and engaged in writing, or in devout meditation, when the assassins crept stealthily to the tent upon their murderous errand. A blanket-curtain, suspended upon pins, formed the door of his tent, and by gently raising a corner of the curtain, the Indians, undiscovered, had a full view of the venerable patriarch, unconscious of lurking danger, and with the calmness of a saint upon his benignant features. They were awe-stricken by his appearance. But this was not all. It was a cool night in September and the count had kindled a small fire for his comfort. Warmed by the flame, a large rattle-snake had crept from its covert, and approaching the fire for its greater enjoyment, glided harmlessly over one of the legs of the holy man, whose thoughts, at the moment, were not occupied upon the grovelling things of earth. He perceived not the serpent, but the Indians, with breathless attention, had observed the whole movement of the poisonous reptile ; and as they gazed upon the aspect and attitude of the count, and saw the serpent offering him no harm, they changed their minds as suddenly as the barbarians of Malta did theirs in regard to the shipwrecked prisoner who shook the viper from his hand without feeling even a smart from its venomous fang. Their enmity was immediately changed into reverence ; and in the belief that their intended victim enjoyed the special protection of the Great Spirit, they desisted from their bloody purpose and retired.* Thenceforward the count was regarded by the Indians with the most profound veneration. The arrival of Conrad Weiser soon afterward afforded every facility for free communication with the sons of the forest,

* This interesting incident was not published in the count's memoirs, lest, as he states, the world should think that the conversions that followed among the Indians were attributable to their superstitions. Mr. Chapman, in his History of Wyoming, has preserved the story—having, as he says, received it from one who was a companion of the count, and who accompanied him, [the author] to Wyoming.

and the count remained among them twenty days. Some time afterward several of the Moravian brethren visited the valley and formed an agreeable acquaintance with the Indians, especially with the chiefs of the Nantikoke tribe, one of whom, eighty-seven years old, was a remarkably intelligent man.* The result was the establishment of a regular mission post there, which was successfully maintained for several years, and until broken up by troubles as extraordinary in their origin as they were fatal to the Indians engaged in them.

The treaty of Aix-la Chapelle, which in 1748 put an end to the French war in Europe, proved to be only a truce between France and Great Britain; and from the movements of the former, it required no remarkable degree of sagacity to foresee that the sword would soon be drawn again, and the contest chiefly waged, and perhaps decided, in the wild woods of America. It was even so. The storm broke forth upon the banks of the Ohio in 1754, and was ended on those of the St. Lawrence in 1763. Preparatory to this contest, the arts of the French, and their Jesuit missionaries, were all put in requisition to secure the friendship and alliance of the Indians. The influence of the Jesuits, among the Indians of the Ohio and upper lakes, was unbounded: and the

* Loskiel.

Shawanese of the Ohio, always haters of the English, were easily persuaded to take up the hatchet at the first sound of the bugle. In anticipation of hostilities, they early invited their brethren, settled in the valley of Wyoming, to join them. These latter were little better disposed towards the English than their brethren deeper in the woods; and but for the new ties that bound the Moravian converts to their church, the invitation would have been promptly accepted.

It was not long, however, before an incident occurred, which not only sundered their Christian relations, but facilitated the removal of all who were able to get away. This incident was a sudden out-break of hostilities between this secluded clan of the Shawanese, and their Delaware neighbors on the other side of the river, the immediate cause of which was the most trivial that can be imagined; in this respect without its parallel in history, unless such parallel is to be found in the celebrated controversy between the virulent factions of the Prasini and the Veniti, in Italy, which began by a distinction of colors in ribands.* Its consequences, too, were the most bloody, for the numbers engaged, of any war, probably, that was ever waged. It happened thus:—On a certain day, the warriors of both clans being engaged

* Vide Dean Swift's "Argument against abolishing Christianity."

in the chase upon the mountains, a party of the Shawanese women and children crossed to the Delaware side to gather wild fruit. In this occupation they were joined by some of the Delaware squaws, with their children. In the course of the day, the harmony of the children was interrupted by a dispute respecting the possession of a large grasshopper, probably with parti-colored wings. A quarrel ensued, in which the mothers took part with their children respectively. The Delaware women being the most numerous, the Shawanese were driven home, several being killed upon both sides. On the return of their husbands from hunting, the Shawanese instantly espoused the cause of their wives, and arming themselves, crossed the river to give the Delawares battle. The latter were not unprepared, and a battle ensued, which was long and obstinately contested, and which, after great slaughter upon both sides, ended in the defeat of the Shawanese, and their expulsion from the valley. They retired among their more powerful brethren on the Ohio, by whom, as already mentioned, they had been invited to remove thither, with them to espouse the cause of the French.

This exploit of the Delawares, becoming noised abroad, went far to relieve them of the reproach under which they had so long been lying, of being "WOMEN."* They were now the principal

* According to Loskiel, a treaty was negotiated between the Iroquois

occupants of the valley—entirely so, indeed, with the exception of the small community of Naticokes who were settled at its lower extremity—and their numbers were rapidly increased by those of their own people who were retreating before the onward march of civilization in the Minisink country of the Delaware. Among these accessions to their community were many from the vicinity of Friedhenshal, Bethlehem, Guadhenthal, Nazareth, Nain, and Gnadenhutten,* the Moravian settlements in the region of the junction, or Forks, of the Delaware and Lehigh. Some of them were converts to the Moravian church; and a constant intercourse was thereafter maintained by way of what is to this day known as the "Indian Walk" across the mountains, between the Indians living at and in the vicinity of Gnadenhutten, and those of Wyoming. As the storm of war with the French drew near, the Indians in their interest began to hover upon the borders of the white settlements, and particularly upon those of the Delaware tribes, which yet adhered to the interests of the English. The Delaware chief at Wy-

and the Delawares in 1755, when the former were soliciting the assistance of the latter, by which the woman's dress of the Delaware nation was shortened so as to reach only to their knees, and a hatchet was given into their hands by way of defence.

* "Huts of Mercy," a settlement founded by the Moravians chiefly for the accommodation and protection of those Indians who embraced their faith.

oming was Tadame, of whom, at this day, but little is known. He was however treacherously murdered by some of the hostile Indians from the northwest; whereupon a general council of the Delawares was convened, and Teedyuscung, of whom mention has already been made, was chosen chief sachem, and duly proclaimed as such. He was residing at Gnadenhutten at the time of his advancement, but immediately removed to Wyoming, which then became the principal seat of the Delawares. Not long afterward a small fort upon the Lehigh, in the neighborhood of Gnadenhutten, was surprised by a party of Indians, and white men disguised as such, its little garrison massacred, the town of Gnadenhutten sacked and burnt,—many of its inhabitants, chiefly Christian Indians, being slain. Numbers of them perished in the flames, while the survivors escaped and joined their brethren at Wyoming.*

It was not long after the actual commencement of hostilities between the English colonists and the French troops, and their Indian allies upon the

* Chapman. It was at about this period of time, according to the same author, that the Nanticokes, never particularly friendly to the English, removed from Wyoming farther up the river to a place called Chemunk [Chemung?] After this removal, hearing that the graves of their fathers, on the eastern shore of Maryland, were about being invaded by the plough-shares of the pale-faces, they sent a deputation back to their native land, who disinterred the remains of their dead, and conveyed them to their new place of residence, where they were again buried with all the rites and ceremonies of savage sepulture. This is a beautiful instance of filial piety, deserving of remembrance.

banks of the Ohio, before Shamokin was attacked by the Indians, and the white settlement destroyed. Fourteen whites were killed, several made prisoners, and the houses and farms plundered. The Delawares now began to waver under the smarting of ancient grievances, and the artful appliances and appeals of the French ; and with the fall of General Braddock and the destruction of his army, they revolted in a body, and went over to the common enemy. They were immediately induced to change their relations, by the strong assurances of the French that the war was in fact undertaken in their behalf, for the purpose of driving away the English, and restoring the red man once more to the full and entire possession of the country of which he had been robbed.*

A sanguinary war, upon the borders both of Pennsylvania and Virginia, immediately followed the secession of the Delawares, and if they were "women," in the popular Indian acceptation, before, they wielded no feminine arms in the new attitude they had so suddenly assumed. Their blows fell thick and fast; their hatchets were red; and their devastations of the frontier settlements were frequent and cruel. Governor Morris wrote to General Shirley on the 3d of December, 1755,

* Chapman. See, also, an interesting journal of Christian Frederick Post, while on a pacific mission to the Delawares and Shawanese, which has been preserved in the appendix to Proud.

—"to our great surprise the Delawares and Shawanese have taken up the hatchet against us, and with uncommon rage and fury carried on a most barbarous and cruel war, burning and destroying all before them, and in a short space of time have been able to lay waste a considerable tract of country, extending a vast length from beyond the Apalaccian Hills in Virginia, to the river Delaware, and it may be expected that they will next fall on Jersey, and perhaps New-York, as they follow the chain of mountains that we call the Blue Hills, which take their rise in New-England."* The storm was as fearful as it was unexpected to the Pennsylvanians; for however much familiarized Virginia and most of the other colonies had become to savage warfare, Pennsylvania, until now, had been comparatively and happily exempt. For more than seventy years a strict amity had existed between the early English settlers and their successors in Pennsylvania and New-Jersey,† and the breaking forth of the war created the greater consternation on that account.

It appears that the Quakers,—a people, by the way, who have at all times manifested a deep solicitude for the welfare of the Indians, and whose benevolent principles and gentle manners have,

* MS. letter from Robert H. Morris, Governor of Pennsylvania, to General Shirley.

† Proud.

in all critical emergencies, more than any thing else, won the red man's confidence,—had previously discovered some uneasiness among the Indians, connected with certain land questions, in respect of which they were not quite clear that injustice had not been done their red brethren of the forest. While, therefore, the government was making such preparations as it could for the common defence, great and persevering efforts were made, under the urgent advisement of the Quakers, to win back the friendship of the Delawares, as also that of the Shawanese. It was the opinion of these good people, as just intimated, that in their revolt the Delawares had been moved by wrongs, either real or fancied,—and if the latter, not the less wrongs to their clouded apprehensions, —in regard to some of their lands. A pacific mission to the Delawares and Shawanese was therefore recommended and strongly urged by them, and the project was acceded to by Governor Morris; but he refused to set the mission on foot until after he had issued a formal declaration of war.* The Quakers were strongly opposed to this measure, and so was Sir William Johnson, who judged that pacific relations might be more easily restored without resorting to a declar-

* Memorial of the Quakers to Governor Denny, who had succeeded Mr. Morris in the government of the Proprietaries in 1756. See Proud, vol. ii. Appendix.

ation, than afterward, and privately remonstrated against it.* Difficulties meantime increased, and the ravages of the frontiers were continued, until the war-path flowed with blood. Governor Morris, in a letter to Sir William Johnson justifying his declaration, said:—"You cannot conceive what havoc has been made by the enemy in this defenceless province, nor what number of murders they have committed, what a vast tract of territory they have laid waste, and what a multitude of inhabitants, of all ages and both sexes, they have carried into captivity. By information of several of the prisoners who have made their escape from them, I can assure you that there are not less than three hundred of our people in servitude to them and the French on the Ohio. At first they appeared in small parties, and committed their outrages where they could do it with more safety to themselves. But of late they have penetrated into the inhabited part of the country in larger bodies, and have defeated several detachments of our armed forces; carried and laid waste whole counties, and spread great terror amongst us."†

The influence of Sir William Johnson and of the Six Nations, with the Delawares, was invoked by the Pennsylvanians, and several of the Chiefs of the confederacy, with Colonel Claus, and Andrew

* Johnson MSS. in the author's possession.

† MS. letter among the Johnson papers.

Montour, Sir William's secretary and interpreter, visited Philadelphia upon that business.* The parent government likewise urged the representatives of the Proprietaries to renew their Indian negotiations, and if possible arrive at a better understanding with them, by defining explicitly the lands that had been actually purchased.†

These pacific dispositions were so far attended with success that two Indian councils were held at Easton, in the Summer and Autumn of 1756. The first, however, was so small, being attended by only twenty-four Indians, that no business was transacted other than the giving and receiving of explanations, and the adoption of such arrangements as it was hoped would lead to a pacific result. The chief and master-spirit of the Indians was Teedyuscung, claiming to be king of the Delawares, and being acknowledged by them as such. He was the bearer of a belt to the Delawares from the Six Nations, urging them to lay down the hatchet,‡ and he claimed to represent ten nations in the council. From the information elicited at

* Memorial of the Quakers, already cited. † Chapman.

‡ Strangely enough Loskiel asserts, repeatedly, that the Delawares and Shawanese had been instigated to these hostilities against the English by the Six Nations. The proof is conclusive,—rendered more conclusive than ever by the Johnson manuscripts,—that the Six Nations did all in their power to assist them, and afterward to aid in the restoration of peace. But the good Moravians always looked with an eye of strong partiality upon the Delawares, and with the opposite feeling upon the Six Nations. I have the manuscript journals of these councils before me at large—and they are long and full.

this council, it appeared that Teedyuscung had been the chief agent in exciting the Delawares and Shawanese to hostilities, and that he had but recently returned from a visit to the French garrison at Niagara, at which place he had been treated with marked attention. Still, in reference to the pacific messages by which he had been invited to the council, he declared "that they had touched his heart, and given him abundance of joy." The discussions were continued several days, in the most amicable spirit, and an arrangement was made by virtue of which Teedyuscung was to visit the remote hostile Indians, and bring them in greater numbers to attend a council to be held in the approaching Autumn. He was not as successful in his efforts to induce the Indians to meet in the proposed council,as it was hoped he would be, yet it took place in November, although it appears to have been confined to the Delawares of the Susquehanna—those of that nation who had previously emigrated to the Ohio, and the Shawanese, not being represented. The council was conducted by Lieutenant Governor Denny on the part of the colony, and by Teedyuscung on behalf of the Indians; and he appears to have managed his case with the energy of a man and the ability of a statesman. If his people had cowered like cravens before the rebukes of the Six Nations, in the council of 1742, their demeanor was far otherwise on this occasion.* Having, by joining the Shawanese and the French, thrown off the vassalage of the Six Nations, and become an independent, as well as a belligerent power, they now met the pale faces, and a deputation of the Six Nations who were present, with the port and bearing of men.

On being requested by the Governor to state the causes of their uneasiness and subsequent hostilities, Teedyuscung enumerated several. Among them were the abuses committed upon the Indians in the prosecution of their trade; being unjustly deprived of portions of their lands; and in the execution, long before, in New-Jersey, of a Delaware chief, named Wekahelah, for, as the Indians alleged, accidentally killing a white man—a transaction which they said they could not forget.†

* At this council, Teedyuscung insisted upon having a secretary of his own selection appointed, to take down the proceedings in behalf of the Indians. The demand was considered extraordinary, and was opposed by Governor Denny. The Delaware chief, however, persisted in his demand, and it was finally acceded to. Teedyuscung therefore appointed Charles Thompson, Master of the Free Quaker School in Philadelphia, as the secretary for the Indians. This was the same Charles Thompson who was afterwards secretary to the Old Congress of the revolution—who was so long continued in that station—and who died in the year 1824, aged 94 years—full of years and honors. The Indians adopted him and gave him a name signifying—" The Man of Truth."

† Weekweela, Wekahela, or Weekquehela, was an Indian of great consideration, both among the Christian and Pagan Indians. He resided, with his clan, upon South river, near Shrewsbury, in East Jersey, and lived in a style corresponding with that of affluent white men. He had a large farm, which was well cultivated and stocked with cattle and horses: his house was large, and furnished after the English manner, with chairs, feather beds, curtains, &c., &c. He had also servants, and was the owner of slaves. He likewise mingled with good society, and was the guest

When the Governor desired specifications of the alleged wrongs in regard to their lands, Teedyuscung replied: "The Kings of England and France have settled or wrought this land so as to coop us up as if in a pen."—"I have not far to go for another instance. This very ground that is under me, (striking it with his foot,) was my land and inheritance; and is taken from me by fraud. When I say this ground, I mean all the land lying between Tohiccon Creek and Wyoming, on the river Susquehanna. I have not only been served so in this government, but the same thing has been done to me as to several tracts in New-Jersey, over the river." When asked what he meant by *fraud*, Teedyuscung replied:—"When one man had formerly liberty to purchase land, and he took the deeds from the Indians, and then dies, and after his death his children forge a deed like the true one, with the same Indian names to it, and thereby take lands from the Indians which

of governors and other distinguished men. Unfortunately, about the year 1728, Captain John Leonard purchased a cedar swamp of some other Indians, which Weekquehela claimed as belonging to him. Leonard disregarded his claim, and persisted in occupying the land. A quarrel ensued, and Weekquehela shot him dead as a trespasser—not, however, upon the disputed territory, but while he was walking one day in his garden. The chief was arrested by the civil authorities, and tried and executed for murder at Amboy. Such is substantially the story as related in Smith's History of New-Jersey. The Indians claimed that Weekquehela's gun went off by accident; and the Six Nations, in a speech delivered at Lancaster in the year 1757, not only affirmed this, but maintained that the Indian went himself and with great grief communicated the circumstance to the widow—surrendering himself up voluntarily to the civil authorities.

they never sold, this is fraud." "Also, when one chief has land beyond the river, and another chief has land on this side, both bounded by rivers, mountains, and springs, which cannot be moved, and the Proprietaries, ready to purchase lands, buy of one chief what belongs to another. This likewise is fraud." "When I had agreed to sell certain lands to the old proprietor by the course of the river, the young proprietors came and got it run by a straight course by the compass, and by that means took in double the quantity intended to be sold." This he thought was fraud. He said the Delawares had never been satisfied with the conduct of the latter since the treaties of 1737, when their fathers sold them the lands on the Delaware. He said that although the land sold was to have gone only "*as far as a man could go in a day and a half from Nashamony Creek*," yet the person who measured the ground did not *walk*, but *ran*. He was, moreover, as they supposed, to follow the winding bank of the river, whereas he went in a straight line. And because the Indians had been unwilling to give up the land as far as the walk extended, the Governor then having the command of the English sent for their cousins the Six Nations, who had always been hard masters to them, to come down and drive them from their land. When the Six Nations came down, the Delawares met them at a great treaty held at the

Governor's house in Philadelphia, for the purpose of explaining why they did not give up the land; but the English made so many presents to the Six Nations, that their ears were stopped. They would listen to no explanation; and Canassateego had moreover abused them, and called them women. The Six Nations had, however, given to them and the Shawanese, the lands upon the Susquehanna and the Juniata for hunting grounds, and had so informed the Governor; but notwithstanding this, the whites were allowed to go and settle upon those lands.* Two years ago, moreover, the Governor had been to Albany to buy some land of the Six Nations, and had described their purchase *by points of compass*, which the Indians did not understand, including lands both upon the Juniata and the Susquehanna, which they did not intend to sell. When all these things were known to the Indians, they declared they would no longer be friends to the English, who were trying to get all their country away from them. He however as-

* In a speech delivered by one of the chiefs of the Six Nations, at a council held with them at Lancaster, in 1757, this last assertion of Teedyuscung was confirmed, as follows:—"Brothers: You desired us to open our hearts, and inform you of every thing we know, that might give rise to the quarrel between you and our nephews and brothers:—That, in former times our forefathers conquered the *Delawares*, and put petticoats on them; a long time after that they lived among you, our brothers; but upon some difference between you and them, we thought proper to remove them, giving them lands to plant and to hunt on, at *Wyoming* and *Juniata*, on *the Susquehanna*; but you, covetous of land, made plantations there, and spoiled their hunting grounds; they then complained to us, and we looked over those lands, and found their complaints to be true."

sured the council that they were nevertheless glad to meet their old friends the English again, and to smoke the pipe of peace with them. He also hoped that justice would be done to them for all the injuries they had received."*

The council continued nine days, and Governor Denny appears to have conducted himself with so much tact and judgment, as greatly to conciliate the good will of the Indians. By his candid and ingenuous treatment of them, as some of the Mohawks afterward expressed it, "he put his hand into Teedyuscung's bosom, and was so successful as to draw out the secret, which neither Sir William Johnson nor the Six Nations could do."† The result was a reconciliation of the Delawares of the Susquehanna with the English, and a treaty of peace, upon the basis that Teedyuscung and his people were to be allowed to remain upon the Wyoming lands, and that houses were to be built for them by the Proprietaries.‡ There were, however, several matters left unadjusted, although the Governor desired that every difficulty should then be discussed, and every cause of complaint,

* In the first edition of this work, I was indebted to Proud for an outline of this speech of the Delaware King; but I have since discovered a manuscript journal of the entire proceedings of this council among the manuscripts of Sir William Johnson. Chapman was in error in supposing it to have been a general council, and that the Ohio Indians were included in the peace.

† Memorial of the Quakers to Governor Denny.

‡ Journal of Christian Frederick Post—note by Proud.

as far as he possessed the power, be removed. But Teedyuscung replied that he was not empowered, at the present time, to negotiate upon several of the questions of grievance that had been raised, nor were all the parties interested properly represented in the council. He therefore proposed the holding of another council in the following spring, at Lancaster. This propositon was acceded to; and many Indians collected at the time and place appointed. Sir William Johnson despatched a deputation of the Six Nations thither, under the charge of Colonel Croghan, the Deputy Superintendent of the Indians; but for some reason unexplained, neither Teedyuscung nor the Delawares from Wyoming attended the council, though of his own appointment. Col. Croghan wrote to Sir William, however, that the meeting was productive of great good in checking the war upon the frontier; and in a speech to Sir William, delivered by the Senecas in June following, they claimed the credit, by their mediation, of the partial peace that had been obtained. The conduct of Teedyuscung on that occasion was severely censured by Sir William, in a speech to the Onondagas, Cayugas, and Senecas; and the latter were charged by the baronet to take the subject in hand, and "talk to him," and should they find him in fault, "make him sensible of it."*

* Manuscripts of Sir William Johnson in the author's possession.

But the Delawares and the Shawanese of the Alleghany and Ohio were yet upon the war-path, and although the horrors of the border warfare were somewhat mitigated by the peace with Teedyuscung, they were by no means at an end. More especially were the frontiers of Virginia exposed to the invasions of the Shawanese. Efforts for a more general pacification were therefore continued, under the auspices of the Quakers. Indeed these people, in whatever related to Indian affairs, formed almost an independent branch of the Pennsylvania government. They enjoyed more of the confidence of the Indians than the officers of the government did; especially of Teedyuscung; and in their great solicitude to protect the red man's interests, they not unfrequently embarrassed the designs and proceedings of the governor.* But the French were strongly posted at Venango and Fort Du Quesne; and they were assiduous and plausible in cultivating the friendship of the Indians, and lavish in their presents. It was consequently a difficult matter to obtain access to the Indian towns thickly studding the more western rivers, or to induce the tribes to open their ears to any body but the French.

A most fitting and worthy agent to bear a message of peace to those Indians, was, however,

* MS. letters of Governor Denny to Sir William Johnson.

found in the person of Christian Frederick Post. He was a plain, honest German, of the Moravian sect, who had resided seventeen years with the Indians, a part of which period had been passed in the valley of Wyoming, and he had twice married among them. He was therefore well acquainted with the Indian character, and was intimately known to many, both Shawanese and Delawares, who had also resided at Wyoming. The service required of him was alike severe and arduous. A dreary wilderness was to be traversed, ravines threaded and mountains scaled; and when these obstacles were surmounted, even if he did not meet with a stealthy enemy before, with his life in his hand he was to throw himself into the heart of an enemy's country—and that enemy as treacherous and cruel, when in a state of exasperation, as ever civilized man has been doomed to encounter. But Christian Frederick Post entered upon the perilous mission with the courage and spirit of a Christian. Accompanied by two or three Indian guides, he crossed the rivers and mountains twice in the summer and autumn of 1758, visited many of the Indian towns, passed and repassed the French fort at Venango, and held a council with the Indians almost under the guns of Fort Du Quesne, where was a garrison, at that time, of about ten thousand men. Far the greater part of the Indians received him with friendship, and his message of peace with gladness. They had such perfect confidence in his integrity and truth, that every effort of the French to circumvent him was unavailing. They kept a captain and more than fifteen soldiers hanging about him for several days, watching his every movement, and listening to all that was said; and various schemes were devised at first to make him prisoner and ultimately to take his life; but although one of his own guides had a "forked tongue," and was seduced from him at fort Du Quesne, yet the Indians upon whom he had thrown himself, with so much confidence and moral courage, interposed for his counsel and protection in every case of danger, and would not allow a hair of his head to be injured. He was charged with messages both from Teedyuscung and Governor Denny. To the former they would not listen for a moment. Indeed that chieftain seemed to be the object of their strong dislike, if not of their positive hate. They would therefore recognize nothing that he had done at Easton; but they received the message of the Governor with the best possible feeling. It was evident from all their conversations with Christian Post, whose Journal is as artless as it is interesting, that they had been deceived by the representations of the French, and deluded into a belief that, while it was the intention of the English to plunder them of all their lands, the

French were themselves actuated solely by the benevolent motive of driving the English back across the water, and restoring the Indians to all the possessions which the Great Spirit had given them.* Convinced by Post of the fraud that had been practised upon their understandings, their yearnings for peace gathered intensity every day. Several times, during his conversations with the chiefs of different towns, as he undeceived them in regard to the real designs of the French, their minds seemed filled with melancholy perplexity. A conviction of what was not wide of the truth flashed upon them, and once at least, the apprehension was uttered that it was but a struggle between the English and French, which should possess their whole country, after the Indians had been exterminated between them. "Why do not the great kings of England and France," they inquired, "do their fighting in their own country, and

* In the course of the speech by one of the Six Nations, delivered at the Council at Lancaster in 1757, cited in a preceding note, it was said in reference to the influence which the French had acquired over the Delawares and Shawanese: "At this time our cousins the Delawares carried on a correspondence with the *French*; by which means the *French* became acquainted with all the causes of complaint they had against you; and as your people were daily incroaching their settlements, by these means you drove them back into the arms of the *French*; and they took the advantage of spriting them up against you, by telling them, '*Children*, you see, and we have often told you, how the *English*, your brothers, would serve you; they plant all the country, and drive you back; so that in a little time, you will have no land; it is not so with us; though we build trading-houses on your land, we do not plant it, we have our provisions from over the great water.'"

not come over the great waters to fight on our hunting grounds?" The question was too deep for honest Christian Frederick Post to answer. However, the inclination of the Indians was decidedly toward the English, and the result of his second embassy, in the autumn of 1758, after encountering fresh difficulties and dangers, was a reconciliation with the Indians of the Ohio country, in consequence of which the French were obliged to abandon the whole of that territory to General Forbes, after destroying with their own hands the strong fortress of Du Quesne.

Great, however, as was the influence of Christian Frederick Post with the western Delawares and Shawanese, he is by no means entitled to the entire credit of bringing about a peace. The efforts of Sir William Johnson were incessantly directed to the same end, and were not without their effect. The fact was, the French were omitting no exertions to win the Six Nations from their alliance with the English. In this design they were partially successful, and the British Indian Superintendent, great as was his influence with the red men, had his hands full to prevent the mass of the Six Nations from deserting him, during the years 1756 and 1757, and joining the French. True, the Mohawks, Oneidas and Tuscaroras maintained their allegiance to the British crown, and were not backward upon the war-path;

but the Onondagas, Cayugas and Senecas, against the strongest remonstrances of Sir William, declared themselves neutral; while large numbers of the Senecas and Cayugas actually took up the hatchet with the western Indians, in alliance with the French.*

The defection probably would have been greater, but for circumstances that occurred at Fort Du Quesne, late in the year 1757, and in the beginning of the following year. These circumstances, which will be presently explained, while they evinced the absence, for a time, of the usual tact and sagacity of the French, had admirably opened the way for Christian Post's mission, also having the effect of at once relieving Sir William Johnson from his embarrassing position in regard to the equivocal attitude of three of the Six Nations. It has been seen that Sir William had interposed, not only directly but through the means of some of his Indians, in producing the partial peace with the Delawares and Teedyuscung. The baronet had also succeeded in forming an alliance with the Cherokees, some of whom had gone upon the war-path in the neighborhood of Fort Du Quesne. These were now likewise exerting themselves to detach the western Indians, as far as might be, from the French.†

It was in this posture of affairs that, late in the

* MSS. of Sir William Johnson. † Idem.

year 1757, a war-party of the Twightwees, (Miamies,) in a frolic close by the fortress of Du Quesne, killed a number of the cattle belonging to the French troops in the fort. In a moment of exasperation, without pausing to reflect upon the consequences, the French fired upon the aggressors, and killed some ten or twelve of their number. The Twightwees were deeply incensed at this outrage, and the western Indians sympathized with them at the loss of their braves. It was not long, probably, before their resolution was taken, not only to withdraw from the French service, but to avenge the untimely fall of their warriors.*

While the Twightwees were thus brooding over this wrong, the Delawares intercepted a French despatch, in which the project was proposed and discussed, of cutting off and utterly exterminating the Six Nations—forming, as they did, so strong a barrier between the French and English colonies. The Indians found some one among themselves to read the document, and they no sooner understood its full purport than they repaired to the fortress in a body, and charged the project home upon the commander. That officer was either confused, or he attempted to dissemble. He like-

* MSS. of Sir William Johnson.

wise tried, but without success, to obtain the document from them. They kept it, and its contents were the occasion of wide-spread consternation among the Indians. But this is not all. In March, 1758, a deputation of the Senecas waited upon Sir William Johnson, with a message from the Delawares, the purport of which was, that the French had recently convened a great council of the north-western Indians at Detroit, at which the same project of exterminating the Six Nations was proposed and discussed. The pretext urged upon them by the French was, that the Six Nations were wrongfully claiming the territory of their western brethren, and were they to be crushed and extinguished, there would be no more difficulty upon the subject. The western Indians would come into the full enjoyment of their own again, without question as to jurisdiction. They therefore proposed that all the Indians should join them "in cutting off the Six Nations from the face of the earth." This proposition startled the Delawares, who, after the council, determined to apprize the Senecas of the plot, and send to them the hatchet which they had recieved from the French to use against the English. They desired the Senecas to keep the hatchet for them, as they were determined not to use it again, unless by direction of their cousins. Having received the message and the hatchet, the Senecas called a council to deliberate upon the subject. The hatchet they had resolved to throw into deep water, where it could not be found in three centuries, and they now came to Sir William with the information, and for counsel. It was a favorable moment for the baronet, and the opportunity was not suffered to pass unimproved. It so happened that the information was in full confirmation of the predictions which Sir William had many times uttered to the Indians, in his efforts to prevent any friendly intercourse between them and the French. These predictions the Senecas, in their present troubles, remembered with lively impressions of the baronet's sagacity; and the result of the interview was an entire alienation of the Senecas and Cayugas from the French.*

On the 19th of April following, the Shawanese and Delawares of Ohio sent a message of peace to Sir William. A council of the Mohawks was immediately convened, at the suggestion of the baronet, and it was determined, in the event of war, that the Shawanese and Delawares should once more find an asylum from the French at Venango and Fort Du Quesne in the valley of Wyoming. But the evacuation, by the French, of the Ohio country, soon afterward, as already mentioned, rendered no such formal removal necessary.† Meantime another and much larger council was

* MSS. of Sir William Johnson.

† Idem.

holden at Easton, late in the autumn of 1758, at which all the Six Nations, and most of the Delaware tribes, the Shawanese, the Miamies and some of the Mohickanders were represented. The number of Indians assembled was about five hundred. Sir William Johnson was present, and the governments of Pennsylvania and New-Jersey were likewise represented. Teedyuscung assumed a conspicuous position as a conductor of the discussions, at which the Six Nations were disposed for a time to be offended—reviving again their claim of superiority. But the Delaware chief was not in a humor to yield the distinction he had already acquired, and he sustained himself throughout with eloquence and dignity.*

The object of this treaty was chiefly the adjustment of boundaries, and to extend and brighten the chain of friendship, not only between the Indians themselves, but between their nations collectively and the whites. It was a convention of much harmony toward the close, and after nineteen days' sittings, every difficulty being adjusted, they separated with great cordiality and good will.†

* Chapman.

† There was yet another council of the Indians held at Easton, in 1761, in which Teedyuscung took an active and eloquent part. He was dissatisfied at Wyoming, although the government of Pennsylvania appear to have fulfilled their contract to build houses for the Indians, at considerable expense. Teedyuscung, however, threatened to leave the place, against which resolution he was strongly urged. The proceedings of this council, at length, are among Sir William Johnson's manuscripts. The results were of but little importance.

CHAPTER IV.

Indefinite grants of lands by the Crown,—Early claim of Connecticut to western lands,—Conflicting grants,—Organization of the Susquehanna Company,—Project of colonizing Wyoming. Objections of the Pennsylvanians,—Conflicting purchases of the Indians,—First attempt to colonize Wyoming,—Frustrated by the Indian Wars,—Resumed in 1762, —First arrival of settlers,—Friendship with the Indians,—Return to Connecticut for the winter,—Opposition of the Proprietaries,—Removal with their families,—Treacherous assassination of Teedyuscung,—First Massacre at Wyoming,—Flight of the survivors,—Case of Mr. Hopkins, —Expedition against the Indians,—Their departure from the valley,—Massacre of the Conestogoe Indians by the Paxtang zealots,—Disgraceful proceedings that ensued,—Moravian Indians settle in Wyalusing,—Remove to Ohio.

Events of a different character now crowd upon the attention. "The first grants of lands in America, by the crown of Great Britian, were made with a lavishness which can exist only where acquisitions are without cost, and their value unknown; and with a want of provision in regard to boundaries which could result only from entire ignorance of the country. The charters of the great Western and Southern Virginia Companies, and of the colonies of Massachusetts Bay and Connecticut, were of this liberal and uncertain character. The charter of the Plymouth Company covered the expanse from the fortieth to the forty-sixth degree of Northern latitude, extending from the Atlantic to the Pacific Ocean."* This charter was granted by King James I., under the great seal of England, in the most ample manner, on the 3d of November, 1620, to the Duke of Lenox, the Marquis of Buckingham, the Earls of Arundel and Warwick and their associates, "for the planting, ruling, ordering, and governing of New-England, in America." The charter of Connecticut was derived from the Plymouth Company, of which the Earl of Warwick was President. This grant was made in March, 1621, to Viscount Say and Seal, Lord Brook, and their associates. It was made in the most ample form, and also covered the country west of Connecticut, to the extent of its breadth, being about one degree of latitude, from sea to sea.† This grant was confirmed by the King in the course of the same year, and again in 1662. New-York, or, to speak more correctly in reference to that period, the New-Netherlands, being then a Dutch possession, could not be claimed as a portion of these munificent grants, if for

* Gordon's History of Pennsylvania.

† Trumbull's History of Connecticut. Colonel Timothy Pickering, in a letter to his son, giving the particulars of the highhanded outrage committed upon him in Wyoming, in 1788, in speaking of these grants, remarks:—"It seems natural to suppose by the terms of these grants, extending to the western ocean, that in early times the continent was conceived to be of comparatively little breadth."

no other reason, for the very good and substantial one that in the grant to the Plymouth Company an exception was made of all such portions of the territory as were "then actually possessed or inhabited by any other Christian prince or State." But the round phraseology of the charters opened the door sufficiently wide for any subsequent claims, within the specified parallels of latitude, which the company, or its successors, might afterward find it either convenient or politic to interpose. And it appears that even at the early date of 1651, some of the people of Connecticut were already casting longing eyes upon a section of the valley of the Delaware. It was represented by these enterprizing men that they had purchased the lands in question from the Indians, but that the Dutch had interposed obstacles to their settlement thereon. In reply to their petition, the commissioners of the United Colonies asserted their right to the jurisdiction of the territory claimed upon the Delaware, and the validity of the purchases that had been made by individuals. "They protested against the conduct of the Dutch, and assured the petitioners that though the season was not meet for hostilities, yet if within twelve months, at their own charge, they should transport to the Delaware one hundred armed men, with vessels and ammunition approved by the magistrates of New-Haven, and should be opposed by the Dutch, they should be assisted by as many soldiers as the commissioners might judge meet; the lands and trade of the settlement being charged with the expense, and continuing under the government of New-Haven."* The project, however, was not pressed during the designated period, nor indeed does it seem to have been revived for more than a century afterward. Many changes of political and other relations had occurred during this long lapse of time. Disputes had arisen between the people of Connecticut and the New Netherlands in regard to boundaries, which had been adjusted by negociation and compromise. The colony of New Netherlands had moreover fallen, by the fortunes of war, under the sway of the British crown. The colonies of New Jersey and Pennsylvania had also been planted. Various additional grants had been given by the crown, and other questions of territorial limits had been raised and adjusted. But in none of these transactions had Connecticut relinquished her claims of jurisdiction, and the pre-emptive right to the lands of the Indians, lying beyond New-York, and north of the fortieth degree of latitude, as defined in the original grant to the

* This quotation is from Gordon. Colonel Pickering, in the letter already cited in a preceding note, addressed to his son, and privately printed for the use of his own family only, supposed that Connecticut did not set up any formal claim to lands west of New-York and New-Jersey, until just prior to the revolution. He was in error.

Plymouth Company. The grant of this Company to Lord Say and Seal and Lord Brook had been made fifty years before the grant of the crown to William Penn, and the confirmation of that grant to Connecticut by royal charter, nineteen years prior to that conveyance.* Unfortunately, moreover, from the laxity that prevailed among the advisers of the crown, in the granting of patents, as to boundaries, the patent to William Penn covered a portion of the grant to Connecticut, equal to one degree of latitude and five of longitude; and within this territory, thus covered by double grants, was situated the section of the Delaware country heretofore spoken of;† as also the yet richer and more inviting valley of Wyoming, toward which some of the more restless if not enterprizing sons of the Pilgrims were already turning their eyes with impatience. Hence the difficulties, and feuds, and civil conflicts, an account of which will form the residue of the present and the succeeding chapter.

The project of establishing a colony in Wyoming was started by sundry individuals in Connecticut in 1753, during which year an association was formed for that purpose, called the Susque-

* Trumbull.

† The specific claim of the Delaware Company, was to the lands between the ranges of the north and south lines of Connecticut, westward by the Delaware river, to within ten miles of the Susquehanna.

hanna Company, and a number of agents were commissioned to proceed thither, explore the country, and conciliate the good will of the Indians. This commission was executed ; and as the valley, though at that time in the occupancy of the Delawares, was claimed by the Six Nations, a purchase of that Confederacy was determined upon. To this end, a deputation of the company, the associates of which already numbered about six hundred persons embracing many gentlemen of wealth and character, was directed to repair to Albany, where a great Indian Council was to be assembled in 1754, and if possible to effect the purchase. Their movements were not invested with secrecy, and the Governor of Pennsylvania,—James Hamilton,—becoming acquainted with them, was not slow in interposing objections to the procedure—claiming the lands as falling within the charter of Penn, and of course belonging, the pre-emptive right at least, to the Proprietaries for whom he was administering the government. Hamilton wrote to Governor Wolcott upon the subject, protesting strongly against the designs of the company. To this letter Wolcott replied, that the projectors of the enterprise supposed the lands in question were not comprised within the grant to William Penn ; but should it appear that they were, the Governor thought there would be no disposition to quarrel upon the subject. Governor Hamilton also addressed General (afterward Sir William) Johnson in relation to the matter, praying his interposition to prevent the Six nations from making any sales to the agents of the Connecticut Company, should they appear at Albany for that purpose; and from the letters and other manuscripts preserved among the papers of the baronet, yet extant, it is certain that he entered fully into the views of the government of Pennsylvania, then and afterward doing all in his power to thwart the Connecticut enterprize.

But these precautionary measures on the part of Hamilton did not defeat the object of the Connecticut Company, although a strong deputation to that end was sent from Pennsylvania to Albany.* A purchase was made by the Connecticut agents, of a tract of land extending about seventy miles north and south, and form a parallel line ten miles east of the Susquehanna, westward two degrees of longitude.† This purchase included the whole valley of Wyoming, and the country westward to the sources of the Alleghany.‡ The Pennsylvania

* The Delegates from Connecticut were, William Pitkin, Roger Wolcott, and Elisha Williams. Those from Pennsylvania were, John and Richard Penn, Isaac Norris, and Benjamin Franklin.

† Trumbull. Since the publication of the first edition of the present work, I have obtained the Deed of this purchase, which will be found in the appendix, containing the names of all the parties to the contract.

‡ Chapman. Another association was subsequently formed in Connecticut, called the *Delaware Company*, which purchased the land of the Indians, east of the Wyoming tract, to the Delaware river. This company commenced a settlement on the Delaware at a place called Coshutunk in

delegates did all in their power to circumvent the agents of the Susquehanna Company, holding several private councils with the chiefs of the Six Nations, and endeavoring to purchase the same lands themselves. In the course of their consultations, Hendrick, the last of the Mohawk kings,* thinking that some reflection had been cast upon his character, became excited, and declared that neither of the parties should have the land. But the Connecticut agents succeeded, as already stated, and the Pennsylvanians also effected the purchase of "a tract of land between the Blue Mountains and the forks of the Susquehanna river."† Strong efforts were subsequently made by the Pennsylvania government, aided by the influence of General Johnson, to induce the Indians to revoke the sale to the Susquehanna Company, and Hendrick was prevailed upon by Johnson to make a visit to Philadelphia upon that business. And in justice to the Pennsylvanians it must be allowed, that they always protested against the legality of this purchase by their rivals—alleging that the bargain was not made in open council, that it was the work of a few of the chiefs only, and that several of them were in a state of intoxication when they signed

1757, which was the first settlement founded by the people of Connecticut within the territory claimed by them west of New-York.

* He fell, bravely fighting under General Johnson, in the battle of Lake George, the following year.

† Chapman.

the deed of conveyance.* It is farthermore true that in 1736 the Six Nations had sold to the Proprietaries the lands upon both sides of the Susquehanna,—"from the mouth of the said river up to the mountains called the Kakatchlanamin hills, and on the west side to the setting of the sun."† But this deed was held by the advocates of the Connecticut purchase, to be quite too indefinite; and besides, as the "hills" mentioned, which are none other than the Blue Mountains, formed the northern boundary not only of that purchase, but in the apprehension of the Indians, of the Colony of Pennsylvania itself, Wyoming valley could not have been included.‡

* MS. letters of Governor Hamilton to General Johnson, in the author's possession. Gordon might be cited to the same purpose; and the same opinion is also supported by Colonel Pickering, who remarks:—"These purchases were not made, I am well satisfied, at any public council, or open treaties of the Indians to whom they belonged, but of little knots of inferior and unauthorized chiefs, indifferent about the consequences, provided they received some present gratifications, of comparatively small value."

† "The lands had already been sold, to the Proprietaries of Pennsylvania in 1730, and that sale enlarged and confirmed by a public deed whose seals were scarce dry. The Indian councils at all times afterward denied the sale (at Albany in 1754.) They disclaimed it in January, 1755, and in November, 1758, at Philadelphia; and, in 1763, they sent a deputation to Connecticut, on hearing that three hundred families proposed to settle these lands, to remonstrate against their intrusion, and to deny the alleged sale; and, in 1771, the Delawares and their derivative tribes, also protested that they had never sold any right to the Connecticut claimants."—*Gordon.*

‡ On the 17th of September, 1718, Sassoon, "King of the Delaware Indians"—so runs the deed,—"and Pokehais, Metashichay, Aiyamaikan, Pepawmaman, Ghettypenceman and Opekasset, chiefs of the said Indians, for and in consideration of two guns, six stroud water-coats, six blankets,

Having succeded in their purchase, the Susquehanna company procured a charter from the government of Connecticut, upon a memorial praying "that they might be formed into a distinct commonwealth, if it should be his Majesty's pleasure to grant it, with such privileges and immunities as should be agreeable to the royal pleasure." The company now consisted of six hundred and seventy-three associates, ten of whom were residents of Pennsylvania; and it was beyond doubt their design to form a separate colony, with a government of its own, subject, not to that of Connecticut, but only to the crown. But the course of subsequent events defeated that object. Still, it was not immediately abandoned, and a meeting of the company was called at Hartford, at which the purchase was divided into shares and distributed among the associates. A messenger had been previously despatched to Pennsylvania, to summon the attendance of the shareholders residing in that province; but he was arrested by the civil authorities, and after the Governor, Morris, had been apprized of the circumstance, and the fresh movements of the company, a messenger was sent to Hartford with a remonstrance against their farther

six duffle match-coats, and four kettles, gave a deed of confirmation of antecedent sales, by their ancestors to William Penn, of all the lands between "the two rivers, Delaware and Susquehanna, from Duck Creek to the mountains on this side Lechay." This deed is certified, among others, by Sir William Keith, at that time gevernor of Pennsylvania.

proceedings. What became of the messenger who was arrested does not appear.

Nothing daunted by the remonstrance, the company pushed forward a number of colonists, accompanied by surveyors and agents, in order to the immediate commencement of the new republic. Unluckily for the enterprise, however, the company arrived in the valley just as the Indians, under the influence of the French, as related in a former chapter, and encouraged by the defeat of Braddock and the fall of Oswego, were beginning to manifest a hostile disposition toward the English. The Nanticokes were the most belligerent in their feelings, and would probably have detained the new comers as prisoners, had it not been for the friendly interposition of Teedyuscung, who had not yet determined to take up the hatchet, although he did so soon afterward. In consequence of this interposition, no injury was inflicted upon the strangers, and they judged wisely in abandoning the enterprise for the time, and returning to Connecticut. The attempt was not renewed until after the general peace with the Indians, concluded at Easton, as heretofore stated, in 1758, nor indeed until after the fall of Canada before the valor of the English and Provincial arms.

The Delaware company commenced a settlement, under favorable circumstances, at a place called Cushetunk, on the river whence the name of their association was derived, in 1757; and in 1758 the Susquehanna Company resumed their preparations for planting their colony in Wyoming. But the unsettled condition of the frontier, notwithstanding the peace then just concluded with the Indians, seemed to render it inexpedient, if not hazardous, for those intending to become colonists to venture at that time so far into the wilderness. These dangers being apparently removed, in the year 1762 a body of settlers to the number of about two hundred pushed forward to the valley, so long the object of their keen desire. They planted themselves down upon the margin of the river, a short distance above its intersection by a fine stream of water, called Mill Creek, flowing from the east; and at a sufficient distance from the Indian towns to prevent any immediate collision of their agricultural interests. The greater part of the valley was yet covered with wood, excepting for short distances close around the Delaware and Shawanese towns, where the trees had been cut away in the slender progress of Indian husbandry. But the new colonists set themselves vigorously at work; a sufficient number of log houses and cabins were erected for their accommodation; and before the arrival of winter, extensive fields of wheat had been sown upon lands covered with forest trees in August.

These adventurers had not taken their families with them; and having now made so favorable a beginning, they secured their agricultural implements and returned to Connecticut.* It has been asserted that the resident Indians were opposed to this intrusion of the pale-faces among them, and that their chief, Teedyuscung, strongly remonstrated against it.† This may be true, but if so, it is equally true that they must have soon laid aside their prejudices, inasmuch as they speedily came to live upon terms of daily intercommunication, and great apparent harmony. But it was not thus with the Pennsylvanians. They looked with displeasure upon such a bold encroachment upon territories claimed as their own, and the most strenuous efforts were again put forth to crush the enterprise. The correspondence between the Executive of Pennsylvania and Sir William Johnson was re-opened, and the influence of the Baronet was exerted upon the Six Nations, to persuade them to disavow the sale of seventeen hundred and fifty-four. Those of the Indians who had not been concerned in the sale, and who on the other hand were doubtless opposed to it, were of course not unwilling to repudiate the transaction; and a deputation of five of their chiefs was sent to Hartford, accompanied by Colonel Guy Johnson, Dep-

* Chapman. † Gordon.

uty-Agent, and an interpreter sent by Sir William. Conferences were held by these chiefs with the Governor of Connecticut and his Council, on the 28th and 30th of May, in the course of which the sale of the land was disavowed as a national transaction. They admitted that a sale had been made, but denied its validity, inasmuch, they averred, as it had not been made according to ancient usage, in a full and open Council, but the chiefs who had signed the deed had been applied to separately, and had acted only in their individual capacities. Governor Fitch, in reply, assured the chiefs that the movements of the company had not been authorised by the government, and with their proceedings it had in fact had nothing to do. For their farther satisfaction, moreover, the Governor informed them that orders had been received from His Majesty, commanding him to use his authority and influence to prevent the intended movement upon the lands in dispute, until the matter should be laid before the King. They were likewise, still farther assured that the company had acquiesced in those orders, and had unanimously agreed that no person should enter upon the lands until His Majesty's pleasure should be known.* With these assurances, the deputies, consisting of one Mohawk, two Onondagas, and two Cayugas,—none

* For the proceedings of these conferences at Hartford, see appendix.

of them chiefs of note,—seem to have been satisfied. But whatever might have been the desire of the shareholders of the company, the individuals who had resolved to emigrate gave little attention to their stipulations with the Governor; and their advance was met by a series of unheeded proclamations, and followed by the powerless remonstrances of the sheriff and magistracy residing in Northampton county, on the Delaware, to which the valley of Wyoming was held to belong, the seat of justice of which was at Easton. Nor was this all. In the course of the same year, the Proprietaries of Pennsylvania made a case, and took the opinion of the Attorney General of the crown,* as to the right of Connecticut to the territory she was claiming. That officer was clear in his opinion against Connecticut—holding that, by virtue of her adjustment of boundaries with New-York, she was precluded from advancing a step beyond. But the Susquehanna company was not idle. Colonel Eliphalet Dyer, a leading associate, and a man of energy and abilities, was dispatched to England, charged likewise with a "case," carefully prepared, which was presented to the consideration of eminent counsel in London, who came to a directly opposite conclusion.† Each

* Mr. Pratt—afterward Lord Camden.

† The author has obtained a collection of Colonel Dyer's correspondence while abroad upon this mission. His letters prove his diligence, and his perseverance, in prosecuting his business, but are not historically important.

party, therefore, felt strengthened by those conflicting legal opinions, and both became the more resolute in the prosecution of their claims.

Meantime fresh scenes were opening in the disputed territory itself, as painful as unexpected. Notwithstanding a proclamation issued by Governor Fitch, eight days after the conferences with the Indians were ended, forbidding the people of Connecticut from trespassing upon the disputed territory, the pioneers who in the summer of 1762 had commenced their operations in Wyoming, returned to the valley to resume their labors early in the ensuing spring, accompanied by their families, and with augumented numbers of settlers. They were furnished with an adequate supply of provisions, and took with them a quantity of live stock, black cattle, horses, and pigs. Thus provided, and calculating to draw largely from the teeming soil in the course of the season, they resumed their labors with light hearts and vigorous arms. The forests rapidly retreated before their well-directed blows, and in the course of the summer they commenced bringing the lands into cultivation on the west side of the river. Their advancement was now so rapid, that it is believed the jealousies of the Indians began to be awakened. At least, notwithstanding the claims which the Six Nations had asserted over the territory, by virtue of which they had sold to the Susquehanna Company, Teedyuscung and his people alleged that they ought themselves to receive compensation also. Sir William Johnson had indeed predicted as much in a letter addressed to Governor Fitch, in the preceding month of November, in which he said:—"I cannot avoid giving you my sentiments, as I formerly did, that the Indians insist upon the claims of the people of Connecticut to lands on the Susquehanna, as unlawful, and the steps taken to obtain the same to be unjust, and have declared themselves determined to oppose any such settlement. I am therefore apprehensive any farther attempt at an establishment there, will not only be severely felt by those who shall put the same in execution, but may, (notwithstanding all my endeavors to the contrary,) be productive of fatal consequences on our frontiers."*

Thus matters stood until early in October, when an event occurred which broke up the settlement at one fell blow. It has already been seen that at the great council held at Easton, in 1758, the Six Nations had observed with no very cordial feelings, the important position which Teedyuscung had attained in the opinion of the whites, by the force of his talents and the energy of his character. Long accustomed to view the Delawares and their

* MSS. draught of the letter in the author's possession.

derivative tribes as their *subjects*, the haughty Mengwes could not brook this advancement of a supposed inferior; and the reflection had been rankling in their bosoms ever since the meeting of that council, until it was determined to cut off the object of their hate. For this purpose, at the time above mentioned, a party of warriors from the Six Nations came to the valley upon a pretended visit of friendship, and after lingering about for several days, they in the night time treacherously set fire to the house of the unsuspecting chief, which, with the veteran himself, was burnt to ashes. The wickedness of this deed of darkness was heightened by an act of still greater atrocity. They charged the assassination upon the white settlers of Connecticut, and had the address to inspire the Delawares with such a belief. The consequences may readily be anticipated. Teedyuscung was greatly beloved by his people, and their exasperation at "the deep damnation of his taking off," was kindled to a degree of corresponding intensity.

The white settlers, however, being entirely innocent of the transaction,—utterly unconscious that it had been imputed to them,—were equally unconscious of the storm that was so suddenly to break upon their heads. Their intercourse with the Indians, during the preceding year, had been so entirely friendly, that they had not even provided themselves with weapons of self-defence; and although there had been some slight manifestations of jealousy at their onward progress, among the Indians, yet their pacific relations, thus far, had not been interrupted. But they were now reposing in false security. Stimulated to revenge by the representations of their false and insidious visiters, the Delawares, on the 14th of October, rose upon the settlement, and massacred about thirty of the people, in cold blood, at noonday, while engaged in the labors of the field. Those who escaped ran to the adjacent plantations, to apprize them of what had happened, and were the swift messengers of the painful intelligence to the houses of the settlement, and the families of the slain. It was an hour of sad consternation. Having no arms even for self-defence, the people were compelled at once to seize upon such few of their effects as they could carry upon their shoulders, and flee to the mountains. As they turned back during their ascent to steal an occasional glance at the beautiful valley below, they beheld the savages driving their cattle away to their own towns, and plundering their houses of the goods that had been left. At nightfall the torch was applied, and the darkness that hung over the vale was illuminated by the lurid flames of their own dwellings,—the abodes of happiness and peace in the morning. Hapless indeed was the condition of the fugitives. Their number amounted to several hundreds—

men, women and children,—the infant at the breast,—the happy wife a few brief hours before, —now a widow, in the midst of a group of orphans. The supplies, both of provisions and clothing, which they had secured in the moment of their flight, were altogether inadequate to their wants. The chilly winds of autumn were howling with melancholy wail among the mountain pines, through which, over rivers and glens, and fearful morasses, they were to thread their way sixty miles, to the nearest settlements on the Delaware, and thence back to their friends in Connecticut a distance of two hundred and fifty miles. Notwithstanding the hardships they were compelled to encounter, and the deprivations under which they labored, many of them accomplished the journey in safety, while others, lost in the mazes of the swamps, were never heard of more.

Thus fell Teedyuscung, who, with all his faults, was yet one of the noblest of his race. Yet his character stands not well in history,—not as well, by any means, as it deserves. That he was a man of talents and courage, there can be no question, but withal he was greatly subject to the constitutional infirmities of his race,—unstable in his purposes, and a lover of the fire-waters,—the enemy which, received to the lip, steals away the brain alike of the white man and the red. It has already been seen that he was early a convert,—

and apparently a sincere one,—to the christian faith of the missionaries. But his faith was too weak to withstand the influence of ambition ; and when elevated to the supreme chieftainship of the scattering tribes of his nation, his behavior was such as to cause the good missionaries to tremble for his safety, seeing that he became " like a reed shaken by the wind."* Hitherto, for many years, his nation had been down-trodden by the Iroquois ; but when they determined once more to assert their own manhood, and to grasp the hatchet presented them by the French, electing Teedyuscung their king, as he had been their energetic champion in the councils, before, he now became, as he was called, " The Trumpet of War."† He did not, however, long continue upon the war path, but, as has been seen in the preceding chapter, became an early advocate and ambassador of peace, although his sincerity in this respect was questioned by the Moravian clergy, and likewise by Sir William Johnson. Still it must be recorded in his behalf that he appears never to have entirely forfeited the confidence of the Quakers. They were indeed opposed to the declaration of war against the Indians by Governor Hamilton—believing that the difficulties with them might have been healed by a more pacific course. And

* Loskiel. † Idem.

in this view they had the concurrence of Sir William Johnson. But in regard to the character of Teedyuscung, the sympathies of the baronet were with his own Indians—the Six Nations. They hated, and finally murdered him, and Sir William loved him not. Yet in his correspondence, while he labored to detract somewhat from the lofty pretensions of the Delaware Captain, the baronet has conceded to him enough of talent, influence, and power among his people, to give him a proud rank among the chieftains of his race.* Certain it is, that Teedyuscung did much to restore his nation to the rank of MEN, of which they had been deprived by the Iroquois, and great allowances are to be made on the score of his instability of conduct, from the peculiar circumstances under which he was often placed. In regard to his religious character and professions, his memory rests beneath a cloud. There were seasons, according to the records of the faithful missionary in which he gave signs of penitence and reform. After his withdrawal from the war, he resided for a considerable time in the neighborhood of Bethlehem, with about one hundred of his warriors, and the Brethren did all in their power for his reclamation. Occasional appearances of contrition at times inspired hopes of success. "As to externals," he once

* MSS. Letters of Sir William Johnson to Governor Denny, and a very long one to Major General Abercrombie, in the author's possession.

said, "I possess everything in plenty; but riches are of no use to me, for I have a troubled conscience. I still remember well what it is to feel peace in the heart, but I have now lost all." Yet he soon turned back. All hopes of his case were lost; and in recording his death, the benevolent Loskiel briefly says—" he was burnt in his house at Wajomick, without having given any proof of repentance."*

Among the individual incidents marking this singular tragedy was the following:—Some of the fugitives were pursued for a time by a portion of the Indians, and among them was a settler named Noah Hopkins,—a wealthy man from the county of Duchess, in the State of New-York, bordering upon Connecticut. He had disposed of a handsome landed patrimony in his native town, Amenia, and invested the proceeds as a shareholder of the Susquehanna Company, and in making preparations for moving to the new colony. Finding, by the sounds, that the Indians were upon his trail, after running a long distance, he fortunately

* Major Parsons, who acted as secretary to the conference with Teedyuscung in 1756, described him as "a lusty raw-boned man, haughty, and very desirous of respect and command." He was however, something of a wit. A tradition at Stroudsburg, states, that he there met one day a blacksmith named Wm McNabb, a rather worthless fellow, who accosted him with, "Well, cousin, how do you do?" "Cousin, cousin!" repeated the haughty red man, "how do you make that out?" "Oh! we are all cousins from Adam." "Ah! then, I am glad it is no nearer!" was the cutting reply.

discovered the trunk of a large hollow tree upon the ground, into which he crept. After lying there several hours, his apprehensions of danger were greatly quickened by the tread of foot-steps. They approached, and in a few moments two or three savages were actually seated upon the log in consultation. He heard the bullets rattle loosely in their pouches. They actually looked into the hollow trunk, suspecting that he might be there; but the examination must have been slight, as they discovered no traces of his presence. The object of their search, however, in after-life, attributed his escape to the labors of a busy spider, which, after he crawled into the log, had been industriously engaged in weaving a web over the entrance. Perceiving this, the Indians supposed, as a matter of course, that the fugitive could not have entered there. This is rather a *fine-spun* theory of his escape; but it was enough for him that he was not discovered. After remaining in his place of concealment as long as nature could endure the confinement, Hopkins crept forth, wandering in the wilderness without food, until he was on the point of famishing. In this situation, knowing that he could but die, he cautiously stole down into the valley again, whence five days before he had fled. All was desolation there. The crops were destroyed, the cattle gone, and the smouldering brands and embers were all that remained of the houses. The Indians had retired, and the stillness of death prevailed. He roamed about for hours in search of something to satisfy the cravings of nature, fording or swimming the river twice in his search. At length he discovered the carcass of a wild turkey, shot on the morning of the massacre, but which had been left in the flight. He quickly stripped the bird of its feathers, although it had become somewhat offensive by lying in the sun, dressed and washed it in the river, and the first meal he made therefrom was ever afterward pronounced the sweetest of his life. Upon the strength of this turkey, with such roots and herbs as he could gather in his way, he travelled until,—after incredible hardships, his clothes being torn from his limbs in the thickets he was obliged to encounter, and his body badly lacerated,—he once more found himself among the dwellings of civilized men.*

But this out-break of the Indians put an end to their own residence in Wyoming. On the receipt of the tidings at Philadelphia, Governor Hamilton directed Colonel Boyd, of Harrisburgh, to march at the head of a detachment of militia, and disperse the authors of the massacre. The savages, however, had anticipated the arrival of

* The facts of this little incidental narrative, were communicated to the author by Mr. G. F. Hopkins, printer, of New-York, and a nephew of the sufferer, who died at Pittsfield, (Mass.) at a very advanced age, about thirty years ago. He was a very respectable man.

the troops,—those of them at least who had participated in the murderous transaction,—and withdrawn themselves farther up the river, to the Indian settlements in the vicinity of Tioga. The Moravian Indians resident there, who had taken no part in the massacre, removed toward the Delaware, to Gnaddenhutten. But their residence at this missionary station was short. The horrible massacre of the Canestogoe Indians, residing upon their own reservation in the neighborhood of Lancaster, in December of the same year, by the infuriated religious zealots of Paxtang and Donnegal, filled them with alarm. They repaired to Philadelphia for protection; and as will presently appear, were only with great difficulty saved from the hatchets of a lawless band of white men, far more savage than themselves.

The transaction here referred to was a most extraordinary event, the record of which forms one of the darkest pages of Pennsylvanian history. It took place in December 1763. It was during that year that the great Pontiac conceived the design, like another Philip, of driving the Europeans from the continent. Forming a league between the great interior tribes of Indians, and summoning their forces in unison upon the war-path, he attacked the garrisons upon the frontiers, and the lakes, which were simultaneously invested, and many of them taken. The borders of Pennsylvania, Maryland, and Virginia, were again ravaged by scalping parties, and the frontier settlers of Pennsylvania in particular suffered with great severity. But although the fragments of the Delawares and Six Nations still residing in that Colony did not join in the war of Pontiac, yet, either from ignorance or malice, suspicions were excited against one of the Indian Moravian communities. Availing themselves of this pretext, a number of religionists in the towns of Paxtang and Donnegal, excited to a pitch of the wildest enthusiasm by their spiritual teachers, banded together for the purpose of exterminating the whole Indian race. Their pretext was the duty of extirpating the heathen from the earth, as Joshua had done of old, that the saints might possess the land. The Canestogoes were the remains of a small clan of the Six Nations, residing upon their own reservation, in the most inoffensive manner, having always been friendly to the English. The maddened zealots fell upon their little hamlet in the night, when, as it happened, the greater portion of them were absent from their homes, selling their little wares among the white people. Only three men, two women and a boy, were found in their village. These were dragged from their beds, and stabbed and hatcheted to death. Among them was a good old chief named Shehaes, who was cut to pieces in his bed. The dead were scalped, and their houses burnt. This infamous procedure took place on the 14th of the month.

Hearing of this deplorable act, the magistrates of Lancaster collected the residue of the helpless clan, men women and children, and placed them in one of the public buildings of the town for their protection. But on the 27th, a band of fifty of the fanatics went openly into the borough, and proceeding to the work-house where the Indians had been placed, broke open the doors, and with fury in their countenances recommenced the work of death. Nor did the people of Lancaster lift a finger, or the magistrates interfere, for their defence. "When the poor wretches saw they had no protection, and that they could not escape, and being without the least weapon of defence, they divided their little families, the children clinging to their parents; they fell on their faces, protested their innocence, declared their love to the English, and that, in their whole lives, they had never done them any injury; and in this posture they all received the hatchet. Men, women, and children —infants clinging to the breast—were all inhumanly butchered in cold blood."*

But the vengeance of the fanatics was not satiated. Like the tigers of the forest, having tasted blood, they became hungry for more; and having

* Proud. Vide also Gordon.

heard that the fugitives from Wyoming, feeling themselves unsafe at Gnaddenhutten, had repaired to Philadelphia, the zealots set their faces in that direction, and marched upon the capital for the avowed purpose of putting those Indians to death also. Their numbers increased to an insurgent army. Great consternation prevailed in Philadelphia on their approach. The poor Indians themselves prayed that they might be sent to England for safety; but this could not be done. An attempt was then made by the government to send them to the Mohawk country, for the protection of Sir William Johnson; but the civil authorities of New-York objected, and the fugitives were marched back to Philadelphia. Whereupon the insurgents embodied themselves again, and marched once more upon that capital in greater numbers than before. Another season of peril and alarm ensued, and the Governor hid himself away in the house of Doctor Franklin; but the legislature being in session, and the people, the Quakers even not excepted, evincing a proper spirit for the occasion, the insurgents were in the end persuaded to listen to the voice of reason, and disband themselves. It is a singular fact, that the actors in this strange and tragic affair were not of the lower orders of the people. They were Presbyterians, comprising in their ranks men of intelligence, and of so much consideration that the press dared not disclose their names, nor the government attempt their punishment.* It was indeed believed by some, that the murder of the Indians was by no means the chief end of their design; but that, taking advantage of the wide-spread consternation they had produced, they intended to overturn the government, and revolutionize the colony.†

After these disorders were quieted, and the Indian Moravians had had time to look about for a place of retreat, they removed to a place called Mahackloosing—or Machwihilusing—the Wyalusing of later times,—situated upon the banks of the Susquehanna, sixty miles above Wyoming. The missionaries had hastened to this place before; but it had been deserted in the late war—the newcomers finding the old huts yet standing.‡ Here "they built a considerable village, containing at one period more than thirty good log houses, with shingled roofs and glazed windows, a church and school-house, not inferior to many erected by wealthy farmers." They also turned their attention earnestly to agricultural pursuits, clearing and enclosing large tracts of upland and meadow. They resided at this place several years very happily; but were ultimately induced to join the Moravian Indians beyond the Ohio.§

* Proud—Gordon. † Loskiel
‡ Loskiel. § Proud—Gordon.

CHAPTER V.

Attempt of the Susquehanna Company to recolonize,—Pennsylvania claims the territory again, and leases the valley to Ogden and his associates,—Rival settlements,—Civil War,—Ogden besieged,—Arrests of the Connecticut people,—Situation,—Hostilities resumed,—Ogden draws off,—The Colony advances,—Propositions for an adjustment,—Rejected by Governor Penn,—Expedition of Colonel Francis,—His retreat,—Additional forces raised by Penn,—Ogden captures Colonel Durkee,—Connecticut settlers negotiate, and leave the valley,—Bad Faith of Ogden,—Lazarus Stewart,—Susquehanna Company reoccupy the valley,—Ogden returns with forces,—Both parties fortify,—Ogden besieged,—Surrenders,—Penn applies to General Gage,—Request denied,—Reinvaded by Ogden,—Yankees taken by surprise,—Captured in the field,—Their fort taken,—Arrest of Lazarus Stewart,—Rescued,—Returns to Wyoming and recaptures the fort,—Ogden reappears,—Both parties fortify,—A skirmish,—Nathan Ogden killed,—Sensation among the Pennsylvanians,—Lazarus Stewart draws off, and Ogden retains the valley, and commences planting a colony,—Sudden descent of Zebulun Butler with a strong force,—Ogden again besieged,—Escapes to Philadelphia by stratagem for succors,—His reinforcements defeated,—Ogden is wounded,—The fort surrenders to the Yankees.

Six years intervened before the Susquehanna Company attempted to resume their operations in the fair valley of Wyoming. But in the meantime the Proprietaries of Pennsylvania, taking advantage of a grand Indian council assembled at Fort Stanwix, in the autumn of 1768, had attempted to strengthen their claim to the disputed territory by a direct purchase from the Six Nations.

This object was of no difficult attainment, as the Indians might doubtless have been persuaded to sell that, or almost any other portion of disputed territory, as many times over as white purchasers could be found to make payment. In a word, the Pennsylvanians were successful, and took a deed of the territory from some of the chiefs, in November, 1768.

But, nothing daunted by this movement, the Susquehanna Company called a meeting, and resolved to resume the settlement, by throwing a body of forty pioneers into the valley in the month of February 1769, to be followed by two hundred more in the Spring. Indeed the association, in order to strengthen their power as well as their claims, and to expand their settlements, now appropriated five townships, each five miles square, and divided into forty shares, as free gifts to the first forty settlers in each township.* Many parts of the flats, or bottom lands, were of course already clear of wood, and ready for cultivation. An appropriation of two hundred pounds was made for the purchase of agricultural implements; regulations for the government of the colony were drawn up, and a committee appointed to carry them into effect.†

* Letter of Colonel Pickering to his son.

† This committee consisted of Isaac Tripp, Benjamin Follet, John Jenkins, William Buck, and Benjamin Shoemaker.

The Pennsylvanians, for once, anticipated the people of Connecticut. No sooner had they heard of the renewed movements of the Susquehanna Company, than they made preparations for the immediate occupation of the valley themselves. To this end, a lease of the valley for seven years was given to Charles Stuart,* Amos Ogden, and John Jennings, conditioned that they should establish a trading-house, for the accommodation of the Indians, and adopt the necessary measures for defending themselves, and those who might proceed thither under their lease. Mr. Stewart, a gentleman of talents, enterprise and wealth, had been extensively and successfully engaged in taking up and leasing lands under the new purchasers, from the Indians, of the Pennsylvanians, and was at the time Deputy Surveyor General of the province. By him the valley was divided and laid out

* Of New-Jersey: afterward Colonel Stewart of the continental army. An early and active promoter of the Revolution, he was among the first of his compatriots at a convention of the leading gentlemen of the colony at Trenton, to take a bold and decided stand against the crown; and on the commencement of hostilities, had the command of the second regiment of the Jersey line tendered him, that of the first being given to Lord Sterling. He was shortly afterward appointed by congress to the staff of Washington, as commissary General of Issues, which station he filled till the termination of the war.—He was a member of the congress; of the convention; also of that of 1784—1785; and on the organization of the government under the constitution, was offered by Washington the Surveyor Generalship of the United States, an appointment which he declined, chiefly, from the occupation of his time, in the prosecution of what he conceived to be the legal and equitable claims of himself and associates to the manors of Wyoming.

into two manors, that portion of it lying upon the eastern side, including the Indian town of Wyoming, being called the "Manor of Stoke," and the western division the "Manor of Sunbury." In January, 1769, the lessees, with a number of Colonists, proceeded to the valley, took possession of the former Connecticut improvements, and erected a block-house, for their defence, should their title and proceedings be disputed. The party of forty from Connecticut pressed close upon the heels of Stewart and Ogden, and sat down before their little garrison on the 8th of February. It was a close investment, all intercourse between the besieged and their friends, if they had any, in the surrounding country, being cut off. Having heard of the approach of the Connecticut party, however, Charles Stewart and his associates despatched a messenger to Governor Penn, stating that they had but ten men in the block-house, and requesting assistance. But after waiting a sufficient length of time without receiving reinforcements, the besieged had recourse to stratagem to accomplish what they could not effect by power. Under the pretext of a consultation, to the end of an amicable adjustment of the question of title, three of the Connecticut party, viz: Isaac Tripp, Vine Elderkin, and Benjamin Follet, were induced to enter the garrison, where they were immediately arrested by Jennings, who was sheriff of Northampton

County, conveyed to Easton, and there thrown into prison. Their rescue would have been attempted, but for the fear of endangering their lives. However, the prisoners were accompanied to Easton by the whole of both parties; and the key of the prison was scarcely turned upon them before bail was given for their good behaviour, and the Connecticut party retraced their steps to Wyoming, where their labors were resumed with characteristic energy. Finding that the numbers of the emigrants were increasing, Jennings made another effort to arrest their persons and proceedings in March. The posse of the county, together with several magistrates, were ordered upon the service, and they again marched upon Wyoming in an imposing array. The Connecticut people had prepared a block-house hastily for defence; but the doors were broken by Jennings, who succeeded in arresting thirty-one persons, all of whom, with the exception of a few who effected their escape while marching through a swamp, were taken to Easton, cast into prison as before, — and again admitted to bail, just in season to return once more to Wyoming with a party of two hundred recruits who now joined them from the Susquehanna Company. Thus reinforced, their first work was to build a fort upon a convenient site, protected by the river on one side, and a creek and morass upon another. It was a regular military defence, consisting of a strong block-house, surrounded by a rampart and entrenchment. In the immediate neighborhood of the fortress,—called Fort Durkee, in honor of the officer elected to its command,—they erected about thirty log-houses, with loop-holes through which to fire in the event of an attack. But they had no immediate cause to try the strength of their defences, although Jennings and Ogden were at the moment raising forces to march against them. They arrived in the valley on the 24th of May; but the works of the Connecticut boys appeared too formidable to justify an attack by so small a number of men as they had the honor to command. Jennings and Ogden therefore returned to Easton, and reported to the Governor that the power of the county was inadequate to the task of dispossessing the Connecticut settlers, who now numbered three hundred able-bodied men.

For a short season the latter were left to push forward their improvements without molestation, during which state of repose the company commissioned Colonel Dyer and Major Elderkin to proceed to Philadelphia and endeavor to negotiate a compromise on the question of title. But the proposition, which was for a reference of the whole matter in dispute, either to an arbitrament or a court of law, was rejected by Governor Penn; and an armed force, under the command of Colonel Francis, was detached to Wyoming, with orders to demand a surrender of the fort and garrison. The summons was not obeyed; and the Colonel, as the Sheriff of Northampton had done before him, after surveying the works, and the other preparations for his reception, should he attempt an assault, arrived at the conclusion that his force likewise was inadequate to the enterprise. He therefore retreated, and upon a representation of the facts to the Governor, a more formidable expedition was immediately set on foot. Mr. Sheriff Jennings was directed to assemble the power of Northampton county in stronger array than before, and to march against the intruders, well furnished with small arms, a four-pounder, and an abundant supply of fixed ammunition. He was carefully instructed by Govenor Penn, however, to avoid, if possible, an effusion of blood. Having knowledge of the approach of Jennings, Ogden, with a band of forty armed men, anticipated his arrival by dashing suddenly among the houses of the settlement, and making several prisoners — among whom was Colonel Durkee. These he secured and carried away—thus weakening the forces of the settlers, and perchance disheartening them by the loss of their principal officer. Durkee was taken to Philadelphia and closely imprisoned. Two days after his capture, Jennings arrived before the fort with two hundred men in arms, and commenced a parley with the garrison, during which Ogden and his company were busy in driving away their cattle and horses found grazing in the fields. On the following day Jennings commenced the erection of a battery upon which his ordnance was to be mounted. These preparations beginning to wear a more serious aspect, the garrison proposed a negociation. The result was a capitulation, by which the settlers agreed to surrender the fort and contiguous buildings. All the colonists from Connecticut, but seventeen, were to return. These seventeen men, with their families, were to be allowed to remain and harvest the crops upon the ground. They were likewise to hold possession of the lands and improvements in the name of the Company, until the pleasure of his Majesty should be known in regard to the rival claims of the parties. The articles of capitulation, drawn out in due form, were carried into effect by the settlers; but Ogden behaved in bad faith. The people, with the exception of the seventeen who were to remain, as before mentioned, had no sooner departed from the valley than Ogden commenced an indiscriminate system of plunder. All their live stock was seized and driven away; their houses were stripped; and, in a word, deprived of the means of subsistence, the seventeen, with their families, were compelled to wend their way back to Connecticut.

Early in the ensuing year, demonstrations of a yet more belligerent character were put forth by the claimants under the Susquehanna Company. It has been noted at a former page, that there were several share-holders of the Company residing in Pennsylvania. In the month of February, 1770, therefore, a gentleman, named Lazarus Stewart led a number of men from Lancaster into the Wyoming valley, who were joined on their progress by a body of people from Connecticut. They were all armed, and Fort Durkee, garrisoned by only eight or ten men, was taken without opposition. Ogden himself was absent at the time, and the victors proceeded to his house and captured the piece of ordnance already mentioned. On hearing of these transactions, Ogden hastened back to Wyoming, accompanied by about fifty men, by whom he garrisoned his own house, (a formidable block-house,) and commenced adding to its strength. On the 28th a detachment of fifty men was sent against him, with a view of carrying the stockade by assault and taking him prisoner. He had a deputy sheriff with him, however, who, at the head of a strong party, sallied out for the purpose of arresting the assailants. A smart skirmish ensued, during which several of the Connecticut people were wounded, and one man killed. Finding that Ogden's men could fire upon them from his house, without exposing themselves to danger, the Connecticut people retreated, and as Colonel Durkee had returned from Philadelphia, a regular siege of Ogden's fortress was determined upon. A battery was erected over against him on the opposite bank of the river, upon which the four-pounder was mounted, and briskly played upon Ogden for several days, without making much impression on his defences. Durkee's men then determined to bring the enemy to closer quarters, for which purpose they were arranged in three divisions, and marched out with drums beating and colors flying, to within musket shot of the block-house. Three breast-works were rapidly constructed, from which the firing was again commenced, and briskly returned. After five days of desultory firing on both sides, a party of the besiegers advanced under Ogden's guns, with great intrepidity, and set fire to one of his outworks, which was consumed, together with a large quantity of goods contained therein. Ogden had again called upon Governor Penn for reinforcements; but as these were not forthcoming, the contest relaxed. Colonel Durkee despatched a flag to Ogden, requesting a conference, which was acceded to, and he surrendered upon terms similar to those which had been granted to the Connecticut people the season before. He had no improvements or land to protect; but the stipulation was that he should withdraw himself and all his party from the valley, excepting six men, who were to remain to guard his house and preserve his property. After his retreat, however, the evil which he had done the people from Connecticut, the season before, was requited upon his own head. His property was seized by the Yankees, and his house burnt.* It was believed that Governor Penn would have attempted his relief but for his own unquiet position just at that time—the Boston massacre having given an impulse to the spirit which not long afterward broke forth in the war of the Revolution. Thus situated, the Governor called upon General Gage, then commanding the forces of the crown at New-York; but the General replied that he thought the character of the dispute was such that it would be highly improper for the King's troops to interfere.

Failing thus in the application for the aid of his majesty's troops, Governor Penn issued another proclamation on the 28th of June, forbidding any settlers from planting themselves down upon the disputed territory, unless by consent of the lessees, Stewart and Ogden. The energies of the government were likewise put in exercise to raise a force adequate to the work of carrying the proclamation

* Among the prisoners found in the block-house after the capitulation, were eight men from New-England, and three Germans, who had never before been in Wyoming, and who mistook Ogden's house for the fort of the opposite party. The number of killed and wounded during the siege is not known.—*Chapman.*

into effect. It appears to have been a hard matter, however, to enlist troops for the service. The summer passed away before the expedition was on foot, and the entire body numbered only one hundred and forty men.* But the deficiency of numbers was made up by the courage and skill of their leader, who was none other than Captain Ogden himself. Taking the route of the Lehigh, and the old "Indian Walk," this enterprising man arrived with his forces upon the crest of the mountain overlooking the settlement, on the 22d of September. He was well aware that his band of one hundred and forty men would stand but a poor chance with the Connecticut boys, unless he could take them by surprise. To this end, therefore, he had advanced with so much circumspection that the colonists were entirely ignorant of his approach. By the aid of his telescope he observed the movements of the settlers in the morning, until, utterly unconscious of danger, they went forth in small squads, to engage in the labors of their field. Then separating his own men into divisions equal to the number of the laboring parties, Ogden descended into the valley, and stole upon them with such admirable caution, that many of them were made prisoners almost before they

* Colonel Pickering attributes the difficulty of raising troops to march against Wyoming, on every application, not only to the unpopularity of the Proprietaries, but to the influence of the Quakers, to whom war was always abhorrent. Vide, letter to his son.

knew of their danger. Those who escaped ran to the fort and gave the alarm. The women and children from the houses immediately collected within the fort for safety, while Ogden drew off into a gorge of the mountain, where his prisoners were made secure and sent off to Easton under a strong escort. Within the garrison all was confusion during the day, while Ogden, yet too weak to hazard another attack, kept in his concealment, trusting to chance or stratagem to direct his next movement. Every thing worked entirely to his satisfaction. The garrison, finding that they had provisions for a siege, resolved to send an express, under cover of the night, to their brother colonists of Coshuntunk for aid. But the messengers detached upon this service, supposing that Ogden would guard the path leading to the Delaware colony, resolved upon taking a route less exposed —and by doing so they threw themselves directly into his camp. From these unfortunate messengers Ogden extracted such information touching the situation of affairs within the fortress, as determined him at once to make a night attack. It was a wise resolution. Crowded with men, women, and children, the little fort was in no condition for repelling an assault, and the result was, a surprise and complete success. The movements of the assailants were conducted with so much secrecy, that the sentinel was knocked down before he saw aught of alarm ; the door of the block-house was easily forced ; and after a short affray, in which the belligerents were tumbling over women and children, and during which several persons of the garrison were killed, the fort surrendered. In the course of the melée, Captain Zebulon Butler would have been killed by a bayonet, but for the interposition of Captain Craig, one of Ogden's officers, who arrested the weapon, and prevented farther bloodshed. The greater portion of the prisoners were sent to Easton for imprisonment, while Butler and a few of the chief men were ordered to Philadelphia. Ogden then plundered the fort, and all the houses of the settlement, of whatever he could find of value, and withdrew to the larger settlements beyond the mountains—leaving a garrison to retain possession of the fort during the winter.

But it was shortly determined by the fortunes of war, that this oft-contested position should again change hands. After the burning of Ogden's house, as already mentioned, warrants were issued by the Judges of the Supreme Court of Pennsylvania, directing the arrest of Lazarus Stewart, Zebulon Butler, and Lazarus Young, for the crime of arson. Stewart was taken at Lebanon ; but some of his partizans in the neighborhood, hearing of his arrest, immediately repaired thither for his rescue. On their approach he knocked down the officer in whose charge he had been placed, and joined his friends, whom he shortly led back to Wyoming, though, as it would appear, in profound secrecy. Meantime, as the settlers from Connecticut had been completely dispersed by Ogden in the autumn, the garrison left by him at Fort Durkee saw no necessity for keeping an over-vigilant watch. The result of their negligence should serve as a caution to soldiers as well in peace as in war; since it happened that at about three o'clock on the morning of December 18th, this little isolated garrison was awakened from a deep and quiet slumber by an unceremonious visit from Stewart, at the head of twenty-three Lancastrians, and half a dozen Connecticut boys, who had already taken possession of the fort, and were shouting "Huzzah for King George!" The garrison consisted of but eighteen men, exclusive of several women and children. Six of the former leaped from the parapet and escaped naked to the woods. The residue were taken prisoners; but were subsequently driven from the valley, after being relieved of such of their movables as the victors thought worth the taking. Stewart and his men remained in the fort.

These bold and lawless exploits of Stewart created a strong sensation in the minds of the Proprietaries' government. Another warrant for his arrest was issued by the Supreme Court, and the Sheriff of Northampton was directed to proceed with the power of his county once more to Wyoming, and execute the writ. He arrived before the fort with his forces on Saturday the 18th of January, 1771, and demanded admittance, which was refused—Stewart declaring that Wyoming was under the jurisdiction of Connecticut, to whose laws and civil officers only he owed obedience. The parley continued until nightfall, when the sheriff retired to a new block-house which Amos Ogden and his brother Nathan with their followers were building. This work was completed on Sunday; and on Monday Nathan Ogden accompanied the sheriff and his posse once more in front of Fort Durkee, to demand the surrender of Stewart. Another refusal ensued, whereupon Ogden commenced firing upon the fort, which was promptly returned. Ogden fell dead, and several of his men were wounded. The body being secured, the party returned to the block-house, and the residue of the day was occupied by Amos Ogden and the sheriff in devising what next was to be done. But the entire aspect of the siege was changed the ensuing night, by the silent evacuation of the fort by Stewart and forty of his men, leaving only twelve men behind, who quietly surrendered to the sheriff the next day, and were marched across the mountains to

Easton. Amos Ogden remained in the fort, and persuaded many of his former associates again to join him, and attempt once more to colonize this vale of beauty and trouble. The death of Nathan Ogden was regarded by the authorities of Pennsylvania as the greatest outrage that had thus far marked this most singular and obstinate contest; and a reward of three hundred pounds was offered for the apprehension of Lazarus Stewart. But he was not taken.

The valley now had rest for the comparatively long period of six months, during which time the settlers of Ogden had increased to the number of eighty-two persons, including women and children. Their repose and their agricultural occupations were, however, suddenly interrupted on the 6th of July, by the descent from the mountains of seventy armed men from Connecticut, under the command of Captain Zebulon Butler, who had been joined by Lazarus Stewart at the head of another party. There object was to regain the possession of the valley, and they set themselves at work like men who were in earnest. During the season of repose which Ogden had enjoyed, he had abandoned Fort Durkee, and built another and stronger defence, which he called Fort Wyoming. The forces of Butler and Stewart were rapidly augmented by recruits from Connecticut; and several military works were commenced by the besiegers, to hasten the reduction of Ogden's garrison. For this purpose two redoubts were thrown up, one of them upon the bank below Fort Wyoming, and the other upon a bold eminence above, projecting almost into the river, and entirely commanding the channel. Two entrenchments were likewise opened, and the fort was so completely invested that communication with the surrounding country was entirely cut off. But Ogden's garrison was well supplied with provisions and ammunition ; and his work too strong to be taken without artillery. Thus circumstanced, he conceived the bold design of escaping from the fort by stratagem, and proceeding in person to Philadelphia for reinforcements—instructing his troops in any event to retain the post until his return. His plan was executed with equal courage and skill. On the night of July 12th he made up a light bundle to float upon the surface of the river, upon which he secured his hat. Connecting this bundle with his body by a cord of several yards in length, he dropped gently into the stream and floated down with the current—the bundle, which presented much the most conspicuous object, being intended to draw the fire should it be discovered. It was discovered by the sentinels, and a brisk fire directed upon it from three redoubts. But as it appeared to hold the even tenor of its way without interruption from the bullets, the firing ceased, and the bundle and its owner escaped—the latter untouched, but the former and less sensitive object pierced with several bullets.

John Penn having retired from the colony, the office of the Executive had now once more devolved upon the Honorable James Hamilton, President of the Council. Ogden arrived at Philadelphia without delay, and on a representation of the situation of affairs at Wyoming, vigorous efforts were set on foot for the succour of the besieged. A detatchment of one hundred men was ordered to be raised to march upon the rebellious settlers, with the sheriff of Northampton, but under the command of Colonel Asher Clayton. The detachment was to be divided into two companies, the one commanded by Captain Joseph Morris, and the other by Captain John Dick. They were to march to the scene of action by different routes, and at different times. But, as before, great difficulty was experienced in raising the men; and Captain Dick, who was to march first, was compelled to advance with only thirty-six men, encumbered by pack-horses and provisions not only for the whole division, but also for the relief of the besieged. The Connecticut forces, however, although maintaining the siege closely, were too vigilant to be taken by surprise. They had become aware of Ogden's escape and movements, and were apprised of the advance of Captain

Dick, for whose reception every needful preparation was made. Suddenly, therefore, on approaching the fort he was to relieve, he found himself in the midst of an ambuscade. At the first fire his men ran to the fort for protection, but sixteen of them together with the entire stock of provisions, fell into the hands of the Connecticut forces. Ogden was of the number who succeeded in entering the fort, as also did Colonel Clayton. This affair happened on the 30th of July. Elated by their success, the assailants now pressed the siege more closely than before, until the 10th of August, keeping up a daily fire whenever any person of the garrison appeared in view.

On the 11th Captain Butler sent a flag demanding a surrender; but as the besieged had contrived to despatch another messenger to Philadelphia, with an account of Dick's misfortune, and praying for farther assistance, and as the government was endeavoring to raise and send forward another body of one hundred men, they refused the summons, and the firing was resumed. Butler had no artillery, and a wooden cannon was constructed from a gnarled log of pepperidge, by a colonist named Carey, and mounted upon his battery. But it burst asunder at the second discharge. Still, the contest was closely maintained until the 14th, when, having been long upon short allowance, disappointed in not receiving the promised reinforcements, and their provisions being entirely exhausted, the garrison surrendered. The articles of capitulation were signed by Zebulon Butler, Lazarus Stewart and John Smith, on the part of the besiegers, and by Colonel Asher Clayton, Joseph Morris and John Dick, in behalf of the Proprietaries. The stipulations were, "that twenty-three men might leave the fort armed, and with the remainder unarmed, might proceed unmolested to their respective habitations; that the men having families might abide on the debateable land for two weeks, and might remove their effects without interruption; and that the sick and wounded might retain their nurses, and have leave to send for a physician."*

It afterward appeared that at the time of the surrender, a detachment of sixty men had arrived within ten miles of the fort, commanded by Captain Ledlie; but having heard of the surrender, the Captain wisely concluded to make a different disposition of his company. Numbers of the garrison were wounded during the siege, among whom was Amos Ogden, severely. While he was leaning upon the arm of one of his subalterns, William Ridyard, the latter was struck by a ball, and killed instantly. The loss of the Connecticut forces, in killed and wounded, was a matter which appears not to have been divulged. By the terms

*Gordon.

of the capitulation, Ogden and his party were all to remove from Wyoming.*

In the month of September following, Mr. Hamilton gave a detailed account of these proceedings to the legislature—informing that body that the intruders had burnt the block-house, and were fortifying themselves upon a more advantageous position. It was determined by the council that a correspondence should be opened with the Governor of Connecticut upon the subject, which was accordingly done. The President informed Governor Trumbull that the intruders had assumed to act under the authority of the state of Connecticut. The latter replied cautiously, denying that the Connecticut people were acting under any directions from him, or from the General Assembly—neither of whom would countenance any acts of violence for the maintenance of any supposed rights of the Susquehanna Company.

Thus closed the operations of the respective parties for the year 1771. The Connecticut colonists increased so rapidly, and prepared themselves so amply for defence, that the Pennsylvania forces were all withdrawn, and the Susquehanna Company left in the quiet possession of the valley.

* Gordon asserts that during this seige, Butler proposed to Colonel Clayton that the rights of the respective claimants should be determined by combat, between thirty men to be chosen from each side. But the proposition was rejected.

CHAPTER VI.

Government of Wyoming—Thoroughly democratic,—Attempted mediation with the Pennsylvanians—Failure—Opinions of English counsel,—Connecticut asserts jurisdiction,—Opposition of Governor Penn,—Proclamations,—Season of repose,—Another Civil War,—Destruction of the Connecticut settlement on the West Branch,—Interposition of Congress,—Not heeded,—Expedition and repulse of Colonel Plunkett,—Relinquishment of the contest,—War of the Revolution,—Letting loose of the Indians,—Defenceless situation of Wyoming,—Invasion by the tories and Indians,—Hasty preparations for defence,—The colonists resolve to attack,—The Battle and Massacre,—The Capitulation,—Ravaging of the valley,—Vindication of Brant,—Cruelties of the tories,—Flight of the people,—Vindication of Colonel Zebulon Butler,—His character,—Vindication of Colonel Dennison,—Captain Spalding,—Second invasion,—Affair of Colonel Powell,—Sullivan's Expedition,—Subsequent battles and skirmishes with the Indians.

Thus far the government of the Connecticut settlers—that is to say, all the government that was exercised,—had been of a voluntary and military character. But the cessation of all opposition to the proceedings of the Susquehanna Company, for the time, on the part of Pennsylvania, rendered the longer continuance of martial law inexpedient, while by the rapid increase of the population it became necessary that some form of civil government should be adopted. The increasing irritation existing between the parent government and the colonies, already foreshadowing an approaching appeal to the *ultima ratio regum*, had taught the directors of the company that a charter for a new and distinct colonial government from the crown, was not to be expected. In this exigency, the company applied to the General Assembly of Connecticut, to have their Wyoming settlements taken under the protection of the colony until the pleasure of his majesty should be known. But the General Assembly was in no haste to extend its ægis over so broad a territory, at so great a distance from home.* They therefore advised the company in the first instance to attempt an amicable adjustment of their difficulties with the Proprietaries of Pennsylvania; offering to undertake the negotiation in their behalf. In case of a failure to obtain a just and honorable arrangement, the General Assembly next suggested a reference of the whole subject to the king in council. Meantime, while they wished the colony God speed, they advised them to govern themselves by themselves, in the best manner they could.

Pursuant to this advice, the inhabitants of the valley proceeded to elect a government of their own; and the institutions established by them were the most thoroughly democratic, probably, of any government that has ever existed elsewhere

* The territory claimed by the Susquehanna Company, extended one hundred miles north and south, and one hundred and ten miles west of the river.

among civilized men. "They laid out townships, founded settlements, erected fortifications, levied and collected taxes, passed laws for the direction of civil suits, and for the punishment of crimes and misdemeanors, established a militia, and provided for the common defence and general welfare of the colony."* The supreme legislative power was vested directly in the people, not by representation, but to be exercised by themselves, in their primary meetings and sovereign capacity. A magistracy was appointed, and all the necessary machinery for the government of towns, according to the New-England pattern, organized and put in motion. Three courts were instituted, all having civil and criminal jurisdiction; but the Court of Appeals, called the Supreme Court, to which every case might be carried, was formed, like their legislature, of the people themselves in solemn assembly convened.

Under this government the people lived very happily, and the colony advanced with signal prosperity for two years. During this time the General Assembly of Connecticut had made an honest effort to negotiate a settlement between the Company and the Proprietaries of Pennsylvania, but in vain. An able commission had been sent to Philadelphia, consisting of Colonel Eliphalet Dyer,

* Chapman.

Doctor Johnson and J. Strong; but Governor Penn would not listen to their propositions, although they were of the most equitable description. Upon this refusal, even to acknowledge the commission, the General assembly caused a case to be made up and transmitted to England for the ablest legal opinions that could be obtained. This case was submitted to Edward, afterward Lord Thurlow, Alexander Wedderburn, Richard Jackson, and J. Dunning,—all famous for their learning in the law, who gave a united opinion in favor of the Company. Thus fortified, the General Assembly of Connecticut took higher ground, and perceiving how greatly the colony was flourishing, in October, 1773, they passed a resolution asserting their claim to the jurisdiction of the territory, and their determination in some proper way to support the claim.* The Company now renewed their application to be taken into the Colony of Connecticut, in which request the General Assembly acquiesced, and the entire territory was erected into a chartered town, called Westmoreland, and attached to the county of Litchfield. The laws of Connecticut were extended over the settlement; representatives from Westmoreland were admitted to sit in the General Assembly;† and Zebulon Butler and Nathan Denniston were regularly com-

* Trumbull.

† Idem.

missioned justices of the peace. All necessary regulations for the due administration of the local affairs of the settlements were made; new townships were opened and entered upon by emigrants, and the colony advanced with unprecedented prosperity. Govornor Penn and his Council beheld these movements with high displeasure, and sundry proclamations were issued forbidding the people to obey the laws and authorities of Connecticut; but these paper missives were no more regarded than would have been an equal number of vermilion edicts from the Emperor of China.

Two years more of repose were enjoyed by the colonists of the Company, during which they flourished to a degree that could scarcely have been anticipated by their principals. The valley was laid out into townships five miles square, and under the hand of industry, the teeming soil soon made it to smile in beauty like a little paradise. The town immediately adjoining the Wyoming Fort, was planted by Colonel Durkee, and named WILKESBARRE, in honor of John *Wilkes* and Colonel *Barré*, as heretofore mentioned. But in the autumn of 1775, just at the moment when the Hercules of the new world was grappling with the giant power of Great Britain, the torch of civil war was again lighted by the people of Pennsylvania. Among the settlements of the Connecticut people, which had been pushed beyond the confines of the valley of Wyoming, was one upon the West Branch of the Susquehanna, uniting with the main stream at Northumberland, about sixty miles below. On the 28th of September, 1775, this plantation was attacked by a body of the Northumberland militia, who, after killing one man, and wounding several others, made prisoners of the residue of the settlers, and conducted them to Sunbury, where they were thrown into prison. The tedium and vexation of their confinement was measurably relieved for a season, however, by the drollery of one of their number,—an active and vivacious young man named Benjamin Bidlack, of whom more will be related hereafter. He was not only, like the Yorick of Hamlet, "a fellow of infinite humor," but athletic and strong—at least as strong as the *shorn* Samson. And as with Samson, the Philistines into whose hands he fell would fain, from day to day, bring Bidlack forth to make them sport. He sang capital songs, among which was one called "The Swaggering Man," each verse ending—

"And away went the swaggering man."

This was a favorite song with the captors, and they urged him repeatedly to sing it—which he very cheefully did—for he was as full of fun as any of them—insisting, however, that they must enlarge their circle, and give him space "to *act* the part." And this he did to admiration—at least in one instance. Having by his conduct allayed all suspicion of sinister intentions, and induced his guards to give him ample room wherein to exercise his limbs while singing their favorite song, as he sang the last line—

"And away went the swaggering man,"

suiting the action to the words, he sprang from the circle like a leaping panther, and bounded away with a fleetness that distanced competition, and gained his liberty.

At about the same time when Bidlack and his companions were taken to Sunbury, a number of boats, trading down the river from Wyoming, were attacked and plundered by the Pennsylvanians. These acts of course produced immediate and extreme indignation on the part of the Connecticut colonists

But instead of seizing their arms at once, and rushing to the liberation of their imprisoned friends, they petitioned the Provincial Congress, then in session, to interpose for the adjustment of the controversy. On the 9th of November the petition was considered by Congress, and a conciliatory resolution, with a suitable preamble, was adopted, setting forth the danger of internal hostilities in that critical conjuncture of the affairs of the American colonies, and urging the governments of Pennsylvania and Connecticut to the adoption of the most speedy and effectual measures to prevent such hostilities.*

The voice of Congress, however, was unheeded, and the imprisonment of the settlers from the West Branch was rendered more rigid than before. Apprehensions were moreover excited among the people of Northumberland, that the chafed inhabitants of Wyoming might make a descent upon Sunbury, liberate their friends and fire the town. Whether these apprehensions were caused by actual threats, or by a sense of their own wrong doing, cannot be predicated; but one of the consequences was a proposition, by a Colonel Plunkett of Northumberland, to raise a force and march against Wyoming for its immediate conquest and subjugation. The proposal was listened to by the Governor, and orders were issued to Plunkett to raise the necessary forces, and execute his purpose by the expulsion of the Connecticut settlers.

Plunkett was himself a civil magistrate, as well as a colonel; but in order to impart to the expedition a *civil* rather than a *military* character, the army was called the "Posse" of the county, and the colonel was accompanied by the sheriff. The number of men raised for the service was seven hundred, well provisioned, and amply fur-

* Journals of the old Congress.

nished with military stores, which latter were embarked upon the river in boats.

These formidable preparations gave no small degree of uneasiness to Congress, yet in session in Philadelphia, and resolutions were immediately passed, urging the Pennsylvanians at once to desist from any farther hostile proceedings, to liberate the prisoners that had been taken, and restore all private property that had been detained; and in a word to refrain from any and every hostile act, until the dispute between the parties could be legally decided.* But these resolutions commanded no more respect from the Pennsylvanians, either the government or the people, than the others. Plunkett, who had already commenced his march, pursued his course. Winter, however, was approaching; the boats were impeded in their progress by a swollen torrent, bearing masses of ice upon its surface; and the troops could not of course proceed in advance of their supplies. The advance of the invaders, therefore, was as deliberate as those who were to be attacked could desire.

It was near the close of December when Colonel Plunkett reached the Nanticoke rapids, in the narrow mountain defile through which the Susquehanna rushes on its escape from Wyoming, and the obstructions of which were so great, that the boats could not be propelled any farther. Detach-

* Journals of Congress.

ing a guard, therefore, for the protection of his supplies, the Colonel continued his march by the road on the west side of the river, which winds along by the bases of the mountains, whose rocky battlements at times hang impending over it. After emerging from the gorge, and entering the valley, the prospect, on that side of the river, is at one point nearly intercepted by a large rock projecting from a spur of the Shawanese Mountain, and extending nearly to the edge of the river.

Entering the valley from the south, this rock, or ledge, presents a formidable perpendicular front, as even as though it were a structure of hewn mason-work. The road winds along at the base of the ledge, turning its projection close by the river. The Colonel was somewhat startled as he came suddenly in view of this gigantic defence; nor was his surprise diminished by a second glance, which taught him that the extended brow of the rock had been fortified, while a volley of musketry told him farther, that this most unexpected fortification was well garrisoned.

The whole passage of the defile at the Nanticoke falls presents exactly such a geological conformation as it would delight a Tyrolese population to defend; and the Yankees of Wyoming had not been blind to the advantages which nature had here supplied for arresting the approach of the invader. The fire had been given too soon for much effect;* but it served to throw the forces of Plunkett into confusion, and an immediate retreat behind another mountainous projection, for consultation, was the consequence. The hazard of turning the point of the battlemented Shawanese rock, defended by an enemy of unknown strength, thus securely posted, was too great to be entertained. It was therefore determined, by the aid of a batteau brought past the rapids by land for that purpose, to cross the river and march upon the fort of Wyoming along the eastern shore.

Immediate dispositions were made for executing this change in the plan of the campaign; but on the approach of the batteau to the opposite side with the first detachment of the invaders, headed by Colonel Plunkett himself, a sharp fire from an ambuscade gave unequivocal evidence that their every possible movement had been anticipated. This ambuscade was commanded by Lieutenant Stewart, who had reserved his fire until the invaders were leaping on shore. One man was killed by the first fire, and several others wounded. So warm a reception upon both sides of the river had not been foreseen. The boat was therefore in-

* Gordon affirms that this volley killed one man, and dangerously wounded three others of Plunkett's party. He also states that Colonel Plunkett was at first met in an amicable manner, by a party of the settlers, under one of their leaders, and that he assured them his only object was to arrest the persons named in his warrants, protesting that he would offer violence to no one submitting to the laws.

stantly pushed from the land, and without attempting to regain the shore whence they had embarked, was suffered to drift down the stream and over the rapids, to the fleet of provision boats below. The chivalrous Colonel, being a peace officer, lay down in the bottom of the boat to avoid the shots that were sent after him. His troops on the western side, however, attempted to cover his retreat, by firing at random into the thicket where Stewart had posted his men. By one of these chance shots a man named Bowen was killed at the instant when he was raising himself above the breast-work to fire upon the enemy.

Plunkett's entire force now fell back upon the boats where another council of war took place. To attempt to force the passage of the terrific rock, frowning in its own strength, and bristling with bayonets besides, was evidently impracticable. It could not be carried by assault, for want of two articles,—courage and scaling ladders.—To march around the point the garrison would not allow them. And to avoid the difficulty by threading the ravines of the mountains in the rear on either side, would be a yet more dangerous undertaking, inasmuch as the Yankees might not only use their fire-arms, but also tumble the rocks down upon their heads and ignominiously crush them to death. In addition to all which, it was now evident that even should they be successful in sitting down before the fort of Wyoming, and opening their entrenchments, the works would not be very easily taken; while their own situation, by the destruction of their boats, and the cutting off of their supplies, and in sundry other respects, might be rendered exceedingly uncomfortable. Under such an accumulation of untoward circumstances and forbidding prospects, discretion was wisely esteemed the better part of valor, and the expedition was abandoned.

With this unsuccessful effort "terminated the endeavors of the Executive of Pennsylvania to expel, by force, her troublesome inmates. They had become very numerous, and had extended themselves over a large tract of country, upon which they had planted and built with great success. Possession, by lapse of time, was growing into right, to preserve which, it was obvious, the possessors had resolved to devote their lives. Forcible ejection would therefore be followed with much bloodshed, and wide-extended misery, which would tend greatly to weaken the efforts of the two colonies in the common cause against Great Britain."*

* * * * * * *

For a season after the breaking out of the war of the revolution, Wyoming was allowed a state

* Gordon.

of comparative repose. The government of Pennsylvania was changed by the removal of the Proprietaries, or successors of Penn, and the formation of a new constitution ; and both Connecticut and Pennsylvania had other and more important demands upon their attention than the disputes of rival claimants for a remote and sequestered territory. A census was taken, and the whole population of the several towns of the valley, now acknowledging the jurisdiction of Connecticut, was computed at about two thousand five hundred souls.* Two companies of regular troops were raised, under resolutions of Congress, commanded by Captains Ransom and Durkee, of eighty-two men each. These companies were mustered and counted as part of the Connecticut levies, and attached to the Connecticut line. They were, moreover, efficient soldiers, having been engaged in the brilliant affair of Millstone, the bloody and unto-

* Chapman, who resided in Wyoming at the time he wrote his history, twenty-five years ago, states the number of inhabitants at five thousand,and so does Marshall. But in a recent appeal to the legislature of Connecticut by a committee from Wyoming, drawn up by the Hon. Charles Miner, for more than forty years a resident of that place, the population at that period is stated at 2500. Considering the number of soldiers raised for the regular service there, and the number killed in the massacre, twenty-five hundred seems too small; but in answer to an objection raised by the author, Mr. Miner writes—"In 1773 there were 430 taxables; allowing five inhabitants to each taxable, will give 2150. In 1777, a new oath of allegiance was required by Connecticut of every freeman. We have the recorded list returned by all the justices; the number is 269. Add for these with the army 100, for many in the service were not of age, and it will make 369. Multiply this by six gives 2214 inhabitants. The number did not exceed 2500."

ward battles of Brandywine and Germantown, and in the terrible cannonade of Mud-bank.

Notwithstanding the remoteness of its position, and its peculiar exposure to the attacks of the enemy, rendered more perilous from its contiguity to the territory of the Six Nations, and the readiness with which a descent could be made upon them by the way of the Susquehanna, the people of Wyoming were prompt to espouse the cause of their country, and as early as the first of August, 1775, in town meeting, they voted "that we will unanimously join our brethren of America in the common cause of defending our country." In the month of August in the following year it was voted "that the people be called upon to work on the forts, without either fee or reward from the town." And in 1777 the people passed a vote empowering a committee of inspectors "to supply the soldiers' wives, and the soldiers' widows, and their families, with the necessaries of life."*

But the unanimity asserted in the first resolution cited above must have been a figurative expression, since, unhappily, there were loyalists in Wyoming, as elsewhere. The civil wars, moreover, had left many bitter feelings to rankle in the bosoms of such as had been actively engaged in those feuds. Added to which, in the

* MS. records of Westmoreland, in the possession of Charles Miner.

exuberance of their patriotism, between twenty and thirty suspected citizens were seized by the Whigs, and dragged over the woods and mountains into Connecticut, for imprisonment. Nine of these men were discharged immediately, and in a few days the residue were set at liberty for want of proof to warrant their detention. They all speedily thereafter found their way into the ranks of the enemy in Canada—among the Tory rangers of Sir John Johnson and Colonel John Butler. These points are stated thus minutely, because they are essential to a just understanding of the darker features of the history that is to follow.

The Indians of the Six Nations were not brought actively into the field against the Americans until the summer of 1777. From that moment, the whole extended frontiers of the colonies, reaching from Lake Champlain round the Northwest and South to the Floridas, were harrassed by the savages. Wyoming, however, did not immediately suffer so severely as many other border settlements. Some straggling parties of Indians, it is true, hung about the valley, while General St. Leger was besieging Fort Stanwix; but after a few skirmishes with the inhabitants, they withdrew, and the people were not again disturbed during that year, save in two or three instances in the autumn. On one of these occasions, Mr.—afterward Lieutenant John Jenkins, Jun.,— visiting the upper part of the Wyoming valley, was met by a hostile party, taken to Niagara, and thence to Montreal, whence he was exchanged in 1778. At the time of his capture, the same party of loyalists took prisoner an old man named Fitzgerald. Placing him upon an elevated seat, they required of him a renunciation of his rebel-principles, and an acknowledgment of allegiance to the King, threatening death if he refused. "I am an old man," replied the silvery-headed patriot, "and can live but a few years at most. I would rather die now, and die a friend to my country, than live a few years longer and then die a tory."* It was bravely said, and even the enemy must have regarded the old man with reverence, for their threat was not executed.

But no small degree of uneasiness was created early in 1778, by the conduct of the loyalists yet remaining in the valley. These apprehensions, however, were allayed for a time, by messages of peace received from the Indians. But these messages were deceptive, as was ascertained in March by the confessions of one of them, who, while in a state of partial intoxication, revealed their real purposes. They had sent their messengers to Wyoming merely to lull the inhabitants into such a state of security as would enable them to strike

* Statement of Elisha Harding—Wyoming Memorial to Congress.

a surer blow. The party to which the drunken Indian belonged, was thereupon arrested and detained, while the women were allowed to depart. It was not long before the inhabitants of the outer settlements,—especially those some thirty miles distant, upon the river north,—were grievously annoyed, and many of them clustered in upon the older and larger towns. In April and May, the savages hanging upon the outskirts became yet more numerous, and more audacious, committing frequent robberies, and in June several murders. Thenceforward, " their pathways were ambushed, and midnight was often red with the conflagration of their dwellings."*

There were no settlements contiguous to Wyoming, upon which the people might call for aid in case of sudden emergency. It was not merely an outpost, but was an isolated community, almost embosomed in the country of a savage enemy. To Sunbury, the nearest inhabited post down the Susquehanna, it was sixty miles; through the great swamp, and over the Pokono range of mountains to the settlements on the Delaware, a pathless wilderness, it was also sixty miles. The Six Nations, ever the most to be dreaded upon the war-path, occupied all the upper branches of the Susquehanna, and were within a few hours' sail of the

* Memorial to the Legislature of Connecticut.

plantations.* Thus situated, there had been a conventional understanding between the government and the people of Wyoming, that the regular troops enlisted among them should be stationed there, for the defence of the valley; but the exigencies of the service required their action elsewhere, and not only were they ordered away, but other enlistments were made, to the number, in all, of about three hundred. The only means of defence remaining consisted of militia-men, the greater proportion of whom were either too old or too young for the regular service. And yet upon these men devolved the duties of cultivating the lands to obtain subsistence for the settlements, and likewise of performing regular garrison duty in the little stockade defences which were dignified by the name of forts, and of patrolling the outskirts of the settlements, and exploring the thickets, in order to guard against surprise from the wily Indians, and their yet more vindictive tory allies.

There were some six or seven of those defences called forts, but consisting only of stockades, or logs, planted upright in the earth, and about fourteen feet high, the enclosures within which served also as places of retreat for the women and children in seasons of alarm. They had no artillery

* Memorial to the Legislature of Connecticut.

save a single four-pounder, kept at Wilkesbarré, as an alarm-gun, and their only means of defence, therefore, consisted of small arms, not always in the best order, as is ever the case with militia. Thus weakened by the absence of its most efficient men, and otherwise exposed, Wyoming presented a point of attack too favorable to escape the attention of the British and Indian commanders in the country of the Six Nations, and in Canada. They were also, beyond doubt, stimulated to undertake an expedition against it by the absconding loyalists, who were burning with a much stronger desire to avenge what they conceived to be their own wrongs, than with ardor to serve their king.

Under these circumstances, the ever memorable expedition of Colonel John Butler, with his own Tory Rangers, a detachment of Sir John Johnson's Royal Greens, and a large body of Indians, chiefly Senecas, was undertaken against Wyoming early in the summer of 1778, and, alas! was but too successful. The forces of the invaders are estimated by some authorities at eleven hundred, seven hundred of whom were Indians. Other accounts compute the Indians at four hundred. Opposed to these forces were a company of some forty or fifty regulars, under Captain Hewitt, and such numbers of the militia, heretofore described, as could be hastily collected. Boys and old men, fathers and sons, aged men and grandfathers, were obliged to snatch such weapons as were at hand, and take the field at the warning of a moment. Nor were the so-called regulars under Captain Hewit, regulars in the proper acceptation of the term. The Captain had but recently received his commission, with directions to recruit at Wyoming. He had enlisted these forty or fifty men, who were obliged to find their own arms; and having had but a short and indifferent experience in martial exercise, when the enemy came they were militia men still, though not such in name. The expedition of the enemy moved from Niagara, across the Genesee country,and down the Chemung river to Tioga Point, whence they embarked upon the Susquehanna, and landed about twenty miles above Wyoming—entering the valley through a notch from the west, about a mile below the head of the valley, and taking possession of a small defence called Wintermoot, after the name of its proprietor, an opulent loyalist of that town.* Colonel John

* Among the papers of Colonel Zebulon Butler, Mr. Miner has discovered a document labelled, "A list of Tories who joined the Indians." There are sixty-one names on the list, but of these there were but three New-England men. Most of them were transient persons, or laborers; or men who had gone to Wyoming as hunters and trappers. Six are of one family—the Wintermoots; four were named *Secord;* three were *Pawlings:* three *Lanaways;* and four *Van Alstynes.* It is not believed that there were more than twenty or twenty-five tory families. Nine of them were from the Mohawk valley, who were probably sent thither by the Johnsons to poison the settlement if possible, or as spies. Four of

Butler established his head quarters at this place, and thence, for several days, scouts and foraging parties were sent out, for observation and to collect provisions. The enemy's arrival at Fort Wintermoot, which stood on the bank of the river, was on the 2d of July.

The dark and threatening sayings of a drunken Indian, as already stated, had awakened some suspicions that an attack was meditated by the enemy in the course of the season,and a message had been sent to the head quarters of the continental army early in June, praying for a detachment of troops for their protection. To this request no answer had been received. To fly, however, with their women and children, with an agile enemy upon their very heels, was impossible, even had the thought been entertained. But it was not. "Retirement or flight was alike impossible, and there was no security but in victory. Unequal as was the conflict, therefore, and hopeless as it was in the eye of prudence, the young and athletic men, fit to bear arms, and enlisted for their special defence, being absent with the main army ; yet the inhabitants, looking to their dependent wives, mothers, sisters, little ones, took counsel of their courage, and

them were from Kinderhook ; six from the county of Westchester, (N. Y.) The Wintermoots were from Minisink. There were not ten tory families who had resided two years in Wyoming.—*Letter to the Author from Charles Miner.*

resolved to give the enemy battle."* Having such treasures to defend, in addition to the great pending question of National existence and liberty, they felt strong confidence that they should be able to repel the invader. No sooner, therefore, was the presence of the enemy known, than the militia rapidly assembled at the old defence, "Fort Forty," so frequently mentioned in the preceding narrative of the civil wars, which was situated immediately on the west bank of the river, some three miles north of Wilkesbarré. Small garrisons of aged men were left in the other feeble forts of the colonists, for the protection of the women and children assembled therein, while the majority of those capable of bearing arms, old men and boys, fathers, grand-fathers and grandsons, assembled at Fort Forty, to the number of nearly four hundred.

Colonel Zebulon Butler, heretofore mentioned as a soldier in the French war, and as being placed in the commission of the peace, was now an officer in the continental army, and happening to be at home at the time of the invasion, on the invitation of the people he accepted the command. A council of war was called on the morning of the 3rd of July, to determine upon the expediency of marching out and giving the enemy battle, or of await-

* Memorial to the Legislature of Connecticut.

ing his advance. There were some who preferred delay, in the hope that a reinforcement would arrive from the camp of General Washington. Others maintained that as no advices had been received thence in reply to their application, the messenger had probably been cut off; and as the enemy's force was constantly increasing, they thought it best to meet and repel him at once if possible. The debates were warm; and before they were ended, five commissioned officers, who, hearing of the anticipated invasion had obtained permission to return for the defence of their families, joined them. Their arrival extinguished the hope of present succor by reinforcements from the main army, and the result of the council was a determination for an immediate attack.

As soon as the proper dispositions could be made, Colonel Zebulon Butler placed himself at the head of the undisciplined force, and led them forward, the design being to take the enemy by surprise. And such would probably have been the issue, but for the occurrence of one of those untoward incidents against which human wisdom cannot guard. A scout, having been sent forward to reconnoitre, found the enemy at dinner, not anticipating an attack, and in high and frolicksome glee. But on his return to report the fact the scout was fired upon by a straggling Indian, who gave the alarm. The consequence was, that on the approach of the Americans, they found the enemy in line ready for their reception. Colonel Zebulon Butler commanded the right of the Americans, aided by Major Garratt. The left was commanded by Colonel Dennison, of the Wyoming militia, assisted by Lieut. Colonel Dorrance. Opposed to the right of the Americans and also resting upon the bank of the river, was Colonel John Butler, with his rangers. The right of the enemy, resting upon, or rather extending into, a marsh, was composed principally of Indians and tories, led by a celebrated Seneca chief named *Gi-en-gwah-toh*; or, *He-who-goes-in-the-Smoke.* The field of battle was a plain, partly cleared and partly covered with shrub oaks and yellow pines.

The action began soon after four o'clock in the afternoon, and was for a time kept up on both sides with great spirit. The right of the Americans advanced bravely as they fired, and the best troops of the enemy were compelled to give back. But while the advantages were thus promising with the Americans on the right, far different was the situation of affairs on the left. Penetrating the thicket of the swamp, a heavy body of the Indians were enabled, unperceived, to outflank Col. Dennison, and suddenly like a dark cloud to fall upon his rear. The Americans, thus standing between two fires, fell fast before the rifles of the Indians and tories, but yet they faltered not, until the order of Colonel Dennison to "fall back," for the purpose only of changing position, was mistaken for an order to retreat. This misconception was fatal. The confusion instantly became so great that restoration to order was impossible. The enemy, not more brave, but better skilled in the horrid trade of savage war, and far more numerous withal, sprang forward, and as they made the air resound with their frightful yells, rushed upon the Americans, hand to hand, tomahawk and spear. But the handful of regulars and those who were not at first thrown into confusion did all that men could dare or achieve to retrieve the fortunes of the day. Observing one of his men to yield a little ground, Colonel Dorrance called to him with the utmost coolness—"Stand up to your work, sir!" The Colonel immediately fell.* As the enemy obtained the rear, an officer notified Captain Hewitt of the fact, and inquired, "Shall we retreat, sir?" "I'll be d—d if I do," was his reply—and he fell instantly dead at the head of his little command. The retreat now became a flight, attended with horrible carnage. "We are nearly alone," said an officer named Westbrook—"shall we go?" "I'll have one more shot," said a Mr. Cooper, in reply. At the same instant a savage sprang toward him with his spear, but was brought

* The Rev. John Dorrance, pastor of the Presbyterian church in Wilkesbarré [in 1839] is a grand-son of Colonel Dorrance.

to the ground in his leap, and Cooper deliberately re-loaded his piece before he moved. He was one of the few who survived the battle. On the first discovery of the confusion on the left, Colonel Zebulon Butler rode into the thickest of the melée, exclaiming — "Don't leave me, my children! The victory will yet be ours." But numbers and discipline, and the Indians besides, were against the Americans, and their rout was complete.

During the flight to Fort Forty, the scene was that of horrible slaughter. Nor did the darkness put an end to the work of death. No assault was made upon the fort that night; but many of the prisoners taken were put to death by torture. The place of these murders was about two miles north of Fort Forty, upon a rock, around which the Indians formed themselves in a circle. Sixteen of the prisoners, placed in a ring around a rock, near the river, were held by stout Indians, while the squaws struck their heads open with the tomahawk. Only one individual, a powerful man named Hammond, by a desperate effort, escaped. Seeing one after another of his fellows perish by the bloody hand of the insatiate squaw acting as executioner, Hammond sprang forward suddenly, and rushing through the circle, outstripped his pursuers, and was not retaken.* In a similar ring, a little far-

* Lebbeus Hammond. He afterward removed to Tioga County, (N. Y.) where he lived and died a very respectable citizen.

ther north of the rock, nine persons were murdered in the same way.* It has been said, both in tradition and in print, that the priestess of this bloody sacrifice was the celebrated Catharine Montour, sometimes called Queen Esther, whose residence was at Catharinestown, at the head of Seneca Lake. But the statement is improbable. Catharine Montour was a half-breed, who had been well educated in Canada. Her reputed father was one of the French governors of that province when appertaining to the crown of France, and she herself was a lady of comparative refinement. She was much caressed in Philadelphia, and mingled in the best society.† Hence the remotest belief cannot be entertained that she was the Hecate of that fell night. A night indeed of terror, —described with truth and power by the bard of Gertrude, as the dread hour when—

> —"Sounds that mingled laugh, and shout, and scream
> To freeze the blood in one discordant jar,
> Rung the pealing thunderbolts of war.
> Whoop after whoop with rack the ear assailed,
> As if unearthly fiends had burst their bar;
> While rapidly the marksman's shot prevailed;—
> And aye, as if for death, some lonely trumpet wailed!"

When the numbers are taken into the account, the slaughter on this occasion was dreadful. The five officers who arrived from the continential ar-

* Note in Silliman's Journal, vol. xviii.

† Vide Whitham Marshe's Journal of a treaty with the Six Nations at Lancaster, in 1744.

my on the morning of the battle were all slain. Captain Hewitt, who fell, had a son in the battle with him, aged eighteen. Captain Aholiah Buck and his son, aged only fourteen, were both slain. Anderson Dana, the representative of the valley in the Connecticut legislature, had returned from the session just in season to fight and fall. His son-in-law, Stephen Whiting, who had been married to his daughter but a few months before, went into the battle with him, and was also slain. Two brothers, named Perrin and Jeremiah Ross, were slain in the battle.* There was a large family named Gore, one of whom was with the continental army. Those at home, five brothers and two brothers-in-law, went into the battle, and of these, five were dead upon the field at night, a sixth was wounded, and one only escaped unhurt. Of the family of Mr. Weeks, seven went into the battle, viz: five sons and sons-in-law, and two inmates. Not one of the number escaped. These are but a few instances of many, selected merely for the purpose of showing how general was the rush to the field, and how direful the carnage.†

* Brothers of General William Ross, who is yet living, (1840,) in Wyoming.

† Among the officers killed in the battle, the following names have been preserved. Lieutenant Colonel George Dorrance:—Major Wait Garrett;—Captains Dottrick Hewitt, Robert Durkee,* Aholiah Buck, Asa Whittlesey, Lazarus Stewart, Samuel Ransom,* James Bidlack, ——— Geere, ——— M'Kanachin, ——— Wigdon;—Lieutenants, Timothy Pierce,* James Wells,* Elijah Shoemaker, Lazarus Stewart, 2d, Perin Ross,* Asa Stevens; Ensigns, Asa Gore, ——— Avery. ☞ Those marked (*) were the five who arrived from the Continental army on the morning of the battle.

The closing scene of that memorable drama, was in terrible keeping with the bloody acts which had preceeded. Flushed with victory, the savage Senecas still pursued their victims, filling the valley with their wild screams, and rushing onward in overwhelming numbers. The few Americans who escaped the murderous conflict in the field, fled precipitately to Wilkesbarré Fort, where were gathered women and children, waiting the dread issue of the contest, with breathless anxiety. Their return only added to the dreadful consternation, already prevailing in the Fortress. Siezed with panic, at the idea of being cooped up there, with the certainty of meeting a ruthless destruction, if they remained, they fled to the mountains, and sought refuge in the recesses of a dreary swamp, called afterward, from the numbers who fell there, the "Shades of Death." But an enemy was on their track, familiar with swamps, and expert in threading the deepest fastnesses. They were soon found, when the work of destruction recommenced with a fiercer violence. To the few survivors this was "a night long to be remembered." Behind them they saw the flames spreading destruction through the valley. On one side of them was the battle-field, on which lay their brave brethren weltering in their blood. Around them, the agonizing shriek proclaimed that the dreadful carnage was still going on.

* * * * * * * * *

The fair fields of Wyoming presented a melancholly spectacle on the morning of the 4th. The pursuit of the Indians had ceased the preceding evening with the nightfall, and the work of death was completed by the tragedy at the Bloody Rock. But the sun arose upon the carcasses of the dead —not only dead but horribly mangled—strewn over the plain, from the point where the battle began to Fort Forty. A few stragglers had at first taken refuge in that defence, and by the morning light, all who had not been slain, or who had not betaken themselves to the mountains, had collected within the Fort, before which Colonel John Butler with his motley forces appeared at an early hour, and demanded a surrender. It appears that some negotiations upon the subject of a capitulation had been interchanged the preceding evening, at Wintermoot's. Be that as in may, it was understood that no terms would be listened to by the enemy but that of the unconditional surrender of Colonel Zebulon Butler, and the small handful of regular troops, numbering only fifteen, who had escaped the battle, to the tender mercies of the Indians. Under these circumstances, means of escape for the Colonel and these fifteen men were found during the night. The former succeeded in making his way to one of the Moravian settlements on the Lehigh, and the latter fled to Shamokin.

The little fort being surrounded by a cloud of Indians and tories, and having no means of defence, Colonel Dennison, now in command, yielded to the force of circumstances, and the importunities of the women and children, and entered into articles of capitulation. By this it was mutually agreed that the inhabitants of the settlement should lay down their arms, the fort be demolished, and the continental stores be delivered to the conquerors. The inhabitants of the settlement were to be permitted to occupy their farms peaceably, and without molestation of their persons. The loyalists were to be allowed to remain in the undisturbed possession of their farms, and to trade without interruption. Colonel Dennison and the inhabitants stipulated not again to take up arms during the contest, and Colonel John Butler agreed to use his utmost influence to cause the private property of the inhabitants to be respected.

But the last-mentioned stipulation was entirely unheeded by the Indians, who were not, and perhaps could not be, restrained from the work of rapine and plunder. The surrender had no sooner taken place than they spread through the valley. Every house not belonging to a loyalist was plundered, and then laid in ashes. The greater part of the inhabitants, not engaged in the battle, men, women, and children, had fled to the mountains toward the Delaware; and as the work of destruction was re-commenced, many others followed the example. The village of Wilkesbarré consisted of twenty-three houses. It was burnt, and the entire population fled. No lives were taken by the Indians after the surrender; but numbers of women and children perished in the dismal swamp on the Pokono range of mountains, in the flight which will be presently described. The whole number of people killed and missing was about three hundred.*

Colonel Benjamin Dorrance, yet a resident of Wyoming, a gentleman of character and affluence, was a lad in Fort Forty at the time of its surren-

* Until the publication, year before last, of the Life of Brant, by the writer of the present work, it had been asserted in all history that that celebrated Mohawk chieftain was the Indian leader at Wyoming. He himself always denied any participation in this bloody expedition, and his assertions were corroborated by the British officers, when questioned upon the subject. But these denials, not appearing in history, relieved him not from the odium; and the "monster Brant" has been denounced, the world over, as the author of the massacre. In the work referred to above, the author took upon himself the vindication of the savage warrior from the accusation, and, as he thought at the time, with success. A reviewer of that work, however, in the Democratic Magazine, who is understood to be the Hon. Caleb Cushing of Massachusetts, disputed the point, maintaining that the vindication was not satisfactory. The author thereupon made a journey into the Seneca country, and pushed the investigation among the surviving chiefs and warriors of the Senecas engaged in that campaign. The result was a triumphant acquittal of Brant from all participation therein. The celebrated chief Captain Pollard, whose Indian name is *Kaoundoowand*, a fine old warrior, was a young chief in that battle. He gave a full account of it, and was clear and positive in his declarations that Brant and the Mohawks were not engaged in that campaign at all. Their leader, he said, was *Gi-en-gwah-toh*, as already mentioned in the text, who lived many years afterward, and was succeeded in his chieftaincy by the late *Young King*. That point of history, therefore, may be considered as conclusively settled.

der to Butler and the Indians, and remembers freshly the circumstances. He states that after the capitulation, the British regular troops marched into the fort by the northern or upper gateway, while Gi-en-gwah-toh and his Indians entered at the southern portal. Colonel Dorrance recollects well the look and conduct of the Indian leader. His nostrils distended, and his burning eyes flash ing like a basilisk's, as he glanced quickly to the right, and to the left, with true Indian jealousy and circumspection, lest some treachery or ambuscade might await them within the fort. But the powerful and the brave had fallen. Old age was there, tottering upon his crutches, and widowed women, with their helpless children clinging to their garments —sobbing in all the bitterness of a woe at which the ruthless savages mocked.*

But after all, the greatest barbarities of this celebrated massacre were committed by the tories. Many loyalists, as has been already seen, had months before united themselves with the enemy at Niagara ; and on his arrival at the head of the valley, many more of the settlers joined his ranks.

* "The Hazleton Travellers," by Charles Miner. I shall have frequent occasion to repeat this reference in the succeeding chapter, and it may be well to explain what is the work referred to. It is not a book, but a series of historical essays, or rather colloquies, published by Mr Miner in the village paper of Wyoming, during the years 1837 and 1838. In these papers, the author introduces a party of strangers from Hazleton, who accompany him in an imaginary journey through the valley, and to whom the author is supposed to recount its history in a series of familiar conversations. These papers have been of great value to the author.

These all fought with the most brutal ferocity against their former neighbors, and were guilty of acts of which even this distant contemplation curdles the blood. Of these acts two or three must suffice. During the bloody fight of the 3d, some of the fugitives plunged into the river and escaped to the opposite shore. A few landed upon Monockonock Island, having lost their arms in the flight, and were pursued thither. One of them was discovered by his own brother, who had espoused the side of the crown. The unarmed Whig fell upon his knees before his brother and offered to serve him as a slave forever, if he would but spare his life. But the fiend in human form was inexorable; he muttered "*you are a d—d rebel,*" and shot him dead. This tale is too horrible for belief; but a survivor of the battle, a Mr. Baldwin, whose name will occur again, confirmed its truth to the writer with his own lips. He knew the brothers well, and in August, 1839, declared the statement to be true.*

A tradition is rehearsed, that, long after this unparalled act of fratricide, the murderer, haunted by conscience, wandered back from Canada, whither he had fled, to the spot where the fearful deed was committed, and found there a grave, whence he could almost hear "the voice of his

* Vide also Chapman.

brother's blood" crying yet for vengeance. The legend needs a voucher for its authenticity. But it has nevertheless been wrought into a metrical tale, by one of our country's gifted bards,* with thrilling and powerful effect: The reader will not regret the interruption of the historical narrative while the story is reproduced in measures so spirited and beautiful:—

THE DEATH OF THE FRATRICIDE.

He stood on the brow of the well known hill,
Its few gray oaks moan'd over him still—
The last of that forest which cast the gloom,
Of its shadow at eve o'er his childhood's home;
And the beautiful valley beneath him lay
With its quivering leaves, and its streams at play,
And the sunshine over it all the while
Like the golden shower of the Eastern Isle.

He knew the rock with its clinging vine,
And its gray top touch'd by the slant sunshine;
And the delicate stream which crept beneath,
Soft as the flow of an infant's breath;
And the flowers which leaned to the West wind's sigh,
Kissing each ripple which glided by,
And he knew every valley and wooded swell,
For the visions of childhood are treasured well!

Why shook the old man as his eye glanc'd down
That narrow ravine where the rude cliffs frown,
With their shaggy brows and their teeth of stone,
And their grim shade back from the sunlight thrown?
What saw he there save the dreary glen,
Where the shy fox crept from the eye of men,
And the great owl sat on the leafy limb
That the hateful sun might not look on him?

* Whittier.

Fix'd, glassy, and strange was that old man's eye!
As if a spectre was stealing by!
And glared it still on that narrow dell
Where thicker and browner the twilight fell;
Yet at every sigh of the fitful wind,
Or stirring of leaves in the wood behind,
His wild glance wander'd the landscape o'er,
Then fix'd on that desolate dell once more!

Oh! who shall tell of the thoughts which ran
Through the dizzied brain of that gray old man?
His childhood's home — and his fathers's toil —
And his sister's kiss — and his mother's smile —
And his brother's laughter and gamesome mirth,
At the village school and the winter hearth —
The beautiful thoughts of his early time,
Ere his heart grew dark with its later crime.

And darker and wilder his visions came
Of the deadly feud and the midnight flame,
Of the Indian's knife with its slaughter red,
Of the ghastly forms of the scalpless dead,
Of his own fierce deeds in that fearful hour
When the terrible Brant was forth in power, —
And he clasp'd his hands o'er his burning eye,
To shadow the vision which glided by.

It came with the rush of the battle storm —
With a brother's shaken and kneeling form,
And his prayer for life when a brother's arm
Was lifted above him for mortal harm,
And the fiendish curse, and the groan of death,
And the welling blood, and the gurgling breath,
And the scalp torn off while each nerve could feel
The wrenching hand and the jagged steel!

And the old man groan'd — for he saw, again,
The mangled corse of his brother slain,
As it lay where his hand had hurl'd it then,
At the shadow'd foot of that fearful glen!
And it rose erect, with the death-pang grim,
And pointed its bloody finger at him! —
And his heart grew cold — and the curse of Cain
Burn'd like a fire in the old man's brain!

Oh, had he not seen that spectre rise
On the blue of the cold Canadian skies!
From the lakes which sleep in the ancient wood,
It had risen to whisper its tale of blood,
And follow'd his bark to the sombre shore,
And glared by night through the wigwam door;
And here — on his own familiar hill —
It rose on his haunted vision still!

* * * * * * * *

Whose corse was that which the morrow's sun
Through the opening boughs look'd calmly on?
There were those who bent o'er that rigid face
Who well in its darken'd lines might trace
The features of him who, traitor, fled
From a brother whose blood himself had shed,
And there — on the spot where he strangely died—
They made the grave of the Fratricide!

Among the fugitives who plunged into the river in their flight, was Captain Shoemaker. He was seen and recognized by a loyalist named Henry Windecker, whose family had been supplied with provisions in a time of scarcity by Shoemaker. Windecker now called to him in a friendly manner, assuring him of protection if he would return to the shore. Confiding in the promise of a former neighbor, he did so; but his life was the forfeit of his trust. As he regained the bank, Windecker received him with his left hand, and struck him dead to the earth with the tomahawk held in his right.

There was another case, very similar to the preceding, marked by equal turpitude—that of Wil-Hammond—a brother of the resolute Hammond who escaped from the massacre of the "bloody rock."* Having escaped from the slaughter of the battle-ground to the river, across which he was swimming for the island, he was hailed by a former neighbor, named Secord, now a tory in the ranks of the enemy. Previously to the war they had lived upon terms of the utmost intimacy,—often being engaged in the same labors in the field, and the same sports in the hours of relaxation. Secord's solicitation was of the most friendly kind, calculated at once to dispel all suspicion of treachery, and to inspire confidence. "Is that you, Bill Hammond," said he. "Yes," was the reply. Whereupon Secord advised him to return and promised him protection, to which the other answered, "No: I can swim across the river, and make my escape." "You cannot," rejoined Secord: "the Indians are on the opposite side and will certainly kill you. If you will return, I will claim you as a brother, and secure your life." Deceived by the apparent sincerity of his assurances, Hammond returned to the shore whence he had plunged into the stream. Secord stepped into the edge of the water to recieve him, and as he grasped with his left hand the right of his friend, with his own right hand he buried his hatchet in his head! The scene of diabolical

* There were three brothers of this name in the battle.

treachery was observed by a fugitive named Tubbs, lying close by in concealment, who ultimately escaped and related the revolting circumstances. The body of Hammond floated down the river to Fort Forty, where it was discovered, recognized, and brought to the shore.†

The fugitives generally crossed the mountains to Stroudsburg, where there was a small military post. Their flight was a scene of wide-spread and harrowing sorrow. Their dispersion being in an hour of the wildest terror, the people were scattered, singly, in pairs, and in larger groups, as chance separated, or threw them together, in that sad hour of peril and distress. Let the mind picture to itself a single group, flying from the valley to the mountains on the east, and climbing the steep ascent—hurrying onward, "filled with terror, despair and sorrow;—the affrighted mother, whose husband has fallen;—an infant on her bosom,—a child by the hand,—an aged parent slowly climbing the rugged steep behind them;—hunger presses them severely,—in the rustling of every leaf they hear the approaching savage,—a deep and dreary wilderness before them,—the valley all in flames behind,—their dwellings and harvests all swept away in this spring-flood of ruin,—the star of hope quenched in this blood-shower

† Life of Major Van Campen, of whom, more in the sequel.

of savage vengeance."* There is no work of fancy in a sketch like this. Indeed it cannot approach the reality. There were in one of these groups that crossed the mountain,—those of them that did not perish by the way,—one hundred women and children, and but a single man to aid, direct, and protect them. Their sufferings for food were intense. One of the surviving officers of the battle, who escaped by swimming the river, crossed the mountain in advance of many of the fugitives, and was active in meeting them with supplies. "The first we saw on emerging from the mountains," said a Mrs. Cooper, one of the fugitives, "was Mr. Hollenbach, riding full speed from the German settlement with *bread:* and O! it was needed; we had saved nothing, and were near perishing; my husband had laid his mouth to the earth to lick up a little meal scattered by some one more fortunate."†

Mr. William Searle, whose father, Constant Searle, an aged man, was slain in the battle, being himself unable to go into the engagement because of a wound received in a skirmish with a party of Indians a few days before, was nevertheless obliged to make his way across the mountains, as the

* The Hazleton Travellers.

† Mr. Hollenbach was a survivor of the battle, and in his escape swam the river naked. In this situation he was found by Solomon Hunt, a brother of Mrs. Myers, who also swam the river, preserving his shirt and pantaloons. Giving Hollenbach one of these garments, they proceeded together to Wilkesbarré.—*Note communicated by Rev. Dr. Peck.*

conductor of a party of twelve women and children. Captain Hewitt, commanding the company of new levies in the engagement, who bravely fell, refusing to retreat, was the son-in-law of Constant Searle. Many of the fugitives continued their journey back to Connecticut, ascending the Delaware and crossing over to the Hudson at Poughkeepsie. It was at this place that the first account of the massacre was published ; being collected from the lips of the panic-stricken and suffering fugitives, and full of enormous exaggerations such as the alleged massacre of women and children after the surrender, the burning of forts full of people, &c. None of these tales were true, albeit they found their way into Dr. Thatcher's Military Journal, written at the time, and even into the statelier histories of Gordon, Ramsay, Botta and others. A venerable old lady, Mrs. Bidlack, yet living in August 1839, was one of the captives surrendered at the fort, being then about sixteen years old. She stated to the author that the Indians were kind to them after they were taken, except that they plundered them of every thing but the clothes upon their backs. They then marked them with paint to prevent them from being killed by other Indians—a precaution often adopted by the red men, by whom such marks are always respected.

Great injustice has been done to the character

and conduct of Colonel Zebulon Butler in connection with this tragic affair of Wyoming, by some ill-informed historians who have written upon the subject, as well because he did not attempt to rally the survivors, and make another stand before Fort Wyoming, as on account of his flight. But the idea is preposterous in the mind of any intelligent man who duly considers the circumstances in which he was placed. Who was there to rally? Could the fife and drum pierce the ears of the slain? Could the dead be raised—the ashes of those who had been put to the torture in the flames be revivified by the reading of a regimental order? Full one half of the males of the colony lay stiff in death on the field. Had there been any body to rally, with the least possible chance of success, Zebulon Butler would have been the last man to fly. But there was not, and the enemy had refused quarter to all who belonged to the continental army. It was therefore the duty of Colonel Butler to save himself and the fifteen brave survivors of Captain Hewitt's company.

Zebulon Butler was not an accidental soldier. He had served in the old French war, with gallantry, and his associations with European officers, had added to his imposing form and carriage the manners of a gentleman. His courage and fortitude had moreover been illustrated in the civil wars, for the possession of the territory he was now defending from foreign invasion. An idea of his spirit may be formed by the following incident, connected with the very service that had now resulted so disastrously. It must be borne in mind that he was the commander of a continental regiment in the Connecticut line. When the people of Wyoming began to be alarmed in the spring, he was directed to repair thither, and look into their condition. On the receipt of his report, setting forth the destitution of the valley, at head-quarters, it was alleged that his account was exaggerated. "It is impossible," exclaimed one of the officers,—"it cannot be so." The officer's incredulity was reported to Colonel Butler, who replied, in his next despatch, "A gentleman who had a just regard for his own honor, would not so lightly suspect the honor of another."

When the invasion actually occurred, he was not only unprepared, but was compelled to meet the enemy, greatly superior in numbers, contrary to his own better judgment. The rashness of the brave but undisciplined men hastily collected together compelled him to the hazard of the die. His dispositions for the battle were those of a soldier, his conduct during the battle that of a brave man and skillful officer; and but for the untoward circumstance of the mistaken order which threw his left wing into confusion, the fortunes of the day, notwithstanding the disparity of their relative forces, might yet have been different. He lost no character in the eyes of those who saw the transaction, or in the estimation of those who knew him; and a long and useful life, during which he enjoyed richly the public confidence, is the most unerring test of his character.*

So also has it been with Colonel Dennison, the second in rank on that fatal day, who was in command of the left wing when it broke and fled. He, too, has been censured in history, if not for his conduct in the battle, at least for the capitulation. But as in the case of his commander, these censures have been most unreasonable. The circumstances in which he found himself, when, from the necessary flight of Colonel Zebulon Butler, the command had devolved upon him, were of the most trying description.

It must not be forgotten that they were only the fragments of a shattered and broken militia, and not regular troops, of whom he was in accidental command. By the result of the battle, the entire force and population of the valley were broken and crushed. The thought of farther resistance would have been more than folly,—it would have

* The grave of Colonel Butler is occasionally visited by strangers. The stone has been embellished by some "poet of the wilderness," with the following rustic but pious rhymes:—

"Distinguished by his usefulness,
At home and when abroad;
In court, in camp, and in recess,
Protected still by God."

been madness. It would not have checked for an hour the victorious enemy, but on the other hand would only have exasperated to additional murders. And what officer ever yet succeeded in rallying, and bringing again into a line, a band of flying militia with a cloud of savages upon their heels? When he capitulated, he was in a defenceless stockade fort, filled with women and children, and surrounded by a savage and victorious enemy. But it was not true, as is stated in the books, that when he demanded upon what terms he might be allowed to surrender, the reply was "THE HATCHET"—and that he thereupon capitulated unconditionally, leaving the women and children to a merciless horde of barbarians. On the contrary, the terms he made were honorable, and it was not his fault that the articles were violated in regard to the plundering, and burnings of the Indians. Those terms were in truth drawn up before Colonel Butler left the garrison. Colonel Dennison has been farther censured, and charged with bad faith in joining the expedition of Colonel Hartley, who, having been ordered to Wyoming soon after the devastation, proceeded against the Indian towns farther north upon the Susquehanna. Colonel Dennison, who had stipulated in the capitulation not again to bear arms against his English Majesty, was an active officer under Colonel Hartley; and the circumstance was used as a pretext by the bitter and bloody-minded Walter Butler, for the invasion and massacre of Cherry Valley in the autumn of the same year.* But it was only a pretext. With the single exception that an end was put by Colonel John Butler and Gi-en-gwah-toh to the effusion of blood, every other provision of the terms of that capitulation was disregarded. Every thing, as has been seen, was plundered, the entire settlement subjected to pillage, and instead of the inhabitants being allowed to remain at peace in their possessions, the whole was given up to rapine, and finally to the flames. So that Colonel Dennison, on principles of the most scrupulous honor, and the most delicate propriety, was fully justified in resuming his arms.

Colonel Dennison was one of the early emigrants to Wyoming. He was a native of New-London county; and on the extension of the jurisdiction of Connecticut over the extensive domain comprehended within the town of Westmoreland, a regiment of militia being organized, he was commissioned its colonel. He was a gentleman of highly respectable talents, and of liberal, and it is believed, collegiate attainments. He was regarded by all who served with or knew him, as a brave and faithful officer. After the close of the war, he held various important civil appoint-

* Life of Brant, Vol. I., Chap. xvii.

ments under the authority of Pennsylvania, and died at a very advanced age—as eminent for his sweet and unaffected piety as he had ever been for his patriotism—honored, loved, and wept by all. He had two sons, both of whom were highly respectable citizens ; one of whom died in March, 1843, and the other a few years ago, after having served his country in the state legislature and in Congress, with ability and honor.

The fields of Wyoming were waving with heavy burdens of grain, ripening for the harvest, at the time of the invasion, and no sooner had the enemy retired than considerable numbers of the settlers returned to secure their crops. In the course of their flight across the mountains, a party of the fugitives fell in with Captain Spalding, of the Continental army, at the head of a company of regulars, on their way to assist in the defence of the valley. Being apprized of the melancholy catastrophe that had befallen it, and having no force adequate to engage the invaders who had been left rioting upon the spoils of their conquest, Captain Spalding retraced his steps to Stroudsburg, where he remained for a month, and until it was ascertained that the enemy had retired. He then advanced and took possession of the vale of desolation, where he was soon afterward joined by Colonel Zebulon Butler, who assumed the command of the station, and under whose direction, aided by the returning inhabitants, another fort was erected on the west bank of the river, a short distance below the present borough of Wilkes-barré. This fort was occupied by Captain Spalding, with a small garrison, for upward of two years, during which period numbers of the inhabitants who had escaped came back, rebuilt their houses, and resumed their stations in the settlement.

There was, however, but little repose for the people until the close of the war. The Indians were frequently hovering upon the outskirts, by straggling scouts, and in larger parties, in quest of scalps, prisoners, and plunder. Sometimes they appeared in considerable numbers. In the month of March, 1779, Captain Spalding's fort was surrounded by about two hundred and fifty Indians and painted tories. They commenced an attack upon the fort, advancing upon all except the river side, in a semi-circle, with the intention of storming it. But a brisk fire being opened upon them from the fort with small arms and also a four-pounder, they dispersed—burning such buildings as came in their way, and driving off the cattle. Spalding's garrison made a sally; but the enemy rallied in numbers sufficient to chase them back, though the firing was maintained during the retreat. A small reinforcement being added to the assistance of Spalding, from Fort Wyoming, by Colonel Butler, the pursuit was renewed; but on reaching the edge of the woods, the force of the enemy was found to be so large as to render a farther advance upon him hazardous. The Americans therefore, retired to their defence, but were not pursued. The skirmishing continued two hours and a half; and the enemy succeeded in carrying away sixty heads of black cattle and twenty horses —shooting the field-horses of Colonel Butler which they could not take.* It was evident, from the traces of blood, and other indications, that considerable execution was done; but it was not until two years afterward, that on the escape of a prisoner, the fact was ascertained that the Indian chief commanding the expedition, had been killed—his body being cut in two by a cannon ball.† In the succeeding month of April, as Major Powell was leading a detachment of troops to reinforce the garrison of Wyoming, while threading a defile so narrow that but a single man could pass at a time, and utterly unconscious that a subtle enemy was lurking about his path, he was fired upon from an Indian ambuscade in Laurel Run, near the crest of the first mountain, and six of his men killed, of which number were Captain Davis and Lieutenant Jones. Taken thus fatally by surprise, Powell retreated for a short distance, to bring his men into

* Despatches of Colonel Butler to General Hand.

† Statement of General Ross—Wyoming memorial.

order of battle, — for they had been marching at their ease, without any organization, or much circumspection. The ambuscade was then charged, and after a few scattering fires the Indians were dispersed. The troops immediately entered the valley, taking with them the bodies of the officers who had fallen, which were interred with the honors of war, and an appropriate though rude memorial placed upon their graves.

Toward the close of June, 1771, General Sullivan arrived in Wyoming, with his division of the army destined for the memorable expedition of that year against the country of the Six Nations — the territory of the Cayugas and Senecas in particular. After remaining there a while, all things being ready, Sullivan moved up the river to the mouth of the Tioga, where he was joined by General Clinton's division from the north. General Sullivan's baggage "occupied one hundred and twenty boats, and two thousand horses, the former of which were arranged in regular order upon the river, and were propelled against the current by soldiers with setting-poles, the whole strongly guarded. The horses, laden with provisions for the daily subsistence of the troops, having to march singly in a narrow path, formed a line six miles in length. The flotilla upon the river formed a beautiful spectacle, as they moved in order from their anchorage, and as they passed the fort they exchanged salutes.

The whole scene formed a military display surpassing any which had previously been seen in Wyoming, and was well calculated to make a deep impression upon the minds of those lurking parties of savages that still continued to prowl about the mountains, from the tops of which the pageant was visible for many miles."*

But these wily warriors were neither driven away, nor awed into inaction. It was not long after Sullivan's departure before a brisk action was fought between a detachment of Pennsylvania militia, moving to the north for the protection of the Lackawaxen settlements, and a party of one hundred and fifty Indians, in which the former were defeated, with the loss of between forty and fifty men killed and taken.

Having ravaged the Genesee country, and laid the Indian towns waste by fire and sword, General Sullivan returned to Wyoming in October, and thence to Easton. The Indians, however, followed close upon his rear, and hung upon the borders of Wyoming until the close of the war. Shortly after Sullivan's departure, a detachment of militia from Northampton county, raised for the protection of the borderers, were attacked while on their march to the Susquehanna, and eleven of their number killed outright, and two others mortally wounded.

* Chapman.

The men were surprised while refreshing themselves at a brook, by a party of about forty Indians, led by a white loyalist. The former were commanded by Captain Moyer, whose good conduct after the first fire in part atoned for the high military offence of allowing himself to be surprised. Ten of the Indians were killed, and an eleventh mortally wounded. Still they succeeded in carrying away three white prisoners, all of whom contrived to effect their escape on the following night.

Incidents of a kindred character might be multiplied to an almost indefinite extent; but their recital, from general sameness, would become tedious; suffice it to say, that until the final close of that great struggle for liberty, from the invasion of 1778, Wyoming seemed the object of inextinguishable rancor—of unappeasable hate. There was not an hour's security for the people. Revenge upon Wyoming seemed a cherished luxury to the infuriated savages hovering upon her outskirts on every side. It was all a scene of war, blood, and suffering—owing, in the main, to the unpardonable neglect of the Continental Congress, who, having drawn off the flower of the population for the regular service, neglected, in return, to afford the valley any adequate protection. In the old town records of Westmoreland, at a public meeting, in the latter part of April, 1780, it is recorded that a committee was appointed to aid the people in protecting their settlements, in consequence of the attacks of the enemy. In 1781, a committee was appointed to obtain an abatement of the state tax at Hartford, in consequence of the continued distress. And in 1782, wheat being taken for taxes in the town treasury, it was ordered to be ground and baked into biscuit to be ready for the scouting parties kept up by the town. There was therefore no repose for the inhabitants, but frequent fightings and continual fears. In the course of this harassing warfare there were many severe skirmishes—several heroic risings of prisoners upon their Indian captors—and many hair-breadth escapes—some of which, together with various details of family and individual heroism and suffering, on the great day of slaughter and afterward, will be found narrated in the succeeding chapter.

CHAPTER VIII.

Anecdotes and biographical sketches of the living and the dead of Wyoming,—General Ross, and his family,—Visit to the Field of Battle,—The Monument,—Inspection of the Bones of the Slain,—Process of Tomahawking,—Visit to Mrs. Myers,—Her recollections,—Messrs. Bennet and Hammond,—Heroic Exploit,—Visit to Rev. Mr. Bidlack,—Mrs. Bidlack,—Recollections of both,—The Gore Family,—Story of the Inman family,—The Jenkins family,—Lieut. John Jenkins,—His captivity,—Extracts from his Diary,—Mrs. Jenkins, his widow,—Her recollections,—The Wintermoots,—Mrs. Jenkins's visit to the battle field,—The Blackman family,—Story of Samuel Carey and Zibbera Hibbard,—Story of John Abbot,—The Williams family—Heroic exploit of Sergeant Williams,—Story of the Weeks family, and of the Indian Anthony Turkey,—Story of Major Van Campen,—Life of Mrs. Phebe Young,—The Slocum family,—Story of Frances Slocum, the "Lost Sister."

Considering the extent of the slaughter in the massacre of Wyoming, the number of the survivors of that fatal day yet lingering this side of the grave is much greater than might have been expected. And the still larger number of the immediate descendants of those who fell, yet inhabiting the valley, is also a source of surprise. Both circumstances speak well for the place and the people—proving the salubrity of the climate, and the good taste and domestic habits of those who enjoy it.* It is the author's design in the present chapter, agreeably to an intimation in the last, to

* Reference is here had to the date of the first edition in 1840.

bring out, in bolder relief than could well be done in a general historical narrative, some of the exploits and sufferings both of individuals and families, who were engaged in the scenes that have been described. And of those thus to be noticed, there are several persons of both sexes yet among the living.

One of the most opulent, as well as respectable citizens yet enjoying a green old age in Wilkesbarré, is General William Ross. He is a native of Montville, in the State of Connecticut, and was removed to Wyoming with his father's family, while yet in his childhood, before the war of the Revolution. At the time of the invasion William Ross was sixteen years old. He was not, however, engaged in the battle which resulted so disastrously, having the day before marched with a small scouting party, twelve miles up the river, to a settlement in which the Indians had just committed a savage butchery. In this expedition they killed two Indians, and buried five bodies of their fellow colonists, which had been sadly mangled. But young Ross had two brothers, older than himself, Jeremiah and Perrin, engaged in the battle, the latter of whom was an officer, and both of whom fell. Their father was already dead. On William, therefore, now devolved the care of an aged mother, several sisters, and the widow and children of his brother Perrin. These all made their escape across the mountains to a place of safety, whence, however, the noble-spirited youth returned to the scene of rapine, to save whatever, if any thing might be left, and in all respects to perform his duty. He, among others, was charged with visiting the field of slaughter and burying the dead. The scene was shocking. They discovered two rings in which prisoners had been massacred, within one of which there were nine bodies, and within the other, fourteen. The only bodies recognized, were those of Darius Spofford and Captain Durkee,—the latter being easily identified from the circumstance that he had lost a joint from one of his fingers. Some of the unhappy prisoners were burnt to death on that fatal night by the torture of fire,—the process having been witnessed by Mr. Bennet and his son Ishmael, by Mr. Whitaker, a magistrate, and by Captain Blanchard, who had stationed themselves for purposes of observation, on the opposite bank of the river. They distinctly saw naked white men running around the fires, and heard the cries of agony. They saw the Indians following them in the circle with their spears, mingling their yells of savage delight with the shrieks of their victims.* It was

* Statement of Ishmael Bennet, in the Wyoming Memorial to Congress. "Early the next morning we could see them fixing their scalps on little bows made of small sticks, and with their moccasin awls and a string, were sewing them around the bows, and scraping off the flesh and blood,

more than a month after the event when this visit to the field was made, and General Ross assured Professor Silliman, in the year 1829, that owing to the intense heat of the weather, and probably to the dryness of the air, the bodies were shrivelled, dry, and inoffensive, but with a single exception they could not be recognized. They were buried in a common grave upon the farm now belonging to Mr. Gay. Everything from his father's farm had disappeared, that the invaders could destroy or carry away. But being the only male of his family left, he resolved to honor his name; and the consequence was, that he not only bore up with heroic fortitude against the flood of calamities that had rolled over the valley, but he overcame and rolled them back. The widows and orphans were taken care of; the fortunes of his house retrieved; and he has lived long in the enjoyment of many public honors from the state of his adoption, and discharging every public or private trust confided to him with fidelity.*

A visit to the field where the battle commenced is no farther of special interest than that it enables one to test the descriptive accuracy of the books. The position of the enemy's line when

carefully drying them, and at the same time smoking." [*Elvira Harding's Statement—Wyoming Memorial.*] The squaws, for several days after the battle, ornamented their girdles with the scalps of the slain.

* Written in 1840. General Ross has since deceased.

receiving the attack may be traced, and the tangled morass still exists through which the Indians penetrated to gain the rear of the left wing of the Americans, commanded by Colonel Dennison.

Returning from the battle field, an interesting object for a visit is the monument which the people of Wyoming have commenced building, in honor of their patriotic ancestors who fell upon this consecrated aceldama. It stands upon the eastern side of the highway, about half a mile south of the village of Troy, and near the line where the fury of the battle ceased—not far, moreover, from the spot where, some weeks after the conflict, the remains of the dead were collected and buried. The monument is to consist of a simple obelisk, of perhaps twenty feet in diameter at the base, to be carried up to the height of fifty or sixty feet. The material is an inferior species of granite quarried in the neighborhood. The foundation has been deeply and substantially laid, and the superstructure carried up some ten or twelve feet above the ground. And here the work rests for want of funds. An application was made by the people of Wyoming to the Legislature of Connecticut, for aid in the completion of this work of piety and patriotism. The case was ably presented to, and enforced upon that body, by a committee from Wyoming, at the head of which was Charles Miner—but without present success. It is to be hoped, however, that a renewed application will be more fortunate. The towns in Wyoming during the whole of the war of the Revolution, though not exactly an integral part of Connecticut, yet as much belonged to that state as did New-London, Norwalk, Danbury, or Fairfield. These towns, which were burnt and desolated by the enemy, received remuneration from the state. But neither of them suffered the horrors of Wyoming; and although Wyoming contributed her full proportion of revenue to the treasury of the state, and raised a goodly number of the "Connecticut line," and poured out her best blood like water, and almost swelled the torrent of the Susquehanna with her tears, yet of compensation she never received a dollar. And now that she appeals for a few thousand dollars to perpetuate the remembrance of the martyrs who bled, and of the cause in which they fell, it would be a burning shame—a disgrace which every son of Connecticut should forever feel—to have the petition denied.

At a house near by the monument, preserved, as they should be, with holy care, are such of the bones of the slain as have been from time to time collected. These are to be deposited in a chamber of the monument.

Several of the larger bones—of thighs, and arms, and shoulder-blades, are perforated with bullet-holes—rifle balls, evidently, by the size. Every skull save one bears the mark of the deadly tomahawk, and exhibits the process of the savage operation. The Indians seem not to have struck vertically downward, but by a glancing side blow, chipped out a piece from the crown, of two or three inches diameter. One of the skulls received two strokes of the hatchet; a cut just described upon the crown, and a second in the side of the head, just by the ear.

About midway between the site of Fort Forty and the place where the conflict was begun is the pleasant village of Troy. This is an interesting place, as the enemy appear to have halted in its neighborhood at the close of the massacre. In a field about sixty rods east of the highway is the bloody rock upon which the prisoners were executed by the Indians, during the night of the battle as heretofore described. It has a red, or rather brick-dust appearance on one side, believed by the superstitious to have been caused by blood which winter storms cannot wash nor time wear away.

Fort Forty stood upon the banks of the river, and the spot is preserved as a common—beautifully carpeted with green, but bearing no distinctive marks denoting the purposes for which the ground in those troublous times was occupied. Near the site of the fort, is the residence of Mrs. Myers, a widow lady of great age, but of clear mind and

23

excellent memory, who is a survivor of the Wyoming invasion, and the horrible scenes attending it. Mrs. Myers was the daughter of a Mr. Bennett, whose family was renowned in the domestic annals of Wyoming, both for their patriotism and their courage. She was born in 1762, and was of course sixteen years old at the time of the invasion. She was in Fort Forty when Colonel Zebulon Butler marched out at the head of the provincials against the enemy. Her recollections of all that passed beneath her eye on that occasion are remarkably vivid. The column marched forth three or four abreast, in good spirits, though not unconscious of the danger they were to encounter.* Still, they were not apprized of the odds against them, since the enemy had most skilfully concealed his strength.

Soon after the departure of the provincials, several horsemen galloped up from below, their steeds in a foam, and the sweat dripping from their sides. They proved to be Captain Durkee, Lieutenant Pearce, and another officer, who, having heard of the invasion, had left the detachment of troops to which they belonged, then distant fifty miles, and ridden all night to aid in the defence of their wives, their children, and their homes. "A morsel of

* One of the settlers, a man named Finch, had been shot and scalped two days before, in a gorge of the mountains near the upper section of the valley.

food and we will follow," said these brave men. The table was hastily spread, and they all partook of their last meal. Before the sun went down they were numbered with the dead. The inmates of the fort could distinctly hear the firing from the commencement of the battle. At first, from its briskness, they were full of high hopes. But as it began to change into a scattered fire, and the sounds grew nearer and nearer, their hearts sank with the apprehension that the day was lost, and their defenders on the retreat. The suspense was dreadful, and was sustained until near night-fall, when a few of the fugitives rushed into the fort, and fell down, wounded, exhausted and bloody!

Mrs. Myers was present at the capitulation on the following day, and saw the victorious entrance of the enemy, six abreast, with drums beating and colors flying. The terms of capitulation were fair and honorable, but as the reader has already seen, the Indians regarded them not, and immediately began to rob, plunder, burn, and destroy. Col. Dennison, according to the relation of Mrs. Myers, sent for Colonel John Butler, the British commander. They sat down together by a table on which the capitulation had been written, (yet carefully preserved by Mrs. Myers.) She and a younger girl were seated within the fort close by, and heard every word they uttered. Colonel Dennison complained of the injuries and outrages then enacting by the savages. "I will put a stop to it, sir—I will put a stop to it," said Colonel Butler. But the plundering continued, and Butler was again sent for by Colonel Dennison, who remonstrated sharply with him at the violation of the treaty. "We have surrendered our fort and arms to you," said Colonel Dennison, "on the pledge of your faith that both life and property should be protected. Articles of capitulation are considered sacred by all civilized people." "I tell you what, sir," replied Colonel Butler, waving his hand emphatically, "I can do nothing with them: I can do nothing with them." And probably he could not, for the Indians, in the end, had the audacity to strip Colonel Dennison himself of his hat and rifle-frock, (a dress then often worn by the officers.) Colonel D. was not inclined to submit peaceably to this outrage, but the brandishing of a tomahawk over his head compelled his acquiescence—not, however, until, during the parley, the colonel had adroitly transferred his purse to one of the young ladies present, unobserved by the Indians. This purse contained only a few dollars—but it was in fact the whole military chest of Wyoming.

Mrs. Myers represents Colonel John Butler as a portly, good looking man, of perhaps forty-five, dressed in green, the uniform of his corps, with a cap and plumes. On the capitulation of Fort Forty, as the victorious Butler entered it, his quick eye rested upon a sergeant of the Wyoming troops, named Boyd, a young Englishman, a deserter from the royal ranks, who had been serviceable in drilling the American recruits. "Boyd!" exclaimed Butler on recognising him, "Go to that tree!" "I hope your honor," replied Boyd, "will consider me a prisoner of war." "Go to that tree!" repeated Butler with emphasis. The deserter complied with the order, repaired to the tree, which was without the fort, and at a signal was shot down. Butler drew his white forces away from the valley shortly after the capitulation. But the Indians remained about the settlements, and finished the work of destruction.* In about a week after the battle, the torch was applied to most of the dwelling houses then remaining, and Mrs. Myers saw that of her father, Mr. Bennett, in flames among the number. He, with his family, thereupon fled from the valley to a place of greater security—Mrs. Myers and her sister, Mrs. Tuttle, being among the fugitives.

Mr. Bennett returned to Wyoming early in the

* It has been stated by several authors, that the British Colonel Butler was a kinsman of Colonel Zebulon Butler. But the fact is not so. Colonel John Butler was an opulent gentleman residing in the Mohawk valley, a neighbor and personal friend of Sir William, and afterward of Sir John Johnson. It was his misfortune to be engaged in a branch of the service which has covered his name, in history, with any thing but honor. Still he was a very respectable man, as were many other loyalists. After the close of the war of the revolution, he was retained in the British Canadian service, and died at an advanced age, much respected by those who knew him.

following spring, and was soon afterward captured by a party of six Indians, with his son, then a lad, and Mr. Hammond, a neighbor, while at work in the field. The Indians marched them toward the North, but during the night of the second or third day, their expedition was brought to a sudden and most unexpected close. From a few words dropped by one of the Indians, Mr. Bennett drew the inference that it was their design to murder them. Having requested of the Indian the use of his moccasin awl to set a button, "No want button for one night," was the gruff and laconic reply. He therefore resolved, if possible, to effect an escape, and while the captors had left them a few moments to slake their thirst at a spring, a plan for that purpose was concerted. Mr. Bennett, being in years, was permitted to travel unbound. Hammond and the boy were pinioned. At night they all lay down to sleep, except one of the Indians and Mr Bennett. The latter, having gathered the wood to keep up the fire for the night, sat down, and soon afterward carelessly took the Indian's spear in his hand, and began to play with it upon his lap. The Indian now and then cast a half-suspicious glance upon him, but continued his employment—picking the scanty flesh from the head of a deer which he had been roasting. The other Indians, wearied, had wrapped themselves in their blankets, and by their snoring gave evidence of being in a deep slumber.

The Indian left upon the watch, moreover, began to nod over his supper as though half asleep. Watching his opportunity, therefore, Mr. Bennett by a single thrust transfixed the savage with his own spear, who fell across the burning logs with a groan. Not an instant was lost in cutting loose the limbs of Hammond and the lad. The other Indians were in the same breath attacked by the three, and the result was that five of the tawny warriors were killed, and the sixth fled howling with a hatchet sticking in his back. The victors thereupon returned in triumph to the valley, bearing as trophies the spoils of the slain.

In the pleasant town of Kingston, on the west side of the river, opposite the borough of Wilkesbarré, resides the Rev. Benjamin Bidlack, a clergyman of the Methodist denomination, who, with his lady, are survivors of the memorable scenes of 1778, already described. This venerable man is between eighty and ninety years of age, and of clear and sound mind. He is of a tall and athletic form, of intellectual and strongly marked features and in the full pride of manhood, his presence must have been commanding. Mr. Bidlack was not himself in the battle of Wyoming, not being at home at the time of its occurrence. But he had a brother, Captain James Bidlack, Jr., in that bloody affair, who bravely fell at the head of his company, only eight of whom escaped the horrors of that day. He entered the field with but thirty-two rank and file, twenty-four of whom were slain. His station was near the left wing, but he refused to move from his post, although the greater portion of his comrades had broken and were in full flight. Their father, James Bidlack, senior, was one of the fathers of the settlement; and when the middle-aged portion of their population was drawn away by enlistment in the continental army, the old gentleman commanded a corps of aged men, exempts, and kept garrison in one of their little forts, called Plymouth. Benjamin went early into the regular service. He was with Washington in the vicinity of Boston, in the summer of 1775, and saw the evacuation of the "rebel town" by General Sir William Howe.

His term of enlistment expired in 1777, whereupon he returned to his parental home, and for a season engaged in the most hazardous and fatiguing service of the border. Enlisting again in the regular service, he continued in the army until the effectual conclusion of the war by the brilliant conquest of Lord Cornwallis, at Yorktown, in the siege of which fortress he participated. Speaking of the affair one day, Mr. Bidlack said, "Our batteries played night and day: it was an incessant blaze and thunder—roar and flash. Midnight was lighted up so that you might pick up a glove, almost any where about the works."

In 1789, the year subsequent to the massacre, during a sudden irruption of the Indians, Mr. James Bidlack, the father, was seized and carried into captivity, and did not obtain a release until the end of the war. He also lost another son in batte before the close of the contest. The old gentleman died about the year 1810. It is many years since Benjamin became a minister of the gospel. From his great age he no longer officiates in that capacity, but it is said of his preaching "that he spoke as he had fought, with impressive earnestness and ardent sincerity."

The venerable consort of Mr. Bidlack was eighty-one years of age in the year 1839, and of course must have been twenty at the time of the battle. Her maiden name was Gore, a member of the brave family so many of whom fell in the massacre, as related in a preceding chapter. Five of her brothers and two brothers-in-law went into the battle, and her father, who had been commissioned a magistrate in the preceding spring, by Governor Trumbull, was one of the aged men left for the defence of Fort Forty, while Colonel Butler marched forth to meet the enemy. Five of her brothers were left dead on the field, and a sixth was wounded. She was herself taken prisoner in Fort Wyoming, and one of the Indians placed his mark upon her as a protection. She stated* that after the capitulation the Indians treated the prisoners kindly, although they plundered them of every thing except the clothes they had on. Some of the females, in order to save what they could, arrayed themselves in three or four dresses. On discovering the artifice, however, the Indians compelled them to disrobe, by threats of having their throats cut.

But although enjoying the protection of her Indian captors, such were their apprehensions for the future that Mrs. Bidlack fled from the valley nine days afterward, and crossed the fearful forests and fens of the Pokono mountains to Stroudsburg, taking an infant, a younger sister, with her. Two of her brothers who fell, Asa and Silas, were ensigns. The one who escaped, Daniel, was the lieutenant in Captain Durkee's company, the station of which was the right wing, "a few rods below Wintermoot's fort, close to the old road that led up through the valley. Stepping into the road, a ball struck him in the arm; tearing from his body a portion of his shirt, he applied a hasty bandage. Just at that moment Captain Durkee stepped into the road at the same place. 'Look out!' said Mr. Gore, 'there are some of the sava-

* To the author, on a visit made to Mr. and Mrs. Bidlack, in 1839.

ges concealed under yonder heap of logs.' At that instant a bullet struck Captain Durkee in the thigh. When retreat became inevitable, Mr. Gore endeavored to assist his captain from the field but found it impossible ; and Durkee said, 'Save yourself, Mr. Gore—my fate is sealed.' Lieutenant Gore then escaped down the road, and leaping the fence about a mile below, lay couched close under a bunch of bushes. While there, an Indian sprang over the fence and stood near him. Mr. Gore said he could see the white of his eye, and was almost sure he was discovered. A moment after a yell was raised on the flats below, when the Indian drew up his rifle and fired, and instantly ran off in that direction."* In the gray of twilight, after the fury of the enemy seemed to have spent itself, Gore heard two persons in conversation near the road where he was lying, one of whom, by his voice, he judged to be Colonel John Butler, the enemy's leader. "It has been a hard day for the Yankees," said one of them. "Yes," replied the other, "there has been blood enough shed."

The name of one of Mrs. Bidlack's brothers-in-law, who fell, was Murfee. In the evening the distress of his wife was very great—and rendered still more poignant by the apprehension that he

* Hazleton Travellers.

might have been captured, and would be put to the torture. It was some relief to the bitterness of her anguish to learn on the following day that he had been killed outright. Mrs. Murfee, too, fled to the mountains, and wandered back to her native place,—Norwich, in Connecticut,—where a few days after her arrival among her friends, she gave birth to an infant.

This case of the Gore family is certainly one of the most remarkable in the history of man. Rarely, indeed, if ever, in the progress of the most bloody civil conflicts, has it happened before, or since, that a father and six sons have been engaged in the same battle-field. Five corpses of a single family sleeping upon the cold bed of death together, upon the self same night. What a price did that family pay for liberty!

There was, however, another case nearly parallel, and equally interesting. A brave family resided in the valley named Inman, consisting of the father, mother, and seven sons. The former was too old to go into the fight. Five of the sons went; and two others, one of whom was nineteen years old, and the other quite a lad, would have gone but for the want of arms. It was one of the many untoward circumstances under which the people were suffering, that by the terms of enlistment prescribed by Congress, the regular troops raised in Wyoming were obliged to supply their own arms. Hence, at the time of the invasion, all the best arms of the valley were with the soldiers attached to the continental army. Two of the younger Inmans, therefore, were compelled to remain at home with their aged parents. Two of those who went forth, Elijah and Israel, went to return no more—both having been slain. "Two escaped without injury; and the fifth, hotly pursued, plunged into the river, overheated with exertion, and hid himself under the willows. He might as well have fallen in the fight; for a cold settled upon his lungs, and carried him in a few weeks to his grave."* Of the two brothers who escaped, one, Richard, had the satisfaction of saving the life of his neighbor, Rufus Bennett, from the tomahawk of a stalwart Indian, when in the act of leaping upon him. Bennett and the Indian had both fired without effect, and the latter, with his uplifted tomahawk flashing in the air, was in the act of springing upon him, when the rifle of Richard Inman brought him with a convulsive bound dead within a few feet of his intended victim. But the tale of sorrow in this patriotic family is not yet ended. In common with the other surviving inhabitants of the valley, the parents with their remaining sons escaped to the Delaware. With others, however, toward winter,

* Hazleton Travellers.

they returned for the purpose of sowing their fields with wheat. Soon after the season of snows had set in, one of the young men, Isaac, aged nineteen, imagining that he heard the rustling of a flock of wild turkeys in a neighboring forest, sallied forth with his fowling-piece to bring some of them in—not anticipating that danger was lurking so near. He had not been long in the forest before the discharge of a musket was heard, and the family were shortly expecting his return, laden with the prize of his skill. He came not. A sleepless night was passed, but there was no return. The hearts of his fond parents sank within them at the tidings that the trail of an Indian scouting party had been discovered in the neighborhood. Still hope ever whispered the flattering tale that their young and promising son,—for he was indeed a youth of uncommon grace and beauty,—had been taken a captive, and would perhaps find his way back in the spring. But, alas ! the spring came, and the dissolving snow revealed a sadder tale. The body of the youth was found in the edge of a little creek passing through the farm. He had been shot, and an Indian's war-club lay by his side. His body was cruelly mangled and his light silken hair was yet stained with blood, drawn by the hatchet and scalping-knife.*

> "Death found strange beauty on his manly brow,
> And dashed it out."

* Hazleton Travellers.

Thus perished four of this devoted family in the course of that memorable year.*

The name of Colonel John Jenkins has more than once occurred in the preceding pages. This gentleman was an early emigrant to the valley, and presided at the meeting of the inhabitants in the beginning of the revolutionary troubles, when the patriotic resolutions mentioned in a former chapter, in opposition to the unconstitutional acts of Parliament, were adopted. The old gentleman was an active patriot until after the massacre, when he removed to Orange county in the State of New-York; closing there an honorable and well-spent life. He had a son, Lieutenant John Jenkins, no less a patriot than himself, who had been married shortly previous to the massacre, and who did the cause good service. He was taken prisoner by a band of Indians, while on a reconnoitring party, near Wyalusing, sixty miles above Wyoming, in November, 1777, and carried to Niagara. It happened that, at the same time, the Americans held captive at Albany a distinguished Indian warrior, for whom Colonel John Butler determined to exchange Mr. Jenkins. For this purpose he sent the latter to the American lines, under a strong escort of Indians. But the

* One of the survivors of these melancholy scenes, Colonel Edward Inman, a man of wealth and character, yet, (1839,) resides in the valley, a few miles below Wilkesbarré.

party was short of provisions, and from the fatigues of the march, and other privations, Mr. Jenkins almost perished. Nay, he came near being murdered in one of the drunken carousals of the Indians, and was only saved by the fidelity of a young warrior, whom he had succeeded in securing as his friend. This faithful savage kept himself perfectly sober, in order to the more effectual preservation of the life of his prisoner.

On the arrival of the party in the neighborhood of Albany, it was ascertained that the chief for whom Jenkins was to be exchanged, had died of the small pox. The Indians, greatly incensed at this loss of a favorite warrior, were resolved upon taking Jenkins back with them into captivity, and Jenkins himself believed it was their intention to murder him as soon as they should have withdrawn beyond striking distance from Albany. His release, however was ultimately negotiated, and he made his way back to Wyoming, to the company of his friends, and to the embrace of his young wife, whom he had recently married.

During the latter years of the war, Lieutenant Jenkins was in the habit of keeping a diary, or record of current events in the valley. From this diary a few extracts have been made, which show how constantly the settlers were harrassed by the subtle and ever-active enemy with whom they were obliged to contend ;—

"*January* 11*th*, 1780. A party of men set out to go through the swamp, (across the Pokono range) on snow-shoes, the snow about three feet deep.

"*Feb.* 2*d.*—Two soldiers went to Capowes, and froze themselves badly.

"*Feb.* 7*th.*—Colonel Butler set out for New-England.

"*March* 27*th.*—Bennett and son, and Hammond taken and carried off—supposed to be done by the Indians. The same day Upson was killed and scalped near William Stewart's house, and young Rogers taken.

"*March* 28*th.*—Several scouting parties sent out but made no discoveries of the enemy.

"*March* 29*th.*—Esquire Franklin went to Huntington on a scout, and was attacked by the Indians, at or near his own house, and two of his party murdered—Ransom and Parker.

"*March* 30*th.*—Mrs. Pike came in this day, and informed that she and her husband were in the woods making sugar, and were surrounded by a party of about thirty Indians, who had several prisoners with them, and two horses. They took her husband and carried him off with them, and painted her and sent her in. They killed the horses before they left the cabin where she was. One of the prisoners told her that the Indians had killed three or four men at Fishing Creek.

"Captain Spalding set out for Philadelphia this morning, &c. This day the Indians took Jones, Avery, and Lyon, at Cooper's.

"*April 4th.*—Pike, and two men from Fishing Creek, and two boys that were taken by the Indians, made their escape by rising on their guard of ten Indians — killed three — and the rest took to the woods naked, and left the prisoners with twelve guns and about thirty blankets, &c. These the prisoners got safe to the fort.*

"*May 17th.* — Sergeant Baldwin went to Lackawana, and found a man which ran away from the Indians, and brought him in. He informed that he was taken by a party of ten Indians and one tory, near Fort Allen.† This day the people were alarmed on both sides of the river. William Perry came in from Delaware in the evening, and informed that about sunrise this morning he saw a party of Indians near the Laurel Run, and several parties between that and the fort, by reason of which he was detained until that time in coming in.

"*May 18th.* — Several reconnoitring parties sent out, but made no discoveries except a few tracks in the road near the mountain.

* The true version of this exploit of Pike, will appear a few pages onward, in the story of Major Van Campen.

† Fort Allen was upon the Lehigh river, in the neighborhood of the Moravian settlements, fifty miles south, or southeast of Wyoming.

" *June 10th.* — A party of our men brought in three tories, which they took at Waysock's. These set out from New-York with the intent to travel through the country to Niagara — Bowman and son, Hover and Philip Buck in Company, but (the latter) made their escape when the others were taken.

" *July 11th.* — Bowman, Hover, and Sergeant Leaders, sent to head quarters in order for trial.

" *Monday, Sept. 4th.* — Sergeant Baldwin and Searle came in from a scout, and brought in a horse and a quantity of plunder of different kinds, which they took from a party of Indians near Tunkhannock creek, on Saturday before.

" *Thursday, Sept. 14th.* — Lieutenant Myers, from Fort Allen, came into the Fort, and said he had made his escape from the Indians the night before, and that he had been taken in the Scotch Valley, and that he had thirty-three men with him, which he commanded. He was surrounded by the Indians, and thirteen of his men killed and three taken. This day we heard that Fort Jenkins and Hervey's Mills were burnt.

" *December 6th.* — In the morning a party of tories and Indians took some prisoners from Shawwanee — [west of the river, four miles below Wilkesbarré.] Did no other damage, except taking a small quantity of plunder.

" *December 6th.* — A party of our men sent

after them, and pursued them three days, and gave out.

"*Jan.* 23*d*, 1781.—Captain Mitchell came to Wyoming in order to release Colonel Butler.

"*January* 24*th.*—Captain Selin and myself set out for Philadelphia."

Lieutenant Jenkins was an active officer during the whole contest, and signalized himself in several brisk affairs with the Indians. When General Sullivan marched from Wyoming to lay waste the Genesee country, he selected Lieutenant Jenkins as his guide or conductor. He fought bravely in the battle of Newtown, and after the close of the war, was for many years a surveyor in the Susquehanna and Genesee countries. He became an influential citizen in Wyoming, and held various important offices,—sometimes representing the County of Luzerne in the Legislature of Pennsylvania. He was the leader of the democratic party in that county, and died about the year 1828,—greatly respected by all who knew him.

The widow of Lieutenant, or rather Colonel Jenkins—for, like his father, he had long worn the latter title before his death—Mrs. Berthia Jenkins, yet survives, at the age of eighty six.—For a lady of her years, she is remarkably active, and her mind and memory are still unclouded. It will be borne in mind that on entering the valley, the first halt of Colonel Butler and his Indian allies, was at

Fort Wintermoot, upon the west bank of the river perhaps a mile above the battle field. Mrs. Jenkins, then just married, was in Fort Jenkins, at the time of Butler's arrival, about a mile yet farther to the north. The fidelity of the Wintermoots to the cause of the revolution, had been questioned previous to the arrival of Colonel John Butler, and the erection of their little fort had caused some remark, inasmuch as Fort Jenkins was so near that this additional stockade was hardly deemed necessary. But on the arrival of the enemy, all disguise was thrown off by the Wintermoots, and Colonel Butler with his troops and Indians were received as friends, —showing that there had been a perfect understanding between the parties, and that the suspected family had in fact been plotting the destruction of their own neighbors. A detachment was immediately sent against Fort Jenkins, with a demand for its surrender,—a demand which could not be resisted, as there were only nine or ten persons in the little defence, old and young. Mrs. Jenkins of course became a prisoner. This was on the 2d of July. The battle was on the 3rd, and the moment it was known that the Yankees were marching up to the attack from Fort Forty, the detachment which had taken Fort Jenkins was recalled to the main body. Mrs. Jenkins followed to the distance of half way between the forts, and sat down upon a stump in the field, with an anxious heart, to await the issue. She heard the firing as it commenced and ran along the line from right to left, until it became general. She also heard the war-whoops of the Indians. By and bye the whoopings became more fierce, and the firing broken. Then it was less frequent and more distant, while the yells of the savages grew more frightful, giving "signs of wo that all was lost." The next morning the prisoners from Fort Jenkins were taken down to Wintermoot's. Among them was a Mrs. Gardiner, whose husband had been captured in the skirmish at Exeter two days before. She was now permitted to go down to the enemy, to take leave of him. Mrs. Jenkins, and a Mrs. Baldwin, whose husband was in the battle, with an old man, her father-in-law, carrying a flag, were allowed to go in company with Mrs. Gardiner. Mrs. Baldwin could obtain no tidings of her husband, and returned with a heavier heart than she went. This visit enabled Mrs. Jenkins to take a survey of the battle field; and her descriptions are as vivid as they are shocking. She discovered numbers among the dead, of her late friends and neighbors. In one place there was a circle of the dead, lying as they had fallen, scalped and mangled. In another, were the smouldering embers of a fire, around which were strowed the half-burnt limbs of those who had been put to death by torture.* By some means the liberation of Mrs. Jenkins was effected, and she fled the valley with other fugitives, returning thither eighteen months afterward. It is an interesting fact related by Mrs. Jenkins, that the people of Wyoming were in part dependent upon themselves for their own gun-powder, which the women rudely manufactured by leeching the earth for the salt-petre, and then compounding it with charcoal and sulphur as best they could with such means as were at hand.

There was a brave family named Blackman, residents of the valley, two of whom, then young men, now far down the vale of years, are yet living, — farmers of wealth and character. Their father, being too old to go out upon the war-path, remained within Fort Wyoming during the action, performing his duty, however, as an officer of a veteran corps previously instituted, called the *Reformadoes*. Mr. Blackman's eldest son, Eleazer, went into the battle, with a young man named David Spofford, who, two months before, had been married to his sister,— Lavina Blackman. The two young men together with a brother of Spofford, named Phineas, fought side by side, until David received his death-wound. Falling upon

* Scarse could he footing find in that fowle way,
For many corses, like a great lay stall,
Which murdered men, which therein *strowed* lay
Without remorse, or decent funerall.
Spencer's Faerie Queene.

his brother's arm, he said,—"I am mortally hurt, take care of Lavina!" These were his last words. Other members of the Blackman family did good service during the war, in the valley and elsewhere.

Among the survivors of the massacre, yet lingering in the valley, are Mr. Samuel Carey and Mr. Baldwin. The former was nineteen years old at the time of the battle. He belonged to Captain Bidlack's company, forming a part of the left wing of the line, which was first out-flanked and thrown into confusion. In the flight that ensued, he was accompanied by Zippera Hibbard, his file-leader in the line. Hibbard was also a a young man, remarkable for the height and beauty of his form, as well as for his great strength and superior agility. In all the athletic sports among the settlers he was a leader, and such were his muscular powers, and his feats of running and leaping, that had he lived to engage in the Olympic games of classsic Greece, he would doubtless often have won the crown.

He had just been married at the time of the invasion, and tradition reports the parting scene from his youthful bride to have been one of tender interest. Fear was a stranger to his breast; but there were ties binding him to his home which could not be severed without a severe struggle. He knew, from the superiority of the enemy's force, that the battle would be fought upon unequal terms, and perhaps his mind was clouded with a presentiment that he should not return from the field he was preparing to enter. After adjusting his arms, therefore, he yet for a moment lingered — stepped forward, and back again — paused — and musingly hesitated. At length he ran back to the embrace of his bride, imparted another kiss upon her pale and trembling lips — but spoke not a word, as he tore himself finally away. "The next hour," to quote the words of Charles Miner, "there was not a soldier that marched to the field with more cheerful alacrity."*

But alas! If he had entertained any gloomy forebodings, they were but too fatally realized. In their flight, Hibbard and Carey took to a field of rye, tall, and ready for the sickle. The former being in advance, broke the path for his junior comrade; and in doing so, by the time they had crossed the field, he became fatigued almost to exhaustion. Their object was to escape to the island already mentioned; but the Indians were in hot pursuit, and Hibbard was overtaken just as he had gained the sandy beach, and ere he could reach the stream. He turned to defend himself, but in the same instant fell transfixed by the spear of his dusky pursuer.

* Hazleton Travellers.

Young Carey was more fortunate. Having been less fatigued in the rye field than his companion who had broken the way, he was enabled to continue his flight farther down the river, before he attempted crossing to the island. The Indians, however, watching his movements, swam the river above more rapidly than himself, and he reached the island only to become their prisoner. He was then compelled to recross the river by swimming, and carried back to Fort Wintermoot. This defence had been fired by the enemy themselves, and was yet in flames when Carey reached it. The painfulness of the scene was increased by the sight of the bodies of one or more of his neighbors, which had been thrown upon the burning pile—

"By the smoke of their ashes to poison the gale:"

but whether they had been thus disposed before or after death, he could not tell. He had been stripped to his skin previous to leaving the island, and was threatened with menacing strokes of the scalping knife.

But his life was reserved for another destiny. It appeared that his captor was Captain Roland Montour, of whose mother an account has already been given. After passing the night, bound to the earth, he was accosted the next morning by Col. John Butler himself, who reminded the stripling of a threat he had made on the preceding day, that "he would comb the Colonel's hair," which threat had been repeated to the Tory commander. Montour then came and unbound him, and after giving him some food, led him to a young Indian warrior who was dying. A conversation ensued between the captor and the dying warrior, which Carey did not then understand. It afterward appeared that Montour was negotiating with the young warrior for the adoption of Carey by the Indian's parents, after the custom of those people, as a substitute for the son they were then losing. The dying Indian assented to the arrangement, and the life of the prisoner was saved. He was painted, and received the name of him whose place he was destined to take in the Indian family--Co-con-e-un-quo—of the Onondaga tribe.

On the retreat of the enemy, Carey was taken into the Indian country with them, and handed over to the family of which he had now become a member. But though treated with kindness by the Indians, he was too old to be broken into their habits of life. He sighed for his liberty and the associations of his own kindred and people. His new parents saw that he was not likely to become a contented child, and as consequently the place of the one they had lost was not filled, they mourned their own son even as David mourned for Absalom. Mr. Carey gives a touching account of their sorrow. Often did he hear them, as they awoke at day-break, setting up their pitiful cry for their son. And as the sun sank to rest behind the purple hills at evening, they would repeat the same wailing lament.

He resided with this family in the Indian country more than two years, after which he was taken to Niagara, where he remained until the end of the war, and the surrender of the prisoners. It was on the 29th of June, 1784, that he once more found himself in the bosom of the vale of Wyoming. He subsequently married Theresa Gore, a daughter of Captain Daniel Gore, who was himself in the battle, and five of whose brothers and brothers-in-law were slain, as the reader has already been informed. He has resided in the valley ever since, and although the morning of his life was stormy and sad, yet, surrounded by his sons and daughters and their descendants, its evening is tranquil and serene. There were two other Careys engaged in the action, Joseph and Samuel, both of whom fell. But they were of another family. The family of the Samuel Carey, of whom some account has been given already, were from the county of Dutchess in the State of New-York.

A brief history of another family of sufferers will perhaps be interesting. Among the early settlers of the valley was a respectable man named John Abbott, who, at the time of the invasion, had a family consisting of a wife and nine children.

As has already been stated, more than once, there was but a single field-piece in the valley, which was kept at the little fort of Wilkesbarré, to be used as an alarm gun. On the approach of danger, it was announced from its brazen throat, and the inhabitants obeyed the signal by rallying for the common defence. When the news of the invasion by the Tories and Indians reached Wilkesbarré, Abbott was at work with his oxen upon the flats, whence he was summoned by the well-known sound of alarm. Though as a husband, and the parent of nine young children, the eldest of whom was but eleven years old, all depending upon his labor for support, he might well have been excused from going into battle, yet he sought no exemption. The danger was imminent, and with as much alacrity as his neighbors he hastened to the battle-field. In the retreat he succeeded, by the aid of a comrade, for he could not swim, in crossing to Monockonock Island, and thence to the main land on the east of the river, and was thus enabled to effect his escape.

In the flight of the inhabitants, Mr. Abbott removed his family down the Susquehanna to Sunbury; but having left his property behind — his flocks and herds — he being an opulent farmer for those days — and his fields waving with a rich burden of grain nearly ready for the harvest, he returned to look after the fruit of his labors. This measure was indeed necessary, for the product of his farm was his only dependence for the support of his family. But sad was the spectacle that met his view on his return. His house and his barn had been burnt, his cattle slaughtered or driven away, and his fields ravaged. The gleanings only remained to require his attention. These he attempted to gather, but in doing so, while engaged in the field with a neighbor named Isaac Williams, a young man, or rather youth of eighteen years, of fine promise, they were shot by a party of Indians who stole upon them unawares, scalped, and left dead upon the spot.*

The widow, with her helpless charge, being now entirely destitute, was compelled to seek her way back to Hampton, an eastern town in Connecticut, whence they had emigrated, a distance of more than three hundred miles, on foot — pennyless, heart-broken, and dependent upon charity for subsistence. But the journey was effected without loss of life or limb; and the widowed Naomi was not more kindly received by the people of Bethlehem, on her return from the land of Moab, than were Mrs. Abbot and her infant charge by their former friends and neighbors. She remained at Hampton several years after the troubles were over, and until her sons were grown up. Return-

* This Mr. Abbot built the first house in the borough of Wilkesbarré.

ing then to the valley, and reclaiming successfully the estate of her husband, she settled thereon with her family, married a celebrated wit named Stephen Gardiner, and continued to live there until her decease. Her son, Stephen Abbott, an independent and respectable farmer, still resides upon the eastern margin of the Susquehanna, opposite the site of Fort Forty.

The Williams family, to which Isaac, the young man whose murder in connection with that of Mr. Abbott has just been related, was distinguished for its patriotism and bravery. The father was Thaddeus Williams, and his house stood not far from Fort Wyoming, in the borough of Wilkesbarré. He had a son, Thomas, who was a sergeant in the regular service, and who, with short intermissions, served with distinguished gallantry during the greater part of the war. It was mentioned in the preceding chapter, that in the month of March, 1779, while Captain Spalding was in command of Fort Wyoming, a sudden irruption of tories and Indians took place, by whom the fort was surrounded. Happily, however, a few discharges of the only field-piece in the fortress put them to flight. But the severest battle fought during this irruption was between the Indians and Sergeant Thomas Williams, who happened to be at home on furlough. His father, who had removed back to the valley, with others, after the general desolation the year before, was at this time indisposed, and in bed. The only other male in the house, besides the sergeant, was a younger brother twelve or thirteen years old. The position of Williams's house was such, that the Indians determined to take and destroy it previous to their meditated attack upon the garrison. There were three loaded muskets in the house, and plenty of ammunition. Seeing the Indians approaching his castle, the sergeant made his dispositions for defence. He barricaded the doors, and getting his guns ready, gave his little brother the necessary directions for loading them as often as he fired. He was a man of too much coolness and experience to waste his ammunition. Waiting, therefore, until the Indians had approached very near, Williams took deliberate aim between the logs of which the house was constructed, and brought their leader dead to the ground. With a hideous yell his comrades retreated, dragging away the body. They advanced again, and assaulted the door, which was too well secured easily to yield. Their numbers were now increased, and they in turn fired into the house, through the interstices between the logs. By one of these shots Mr. Williams, the father, was severely wounded in his bed; but the sergeant kept up as brisk a fire as his little brother, who acted his part manfully, could enable him to do, and a second and a third of the savages fell. They again retreated, taking away their slain, and raising their customary death howls. Maddened by their loss, however, they again approached, one of them bearing a flaming brand, with which they were resolved to fire the house. But with deliberate aim the sergeant brought the incendiary to the ground, whereupon the Indians seized his body and drew off, without again returning to the assault. How many more than the four enumerated were slain by the brave sergeant was not known, because the Indians always carry off their dead. Beyond doubt, the lives of the whole family were saved by his intrepidity, and that of his heroic little brother. The sergeant is yet living in the valley, an opulent and respectable farmer.

Another family upon whom the blow fell with great force and severity, was that of Mr. Jonathan Weeks. He resided upon a large farm, with his sons and sons-in-law, about a mile below the borough of Wilkesbarré. He had living with him, at the time of the alarm, his three sons, Philip, Jonathan, and Bartholemew; Silas Benedict, a son-in-law; Jabel Beers, an uncle; Josiah Carman, a cousin; and a boarder, named Robert Bates. These seven men from a single household all seized their arms and hurried to the field. And they all fell with their Captain, whose name was M'Carrican, a man of letters and teacher of the hamlet school. Two days after the battle, a party of twenty Indians visited the house of Mr. Weeks, and demanded breakfast. Having obtained their demand, they next informed Mr. Weeks that he must quit the valley forthwith. The old man remonstrated. "All my sons have fallen," said he with emotion; "and here am I left with fourteen grand-children, all young and helpless." But the dusky conquerors were inexorable: nevertheless, having gorged themselves with blood already, and having moreover satisfied their appetites for the morning, they did not wantonly apply the tomahawk again. The leader of this party was an Indian named Anthony Turkey,—a fellow who had been well known to the settlers as one of the former residents of the valley, when both races lived together in friendship. The appearance of Turkey among the invaders was a source of surprise, because of his former friendship. But he proved as thoroughly savage as the wildest of his race; and notwithstanding his former acquaintance with Mr. Weeks, he would not allow the bereft old man to remain upon his farm. Still, in driving him away, the Indians so far tempered their decree with mercy as to allow him his oxen and wagon, with which he took the sobbing women and their little ones back to the county of Orange, (New-York,) whence they had emigrated to Wyoming. But the Indian leader, Turkey, afterward met the fate he deserved, in this place. Returning with the party of tories and Indians who invaded the valley a second time in March, 1779, as just related in the case of the Williams family, he was shot through the thigh in the engagement which took place on the flats, and before his people could carry him away he was surrounded by the Wyoming boys who called out to him — "Surrender, Turkey, — we won't hurt you." But he refused, and resisted like a chafed tiger, until it became necessary to make an end of him. After the enemy were gone, the lads took the body of Turkey, and set it up-right in a canoe, all painted to their hands, and grinning horribly with the muscular contortions of death. They then placed a bow and arrows in his hand, and sent him adrift, amidst the cheers of men and boys. The canoe, thus freighted, created some sensation as it passed below, and was the cause of several amusing incidents. In one case a man put off in a canoe to take the straggler; but catching a glimpse of the ferocious countenance of the Indian, and fancying that he was drawing his bow to let fly a poisoned arrow, he paddled back to the shore with all convenient expedition,

Yet another case will be briefly related. It is that of a Mr. Skinner, whose baptismal name has not been preserved. Mrs. Esther Skinner died in Torringford, Connecticut, in the year 1831, aged one hundred years. She had been one of the earliest white residents of Wyoming. In the massacre she lost her husband, two sons, and a brother, all of whom fell beneath the tomahawk,—she herself escaping, with six of her children, as it were by a miracle. Her son-in-law was almost the only man of twenty who threw themselves into the river, and attempted to hide themselves beneath the foliage depending from the banks into the water, that escaped. All the others were successively massacred while sustaining themselves in the water by the branches of the trees that dipped into it. He alone was undiscovered. The lone mother travelled back to Torringford, where she led a useful life to its close. She was sometimes cheerful, though a cloud of heaviness, brought on by her sorrows, was never entirely dissipated.

Among the names most intimately connected with the history of Wyoming during the period under review, is that of Moses Van Campen. Major Van Campen,—for such was his legitimate title in the service before the close of the contest,—first served as a private in the year 1777, upon Grand Island, situated in the west branch of the Susquehanna. In the following year he was commissioned a lieutenant, and stationed in the valley of the Susquehanna, between Northumberland and Wyoming, where he erected a small fort for the protection of the scattered settlers of the neighborhood, the inhabitants of which in seasons of alarm took refuge within its walls. Before his little defence had been completed, it was gallantly and succes fully defended against two successive attacks by strong bodies of Indians, whose tomahawks were nevertheless bathed in the blood of several families upon that section of the border.

When, in the year 1779, General Sullivan ascended the Susquehanna and Chemung rivers in his march into the Indian country to avenge the butcheries of Wyoming and Cherry Valley, lieutenant Van Campen was advanced to the post of quarter-master; but being a man of approved courage and activity, well skilled in the subtleties of Indian warfare, his duties were by no means confined to the commissariat. Previous to the battle of Newtown, in which the Indians under Brant, and the American loyalists of Sir John Johnson and Colonel John Butler were signally defeated by the united forces of Sullivan and Clinton, Major Van Campen was sent forward, under the disguise of an Indian warrior, — dressed, painted, and plumed, — to ascertain the numbers and condition of the enemy, — a task which he executed with complete success. Passing their out-posts in the night, he entered their camp, visited their fires, and computed, with sufficient accuracy, the number of the warriors slumbering around them. In the attack upon a division of the enemy, preceding the main battle, by the brigade of General Hand, Major Van Campen was in the advance, contributing actively to the success of that brilliant affair.*

At the close of Sullivan's campaign, a severe attack of bilious fever compelled Major Van Campen to retire from the service, and return to the residence of his father, in the vicinity of his former station below Wyoming, upon the Susquehanna. The savages had been so effectually subdued by the operations of Sullivan, that apprehensions of farther outrages upon the border were measurably allayed, and the scattered inhabitants were preparing to resume their field labors in the spring of the following year with comparative unconcern. Toward the close of March, Major Van Campen left the fort with his father and a brother, to work upon the farm, accompanied also by an uncle and his son, a lad of twelve years of age, and a man named Peter Pence—the uncle having a farm to attend in the same vicinity.

Suddenly, on the 30th of March, while in the field, the Major and his father were attacked by a party of ten Indians, who stole so warily upon them that flight was impossible. The uncle had already been killed upon his own plantation; the lad and Pence being now in company, bound pris-

* For the fullest and best historical narrative of Sullivan's memorable expedition into the Indian country, see the author's Life of Joseph Brant—Thayendanegea, Vol. II.

oners. The Major's father was thrust through the lungs with a spear in the first onset, and his throat instantly cut. The lad, his brother, was likewise struck down with a tomahawk, scalped, and his body cast into a fire blazing near by. As the warrior who had slain the elder Van Campen drew the spear from his body, he made a lunge at the Major, already engaged apparently in a death struggle with another Indian; but not poising his weapon with skill, a slight flesh wound only was inflicted, while the barb became entangled in the clothes of the intended victim. Sated, for the time, with blood, after a brief struggle the savages contented themselves with making the Major a prisoner, and with his youthful cousin, and the man Pence, he was marched away in the direction of the Six Nations' country. In descending the valley of the Susquehanna the Indians had skirted the Wyoming settlements and committed some aggressions. In returning, on the same afternoon, they fell in with a party of four men engaged in making maple-sugar, upon whom they fired—wounding one man, Captain Ransom, who, however, escaped with the others. Encamping at night, after building their fires the prisoners were bound and well secured, the Indians sleeping five upon either side of them. On the second day of their march, while yet in the Wyoming region, they found one Abraham Pike, with his wife and child.

Placing the mark of prisoners upon the latter two, they were suffered to "go" ; but Pike was taken away, and at night they were all bound and guarded as before. Reflecting that they had probably been spared by their captors to grace a war-feast on returning to their villages, in the course of which they would be put to death by torture, Van Campen began now to meditate an escape—a feat, he was well aware, only to be achieved by putting the Indians to death. The daring suggestion was cautiously imparted to his fellow prisoners on the third day of their captivity ; but it was not until the fourth that a reluctant assent was obtained from his associates, Pence and Pike—the lad being too young for a combatant. The sleep of the Indians, it is well known, is very deep and heavy ; and Van Campen's proposal was that on the next night, after waiting until their grim guardians were in a profound slumber, they should contrive to extricate themselves in some way from the cords with which they were bound, and in the next place cautiously disarm the Indians. This effected, Van Campen intended that himself, Pence, and Pike, armed with tomahawks, should each, by as many blows, dispatch three of the sleepers before any of them should have time to to arouse for resistance. Nine of them being thus disposed of and the tenth unarmed, the three could have nothing serious to apprehend from him.

But although the project was obviously well conceived, neither Pence nor Pike would agree to the details beyond the disarming. That object attained, they proposed that one of their number should be stationed with the fire-arms of the Indians, to be removed a few paces from the camp, which should be used with the best possible effect, while the other two were to attack with tomahawks, and ply them as briskly and fatally as possible during the confusion which would ensue on the first discharge of a musket. In this hazardous deviation from his plan Van Campen was obliged to acquiesce; and the duty of firing the muskets, from a point of comparative safety, was assigned to Pence.

Encamping as usual at dark, the Indians were remarkably diligent and attentive in providing an abundance of fuel for the night; and a roaring fire having been built, they all lay down to sleep—the prisoners being carefully bound as before. Providence, however, favored the design of escape, for one of the Indians, while adjusting himself for the night, dropped his knife, without perceiving it, close by Van Campen's feet. Of course the latter failed not to avail himself of this important weapon; and at midnight, perceiving that the warriors were all in a profound slumber, the Major arose, and with the knife quietly severed the cords upon his own limbs and those of his fellow prisoners. He was himself to strike the three Indians upon the right wing, and Pike the two upon the left, while Pence should do such execution as he could with the guns. Just as they were about to strike, the two warriors allotted to Pike awoke; whereupon, like a coward, as he proved to be, he again lay down in his place, as though all was well. Not so Van Campen, who saw that in an instant more all would be lost. Quick as lightning, therefore, he darted upon the two awaking savages, and planting his tomahawk deep into their heads, left them quivering in death. Three more blows, equally well directed, with the rapidity of thought, ended the lives of the three as allotted to him at the first. Pence fired at the same instant, with wonderful judgment and accuracy — killing four of the remaining five. One only was left — a stalwart savage named Mohawk, who sprang to his feet with the discharge of the guns, and uttering the war-whoop, darted to take possession of them. Van Campen sprang after him to defeat his purpose, aiming a blow at his head with a tomahawk, but missing, struck him in the shoulder, or rather in the back of his neck. The Indian pitched forward and fell — and Van Campen's foot slipping at the same instant, he also fell by his side. They clenched, and a struggle of several moments ensued, during which the Major endeavored to dispatch him with his own knife. Mohawk, however, succeeded in disengaging himself, and springing to his feet, plunged into the woods and fled. The transaction was one of surprizing bravery, — of darkness and of blood. Yet it was not unrelieved by an incident, or rather side-act, of a ludicrous character ; for while Van Campen and Mohawk lay struggling, grasped in each other's arms upon the ground as in the hug of death, Pike was attempting to pray, and Pence stood swearing at him for his cowardice.

The victory, however, was complete. Nine of the ten warriors lay before them dead ; and it only remained for the victors to secure the spoils, and wend their way back to Wyoming before Mohawk should be able to return upon them with re-inforcements. Having secured the arms, blankets, and supplies of the dead, taken their scalps, and recovered also those of his father, his uncle, and his brother, Van Campen caused a rude raft to be constructed—for the brave action I have recorded occurred upon the bank of the Susquehanna not far from Tioga,—upon which he embarked with his little party, and in due season they all reached their homes in safety. On their passage, however, they had several alarms, Pike, in every instance, sustaining his character as an arrant coward.*

* And yet this man, Pike, who deceased only a few years ago, lived and died, in the popular estimation, a hero, or rather the hero of the transaction recorded in the text. I have now before me a manuscript narrative, written from the personal relation of Pike, in 1819, by the Rev. Dr. Peck, then of Wyoming, but now of New-York, in which he makes himself the planner and the hero, of the whole affair. But such was not the fact. The account given in the text I have written with the narrative

The Indian, Mohawk, recovered from his wound, and in process of time, by the removal of Van Campen into the neighborhood of his village, they became acquainted. The effect of the wound was such as to contract, or perhaps to destroy, some of the muscles of Mohawk's neck, by reason of which he could never carry his head erect afterward. He was for a time shy of seeing Major Van Campen; but finding that the latter cherished no hostility toward him, he subsequently became his frequent visiter.

Among the residents of Wyoming who long survived the scenes that have been faintly sketched, was Mrs. Phebe Young, a lady eminent for her piety and worth, who died in August, 1839, at the advanced age of ninety years. She retained her faculties of mind and memory until her decease, and as her temperament was cheerful, and her colloquial powers pleasing, her society was courted until she was summoned to depart from the bright spot which for so long a period in her youth she had known literally as a vale of tears. Mrs. Young was a native of the ancient Dutch town of

of Major Van Campen before me. He yet (1844) lives in the western section of New York, a citizen, venerable for his years, and of great respectability. His veracity is not to be questioned; while the character of Pike, through life, was not only questionable, but sometimes bad. He was shrewd, but faithless. It is said of him that he often committed petty larcenies; but when called to an acconnt for them pleaded his soldiership, his sufferings, and his exploits, and the inhabitants were induced by his appeals to shut their eyes to his offences.

Æsopus, in the state of New-York, whence she emigrated to Wyoming at the age of twenty, in the year 1769. There were in Wyoming, at that period, only five white females, including herself. The Indians were then in the quiet possession of the circumjacent country, excepting the sections that had been entered upon by the whites; and the relations of Mrs. Young and her friends with them, were of the most friendly character. Having taken up her residence there thus early, Mrs. Young was of course a participator in all the hardships and deprivations incident to the commencement of a settlement in the woods at a distance so remote from the abodes of civilization. She was also a spectator of, and consequently a sufferer in, the bitter civil feuds which for so many years distracted the valley. On the day of the battle and massacre, while the men were preparing themselves for the contest, and making such hasty dispositions as they could for the security of their families, she, and her children, were furnished by her husband with a canoe, and advised to hasten from the valley down the Susquehanna at once; but she was unwilling to depart until she could learn the result of the impending contest. She therefore took refuge, with her children, in a small house near the river, at the distance of several miles below the battle ground. A portion of the family of Colonel Dennison were with her. As the evening of the fatal day approached, she lulled her children to sleep, and with her friends watched, with a solicitude that cannot be described, until midnight. Then was heard the approaching tramp of horses at full speed. They hastened to the door to receive them, and the tidings were, "all is lost, and the Indians are sweeping down the valley!" Gathering her children from the floor upon which they were dreaming in happy unconsciousness of what had passed, she placed them in a canoe, and launched forth upon the river, to be wafted by its current whither it might. The moon shone sweetly upon the water, and in passing her own house, all was quiet, and the cow stood ruminating by the door. She kept in her canoe, borne rapidly along by the stream, until she arrived in Lancaster county, where resided the friends of her husband, among whom she remained until after the campaign of General Sullivan against the Indian country in 1779. Her return was to a valley of desolation—every person she met was a mourner—the relics of "a people scattered and peeled." Mrs. Young never afterward left Wyoming: nor for many years previous to her decease had she moved beyond the limits of the borough of Wilkesbarré, except on the interesting occasion, three or four years ago, when the common grave of those who fell in the massacre was opened "for the purpose of founding a monument to their memory. All the survivors of the times of Indian troubles were assembled, and Mrs. Young was sent for as one of them. The spectators of what took place on that occasion can never forget it. The bones of slaughtered brothers and fathers, marked with the tomahawk and the scalping-knife and the rifle, were opened to view; and as the vast assembly marched around the grave, the old, who had shared in the sorrows of the first settlers of the valley, wept at the recollection of what they had known, and the young wept in sympathy because they had heard from their fathers' lips the unhappy story of their native valley. Mrs. Young could share largely in the feelings of that occasion, for many of those whose bones were there collected she had personally known as neighbors; but she did not seek to be present. It was only the urgent solicitations of a respected neighbor, who was himself a survivor of the 'Indian troubles,' and the remnant of a family cut off in the massacre, that prevailed and induced her to go. She never left the town again."* For sixty years Mrs. Young never looked upon the world beyond the narrow barriers of Wyoming.

* Tribute to the memory of Mrs. Young, by the Rev. Mr. May, her pastor, published in the London Episcopal Recorder.

CHAPTER VIII.

The Slocum family,—Two of them in the battle of Wyoming,—Perilous Escape of Giles Slocum,—Murder of the elder Slocum and his father-in-law,—Story of the Lost Sister,—Her captivity,—Long-continued efforts for her discovery,—Disappointments,—Found sixty years afterward by Colonel Ewing,—Correspondence,—Visit of the surviving brothers and sister to the Miami country,—The recognition,—Narrative of the lost one,—Refuses to return with her relations,—The visit repeated.

THE Slocum family of Wyoming were distinguished for their sufferings during the war of the revolution, and have been recently brought more conspicuously before the public in connection with the life of a long lost but recently discovered sister. The story of the family opens with tragedy, and ends in romance without fiction.

Mr. Jonathan Slocum, the father of the subject of the present narrative, was a non-combatant,—being a member of the society of Friends. Not so, however, all the members of his family. His eldest son, Giles, was in the battle, as also was his brother-in-law, named Hugh Forsman. The junior escaped to Monockonock island, and though hotly pursued, succeeded in burying himself in the sand and bushes so as to elude discovery until the following day, when he made good his retreat to Fort Forty. While lying thus in concealment, his pursuers fell upon another fugitive whom they slew, notwithstanding his entreaties for mercy. Forsman was a subaltern in Captain Hewett's company, and was one of the fifteen of that corps who escaped the slaughter, and the only man of them who brought in his gun.* Yet the father, feeling himself safe in his pacific principles from the hostility even of the savages, did not join the survivors of the massacre in their flight, but remained quietly upon his farm,—his house standing in close proximity to the village of Wilkesbarré. But his faith had little weight with the Indians, notwithstanding the affection with which their race had been treated by the founder of Quakerism in Pennsylvania,—the illustrious Penn, —and long had the family cause to mourn their imprudence in not retreating from the doomed valley with their neighbors.

It was in the autumn of the same year of the invasion by Butler and Gi-en-gwah-toh, at midday, when the men were laboring in a distant field, that the house of Mr. Slocum was suddenly surrounded by a party of Delawares, prowling about the valley, in more earnest search, as it seemed, of plunder than of scalps or prisoners.—The inmates of the house, at the moment of the

* Wyoming Memorial to Congress.

surprise, were Mrs. Slocum and four young children, the eldest of whom was a son aged thirteen, the second a daughter, aged nine, the third, Frances Slocum, aged five, and a little son aged two years and a half. Near by the house, engaged in grinding a knife, was a youth named Kingsley, assisted in the operation by a lad. The first hostile act of the Indians was to shoot down Kingsley, and take his scalp with the knife he had been sharpening. Kingsley, the father of the youth thus murdered, had been previously taken prisoner by the Indians, and was then in captivity,—Mrs. K. and her child having found a temporary home in the family of the Quaker.*

The girl nine years old appears to have had the most presence of mind, for while the mother ran into the edge of a copse of wood near by, and Frances attempted to secrete herself behind a stair-case, the former at the moment seized her little brother, the youngest above mentioned, and ran off in the direction of the fort. True, she could not make rapid progress, for she clung to the child, and not even the pursuit of the savages could induce her to drop her charge. The Indians did not pursue her far, and laughed heartily at the panic of the little girl, while they could not but admire her resolution. Allowing her to make her escape, they returned to the house, and

* Wyoming Memorial to Congress.

after helping themselves to such articles as they chose, prepared to depart.

The mother seems to have been unobserved by them, although, with a yearning bosom, she had so disposed of herself that while she was screened from observation she could notice all that occurred. But judge of her feelings at the moment when they were about to depart, as she saw little Frances taken from her hiding place, and preparations made to carry her away into captivity, with her brother, already mentioned as being thirteen years old, (who, by the way, had been restrained from attempted flight by lameness in one of his feet,) and also the lad who a few moments before was assisting Kingsley at the grindstone. The sight was too much for maternal tenderness to endure. Rushing from her place of concealment, therefore, she threw herself upon her knees at the feet of her captors, and with the most earnest entreaties pleaded for their restoration. But their bosoms were made of sterner stuff than to yield even to the most eloquent and affectionate of a mother's entreaties, and with characteristic stoicism they began to remove. As a last resort the mother appealed to their selfishness, and pointing to the maimed foot of her crippled son, urged as a reason why at least they should relinquish him, the delays and embarrassments he would occasion them in their journey. Being unable to walk, they would of course be compelled to carry him the whole distance, or leave him by the way, or take his life. Although insensible to the feelings of humanity, these considerations had the desired effect. The lad was left behind, while deaf alike to the cries of the mother, and the shrieks of the child, Frances was slung over the shoulder of a stalwart Indian with as much indifference as though she were a slaughtered fawn.

The long, lingering look which the mother gave to her child, as her captors disappeared in the forest, was the last glimpse of her sweet features that she ever had. But the vision was for many a long year ever present to her fancy. As the Indian threw her child over his shoulder, her hair fell over her face, and the mother could never forget how the tears streamed down her cheeks, when she brushed it away as if to catch a last sad look of the mother, from whom, her little arms outstretched, she implored assistance in vain. Nor was this the last visit of the savages to the domicil of Mr. Slocum. In the month of December following, no Indians having been recently seen in the neigborhood, Jonathan Slocum, with his son William, and Mr. Isaac Tripp, an old man, father of Mrs. Slocum, ventured forth to feed their cattle unattended by a guard. But a horde of savages who had stolen down unobserved from the mountains, were lurking in the neighborhood of the fold, from whom, on descrying them, the little party, with a single exception, attempted in vain to escape. Mr. Tripp, the elder of the three, on being first overtaken, fell, nine times pierced through the body with a spear. A musket ball brought the elder Slocum dead to the ground, and both were scalped and otherwise mangled, while William, with a leg wounded by a spent ball, succeeded in gaining the fort.* That ball he carried in his flesh to the grave, more than half a century afterward.

These events cast a shadow over the remaining years of Mrs. Slocum. She lived to see many bright and sunny days in that beautiful valley — bright and sunny, alas! to her no longer. She mourned for the lost one, of whom no tidings, at least during her pilgrimage, could be obtained. — After her sons grew up, the youngest of whom, by the way, was born but a few months subsequent to the events already narrated, obedient to the charge of their mother, the most unwearied efforts were made to ascertain what had been the fate of the lost sister. The forests between the Susquehanna and the great lakes, and even the more distant wilds of Canada, were traversed by the brothers in vain, nor could any information respecting her be derived from the Indians.† Once, indeed, du-

* Wyoming Memorial to Congress.

† In the Narrative of Colonel Thomas Proctor, a Commissioner deputed by Gen. Knox, then Secretary of War, upon a mission to the Northwestern Indians, in 1791, under date of March 28th, is this entry: — "I was joined

ring an excursion of one of the brothers into the vast wilds of the west, a white woman, long a captive, came to him in the hope of finding a brother; but after many anxious efforts to discover evidences of relationship, the failure was as decisive as it was mutually sad. There was yet another kindred occurrence, still more painful. One of the many hapless female captives in the Indian country, becoming acquainted with the inquiries prosecuting by the Slocum family, presented herself to Mrs. Slocum, trusting that in her she might find her own long lost mother. Mrs. Slocum was touched by her appearance, and fain would have claimed her if she could. She led the stranger about the house and yards, to see if there were any recollections by which she could be identified as her own lost one. But there was nothing written upon the pages of memory to warrant the desired conclusion; and the hapless captive returned in bitter disappointment to her forest home.* In process of time these efforts were all relinquished as hopeless. The lost one might have fallen beneath the tomahawk, or might have proved too tender a flower for transplantation into the wilderness.—

by Mr. George Slocum, who followed us from Wyoming, to place himself under our protection and assistance, until he should reach the Cornplanter's settlement, on the head waters of the Alleghany, for the redeeming of his sister from an unpleasing captivity of twelve years, to which end he begged our immediate interposition."—*Vide Indian State Papers.*

* Story of the Lost Sister, written for children, from authentic materials, by the Rev. J. Todd.

Conjecture was baffled, and the mother, with a sad heart, sank into the grave, as also did the father, believing with the Hebrew patriarch that "the child was not."

The years of a generation passed, and the memory of little Frances was forgotten, save by two brothers and a sister, who, though advanced in the vale of life, could not forget the family tradition of the lost one. Indeed it had been the dying charge of their mother that they must never relinquish their exertions to discover Frances. A change now comes over the spirit of the story. It happened that in the course of the year 1835, Colonel Ewing, a gentleman connected with the Indian trade, and also with the public service of the country, in traversing a remote section of Indiana, was overtaken by the night, while at a distance from the abodes of civilized man. When it became too dark for him to pursue his way, he sought an Indian habitation, and was so fortunate as to find shelter and a welcome in one of the better sort. The proprietor of the lodge was indeed opulent for an Indian,—possessing horses and skins, and other comforts in abundance. He was struck in the course of the evening by the appearance of the venerable mistress of the lodge, whose complexion was lighter than that of her family, and as glimpses were occasionally disclosed of her skin beneath her blanket-robe, the Colonel was impressed with the opinion that she was a white woman. Colonel Ewing could converse in the Miami language, to which nation his host belonged, and after partaking of the best of their cheer, he drew the aged squaw into a conversation, which soon confirmed his suspicions that she was only an Indian by adoption. Indeed she frankly confessed the fact, and proceeded to give her guest a rapid sketch of her life, — a narrative of absorbing interest which made a deep impression upon his mind.

In the course of her statement she mentioned that her family name was Slocum, and that she had been stolen from somewhere in the valley of the Susquehanna. But of circumstances calculated to throw more light upon her early history, or designating the particular section of the Susquehanna country whence she had been torn, she could remember no more. Still, for many months afterward the family at Wyoming were ignorant of the discovery, nor did Colonel Ewing know any thing of them. And it was only by reason of a peculiarly providential circumstance that the tidings ever reached their ears. On Colonel Ewing's return to his own home, he related the adventure to his mother, who, with the just feelings of a woman, urged him to take some measure to make the discovery known, and at her solicitation he was induced to write the following narrative of the case, which he addressed to the deputy postmaster at Lancaster, with a request that it might be published in some Pennsylvania newspaper:—

"*Logansport, Indiana, Jan.* 20, 1835.

"DEAR SIR—In the hope that some good may result from it, I have taken this means of giving to your fellow-citizens, those who are descendants of the early settlers of the Susquehanna, the following information; and if there be any now living, whose name is SLOCUM, to them, I hope the following may be communicated, through the public prints of your place.

"There is now living near this place, among the Miami tribe of Indians, an aged white woman, who a few days ago told me, whilst I lodged in the camp with her one night, that she was taken away from her father's house, on or near the Susquehanna river, when she was very young—say from five to eight years old, as she thinks, by the Delaware Indians, who were then hostile toward the whites. She says her father's name was SLOCUM, that he was a Quaker, rather small in stature, and wore a large brimmed hat—was of sandy hair and light complexion, and much freckled—that he lived about half a mile from a town where there was a fort—that they lived in a wooden house of two stories high, and had a spring near the house. She says three Delawares came to the house in the day time, when all were absent but herself, and perhaps two smaller children ; her father and brothers were absent making hay. The Indians carried her off, and she was adopted into a family of Delawares, who raised her and treated her as their own child. They died about forty years ago, somewhere in Ohio. She was then married to a Miami, by whom she had four children ; two of them are now living—they are both daughters and she lives with them. Her husband is dead—she is old and feeble, and thinks she will not live long.

"These considerations induced her to give the present history of herself, which she never would do before—fearing that her kindred would come and force her away. She has lived long and happily as an Indian—and but for her color, would not be suspected of being any thing else than such. She is very respectable and wealthy—sober and honest. Her name is without reproach. She says her father had a large family, say eight children in all—six older than herself; one younger, as well as she can recollect ; and she doubts not, there are yet living many of their descendants, but seems to think that all of her brothers and sisters must be dead, as she is very old herself—not far from the age of eighty. She thinks she was taken prisoner before the two last wars, which must mean the Revolutionary war, as Wayne's war and the late war have been since that one. She has entirely lost her mother tongue, and speaks only in Indian, which I also understand, and she gave me a full history of herself.

"Her own christian name she has forgotten, but says her father's name was SLOCUM, and he was a Quaker. She also recollects that it was upon the Susquehanna river that they lived—but don't recollect the name of the town near which they lived. I have thought that from this letter you might cause something to be inserted in the newspapers of your county, that might possibly catch the eye of some of the descendants of the Slocum family, who have knowledge of a girl having been carried off by the Indians some seventy years ago. This they might know from family tradition. If so, and they will come here, I will carry them where they may see the object of my letter, alive and happy, though old and far advanced in life.

"I can form no idea whereabout upon the Susquehanna river this family could have lived at that early period, namely about the time of the Revolutionary war—but perhaps you can ascertain more about it. If so, I hope you will interest yourself, and if possible, let her brothers and sisters, if any be alive, if not, their children, know where they may once more see a relative, whose fate has been wrapped in mystery for seventy years, and for whom her bereaved and afflicted parents doubtless shed many a bitter tear. They have long since found their graves, though their lost child they never found. I have been much affected with the disclosure, and hope the surviving friends may obtain, through your goodness, the information I desire for them. If I can be of any service to them, they may command me. In the mean time, I hope you will excuse me for the freedom I have taken with you—a total stranger, and believe me to be, Sir, with much respect,

"Your obedient servant,

"GEO. W. EWING."

The functionary to whom the narrative was addressed, however, having no knowledge of the writer, and supposing that it might be a hoax, paid no attention to it, and the letter was suffered to remain among the worthless accumulations of the office for the space of two years. It chanced then, that the post-master's wife, in rummaging over the old papers while putting the office in order one day, glanced her eyes upon this communication. The story excited her interest, as well it might, and with true maternal feeling, and the active spirit of woman, she resolved to give the document publicity, and sent it to a neighboring journalist for that purpose. And here, again, another providential circumstance intervened. It happened that a Temperance Committee had engaged a portion of the columns of the paper to which the letter of Colonel Ewing was sent, for the publication of an important document connected with that cause, and a large extra number of papers had been ordered for general distribution. The letter was sent forth with the temperance document, and it yet again happened that a copy of this paper was addressed to a clergyman who had a brother residing in Wyoming. Having, from that brother, heard the story of the captivity of Frances Slocum, he had no sooner read the letter of Colonel Ewing, than he enclosed it to him, and by him it was placed in the hands of Joseph Slocum, Esq., the surviving brother.

Any attempt to describe the sensations produced by this most welcome, most strange, and most unexpected intelligence, would necessarily be a failure. This Mr. Joseph Slocum was the child, two years and a half old, that had been rescued by his intrepid sister, nine years old. That sister also survived, as did the younger brother, living in Ohio. Arrangements were immediately made by the former two, to meet the latter in Ohio, and proceed thence to the Miami country, and reclaim the long lost and now found sister. "I shall know her if she be my sister," said the elder sister now going in pursuit, "although she may be painted and jewelled off, and dressed in her Indian blanket, for you, brother, hammered off her finger nail one day in the blacksmith's shop, when she was four years old." While these arrangements were afoot, however, it was judged wise to open a direct correspondence with Colonel Ewing, in order to a more intelligent undertaking of the journey. To this end the following letter was addressed to that gentleman, by Jonathan J. Slocum, Esq., of the Wilkesbarré bar, a son of Joseph, and nephew of "the lost sister."

" *Wilkes Barré, Penn., Aug.* 8, 1837.

" George W. Ewing, Esq.

" Dear Sir,—At the suggestion of my father and other relations I have taken the liberty to write to you, although an entire stranger.

" We have received but a few days since, a letter written by you to a gentleman in Lancaster of this state, upon a subject of deep and intense interest to our family. How the matter should have lain so long wrapped in obscurity we cannot conceive. An aunt of mine—sister of my father—was taken away when five years old by the Indians, and since then we have only had vague and indistinct rumors upon the subject. Your letter we deem to have entirely revealed the whole matter, and set every thing at rest. The description is so perfect, and the incidents (with the exception of her age,) so correct that we feel confident.

" Steps will be taken immediately to investigate

the matter, and we will endeavor to do all in our power to restore a lost relative, who has been sixty years in Indian bondage.

"Your friend and obedient servant,

"JON. J. SLOCUM."

As the reply of Colonel Ewing forms a part of this remarkable history, it is here subjoined:—

"*Logansport, Indiana, Aug.* 26, 1837.

Jon. J. Slocum, Esq. Wilkes Barré.

"DEAR SIR—I have the pleasure of acknowledging the receipt of your letter of the 8th inst., and in answer, can add, that the female I spoke of in Jan. 1835, is still alive; nor can I for a moment doubt but that she is the identical relative that has been so long lost to your family.

"I feel much gratified to think, that I have been thus instrumental in disclosing to yourself and friends, such facts in relation to her as will enable you to visit her and satisfy yourselves more fully. She recovered from the temporary illness by which she was afflicted about the time I spent the night with her in Jan. 1835, and which was, no doubt, the cause that induced her to speak so freely of her early captivity.

"Although she is now, by long habit, an Indian, and her manners and customs precisely like theirs, yet she will doubtless be happy to see any of you; and I myself will take great pleasure in accompanying you to the house. Should you come out for that purpose, I advise you to repair directly to this place; and should it so happen that I should be absent, at the time, you will find others who can take you to her. Bring with you this letter,—show it to James T. Miller, of Peru, (Ind.) a small town not far from this place. He knows her well. He is a young man whom we have raised. He speaks the Miami tongue and will accompany you, if I should not be at home. Inquire for the old white woman, mother-in-law to Brouriette, living on the Missisinewaw River, about ten miles above its mouth. *There you will find the long lost sister of your Father*, and as I before stated you will not have to blush on her account. She is highly respectable, and her name, as an Indian, is without reproach. Her daughter, too, and her son-in-law, Brouriette, who is also a half-blood, being part French, are both very respectable and interesting people—none in the nation are more so. As Indians, they live well, and will be pleased to see you. Should you visit here this fall, I may be absent, as I purpose starting for New York in a few days, and shall not be back till some time in October. But this need not stop you; for although I should be gratified to see you, yet it will be sufficient to learn that I have furthered your wishes in this truly interesting matter.

"The very kind manner in which you have been pleased to speak of me shall be fully appreciated.

"There perhaps are men who could have heard her story unmoved, but for me, I could not; and when I reflected that there was perhaps still lingering on this side of the grave some brother or sister of that ill-fated woman, to whom such information would be deeply interesting, I resolved on the course which I adopted, and entertained the fond hope that my letter, if ever it should go before the public, would attract the attention of some one interested. In this it seems at last, I have not been disappointed, although I had long since supposed it had failed to effect the object for which I wrote it. Like you I regret that it should have been delayed so long,—nor can I conceive how any one should neglect to publish such a letter.

"As to the age of this female, I think she herself is mistaken and that she is not so old as she imagines herself to be. Indeed I entertain no doubt but that she is the same person that your family have mourned after for more than half a century past.

"Your obedient, humble servant,

"GEORGE W. EWING."

All necessary arrangements for the journey having been completed, it was undertaken by the two surviving brothers and their sister; who, accompanied by an interpreter engaged in the Indian country, reached the designated place, and found the lost one. But, alas! how changed! Instead of the fair-haired and laughing girl, the picture yet living in their imaginations, they found her an aged and thorough-bred squaw in every thing but complexion. She was sitting, when they entered her lodge, composed of two large log-houses connected by a shed, with her two daughters, the one about twenty-three years old, and the other about thirty-three, and three or four pretty grand-children. The closing hours of the journey had been made in pensive silence—deep thoughts struggling in the bosoms of all. On entering the lodge. the first exclamation of one of the brothers was—"Oh God! is that my sister!" A moment afterward, and the sight of the disfigured thumb left no doubt as to her identity. The following colloquy, conducted through the interpreter, ensued:

"What was your name when a child?"

"I do not recollect."

"What do you remember?"

"My father, my mother, the long river, the stair-case under which I hid when they came."

"How came you to lose your thumb-nail?"

"My brother hammered it off, a long, long time ago, when I was a very little girl at my father's house."

"Do you know how many brothers and sisters you had?"

She then mentioned them, and in the order of their ages.

"Would you know your name, if you should hear it repeated?"

"It is a long time since, and perhaps I should not."

"Was it FRANCES?"

At once a smile played upon her features, and for a moment there seemed to pass over the face what might be called the shadow of an emotion, and she answered, "Yes!"*

Other reminiscences were awakened, and the recognition was complete. But how different were the emotions of the parties! The brothers paced the lodge in agitation. The civilized sister was in tears. The other, obedient to the affected stoicism of her adopted race, was as cold, unmoved, and passionless as marble. Her two daughters had both been married, but the youngest was a widow. The husband of the other was a half-breed Frenchman, named Brouriette, bearing the rank of "Captain" among his people — a man of cultivated manners and elegant appearance. It required considerable time to overcome the suspicions of the long lost and now found sister, and her family, that the strangers were their

* The Lost Sister.

relatives. They were however at length persuaded to accompany the strangers back to the quarters they had secured, nine miles distant, and pass the night. Yet "before they fully yielded their confidence, it was necessary, in compliance with Indian usage, to give and receive a formal pledge of friendship. To this end, the parties being all assembled, the eldest daughter brought in a clean white cloth, carefully rolled up, and laid it on the stand, and then, through the Interpreter, arose and solemnly presented it as a pledge of their confidence. It contained the hind quarter of a deer, which they had probably just hunted and killed for this very purpose. The brothers and sisters then arose and as solemnly received it as a token of friendship and kindness. But still, they were not satisfied, till the civilized sister had gone and formerly taken possession of the cloth and its contents. They then seemed at ease, and from that moment, gave their new friends their entire confidence."* The ceremony over, the party moved off to the point designated,—the daughters of Frances mounting their spirited Indian horses, which they soon gave evidence that they could manage as well as in the days of chivalry did the rather masculine spouse of Count Robert of Paris, her steed, in the wars of the Holy Land, as de-

* The Lost Sister.

scribed in the brilliant romance of the Crusaders, by Sir Walter Scott.

Neither the acquired stoicism of her adopted race, nor her incommunicative disposition, was entirely overcome by the strangers. Still their persuasions were listened to by degrees, until the old lady was at length induced to relate so much of her history as she could remember, — manifesting no small degree of suspicion, however, on the production of the necessary utensils for reducing the narrative to writing. This narrative was in substance as follows :—

"I can well remember the day when the Delaware Indians came suddenly to our house. I remember that they killed and scalped a man near the door, taking the scalp with them. They then pushed the boy through the door; he came to me and we both went and stood under the stair-case. They went up stairs and rifled the house, though I cannot remember what they took except some loaf sugar and some bundles. I remember that they took me and the boy on their backs through the bushes. I believe the rest of the family had fled, except my mother.

"They carried us a long way as it seemed to me, to a cave, where they had left their blankets and travelling things. It was over the mountain and a long way down on the other side. Here they stopped while it was yet light, and there we staid all night. I can remember nothing about that night, except that I was very tired, and lay down on the ground and cried till I was asleep. The next morning we set out, and travelled many days in the woods before we came to a village of Indians. When we stopped at night, the Indians would cut down a few boughs of hemlock on which to sleep, and then make up a great fire of logs at their feet, which lasted all night. When they cooked any thing, they stuck a stick in it, and held it to the fire as long as they chose. They drank at the brooks and springs, and for me they made a little cup of white-birch bark, out of which I drank. I can only remember that they staid several days at this first village, but where it was, I have no recollection.

"After they had been here some days, very early one morning, two of the same Indians took a horse, and placed the boy and me upon it, and again set out on their journey. One went before on foot, and the other behind, driving the horse. In this way we travelled a long way till we came to a village where these Indians belonged. I now found that one of them was a Delaware Chief by the name of Tuck-Horse. This is a great Delaware name, but I do not know its meaning. We were kept here some days, when they came and took away the boy and I never saw him again, and do not know what became of him.

"Early one morning this Tuck-Horse came and took me, and dressed my hair in the Indian way, and then painted my face and skin. He then dressed me in beautiful wampum-beads and made me look, as I thought, very fine. I was much pleased with the beautiful wampum. We then lived on a hill, and I remember he took me by the hand and led me down to the river-side, to a house where lived an old man and woman. They had once had several children, but now they were all gone — either killed in battle, or having died when very young. When the Indians thus lose all their children, they often adopt some new child as their own, and treat it in all respects like their own. This is the reason why they so often carry away the children of white people. I was brought to these old people to have them adopt me, if they would. They seemed unwilling at first, but after Tuck-Horse had talked with them a while, they agreed to it, and this was my home. They gave me the name of *We-let-a-wash,* which was the name of their youngest child whom they had lately buried. It had now got to be the fall of the year, for chestnuts had come. The Indians were very numerous here, and here we remained all the following winter. The Indians were in the service of the British, and were furnished by them with provisions. They seemed to be the gathered remnants of several nations of Indians. I remember that there was a fort here. In the spring I went with the parents who had adopted me, to Sandusky, where we spent the next summer; but in the fall, we returned again to the fort, — the place where I was made an Indian child, and here we spent the second winter. In the next spring we went down to a large river, which is Detroit River, where we stopped and built a great number of bark canoes. I might have said before, that there was war between the British and the Americans, and that the American Army had driven the Indians around the fort where I was adopted. In their fights, I remember the Indians used to take and bring home scalps, but I do not know how many. When our canoes were all done, we went up Detroit River, where we remained about three years. I think peace had now been made between the British and the Americans, and so we lived by hunting, fishing, and raising corn. The reason why we staid here so long, was, that we heard that the Americans had destroyed all our villages and corn-fields. After these years, my family and another Delaware family removed to Fort Wayne. I don't know where the other Indians went. This was now our home, and I suppose we lived here as many as twenty-six or thirty years. I was there long after I was full grown, and I was there at the time of Harmar's defeat. At the time when this battle with Harmar was fought, the women and children were all made to run north. I cannot remember whether the Indians took any prisoners, or brought home any scalps at this time. After the battle, they all scattered to their various homes, as was their custom, till gathered again for some particular object. I then returned to Fort Wayne again. The Indians who returned from this battle were Delawares, Pottawatamies, Shawanese, and Miamis. I was always treated well and kindly; and while I lived with them, I was married to a Delaware. He afterwards left me and the country and went west of the Mississippi. The Delawares and the Miamis were then all living together. I was afterwards married to a Miami, a chief, and a deaf man. His name was Che-por-on-wah. After being married to him, I had four children — two boys and two girls. My boys both died while young. The girls are living and are here in this room at the present time. I cannot recollect much about the Indian wars with the whites, which were so common and so bloody. I well remember a battle and a defeat of the Americans at Fort Washington, which is now Cincinnati. I remember how Wayne, or "Mad Anthony," drove the Indians away and built the Fort. The Indians then scattered all over the country, and lived upon game which was very abundant. After this they encamped all along on Eel River. After peace was made, we all returned to Fort

Wayne, and received provisions from the Americans, and there I lived a long time. I had removed, with my family, to the Missisineway river sometime before the battle of Tippecanoe. The Indians who fought in that battle were Kickapoos, Pottawatamies and Shawanese. The Miamis were not there. I heard of the battle on the Missisineway, but my husband was a deaf man and never went to the wars, and I did not know much about it."

"Was you ever tired of living with the Indians?"

"No. I had always enough to live on, and to live well. They always used me very kindly."

"Did you ever know that you had white relations who were seeking you for so many years?"

"No. No one told me, and I never heard of it. I never thought any thing about my white relatives, unless it was a little while after I was taken."

"But we live where our father and mother used to live on the banks of the beautiful Susquehanna, and we want you should return with us. We will give you of our property, and you shall be one of us, and share all that we have. You shall have a good house, and every thing you desire. O do go back with us."

"No I cannot. I have always lived with the Indians. They have always used me very kindly. I am used to them. The Great Spirit has always allowed me to live with them, and I wish to live and die with them. Your *Wah-puh-mone,* (looking-glass,) may be larger than mine, but this is my home. I do not wish to live any better, or any where else, and I think the Great Spirit has permitted me to live so long, because I have always lived with the Indians. I should have died sooner if I had left them. My husband and my boys are buried here, and I cannot leave them. On his dying day my husband charged me not to leave the Indians. I have a house, and large lands, two daughters, a son-in-law, three grand-children, and every thing to make me comfortable. Why should I go, and be like a fish out of the water?"

"And I," said Brouriette, her son-in-law, "know all about it. I was born at Fort Harrison, about two miles from Terre Haute. When I was ten years old, I went to Detroit. I was married to this woman about thirteen years ago. The people about here, and at Logansport, and at Miamisport, have known me ever since the country has been settled by the whites. They know me to be industrious, to manage well, and to maintain my family respectably. My mother-in-law's sons are dead, and I stand in their place to her. I mean to maintain her well as long as she lives, for the truth of which you may depend on the word of Capt. Brouriette."

"What Capt. Brouriette says," added the old

lady, "is true. He has always treated me kindly, and I am satisfied with him—perfectly satisfied,—and I hope my connexions will not feel any uneasiness about me. The Indians are my people. I do no work. I sit in the house with these my two daughters, who do the work, and I sit with them."

"But will you at least, go and make a visit to your early home, and when you have seen us, return again to your children?"

"I cannot. I cannot. I am an old tree. It cannot move about. I was a sapling when they took me away. It is all gone past. I am afraid I should die and never come back. I am happy here. I shall die here and lie in that grave-yard, and they will raise the pole at my grave with the white flag on it, and the Great Spirit will know where to find me. I should not be happy with my white relatives. I am glad enough to see them, but I cannot go. I cannot go. I have done."

"When the whites take a squaw," said Brouriette, with much animation, as if delighted with the decision of the old lady, "they make her work like a slave. It was never so with this woman. If I had been a drunken, worthless fellow, this woman could not have lived to this age. But I have always treated her well. The village is called Deaf Man's Village after her husband. I have done."

The eldest daughter, whose name is *Kick-kese-qua*, or "*cut-finger*," assented to all that had been said, and added that "the deer cannot live out of the forest."

The youngest daughter, *O-show-se-quah,* or "*yellow leaves,*" confirmed all, and thought that her mother could not go even on a visit, "because," said she, "the fish dies quickly out of the water."

The brothers and sister returned, unable to win back their tawny sister from her wilds even long enough to make them a visit. She was not just what their hopes had painted; but she was all that an Indian could be in her circumstances. Yet their love for her was not quenched.*

* The whole of this simple narrative, is taken verbatim, from Mr. Todd's little book — he, of course drawing the statement from the memoranda written at the time of the interview, by the Messrs. Slocums,

CHAPTER IX.

Continuation of the History,—The State Government succeeds that of the Proprietaries,—Conduct of the State to the heirs of Penn,—The State claims the title to the Wyoming lands,—Appeals to Congress,—A Commission appointed,—Decision in favor of Pennsylvania,—Dissatisfaction of the people,—State troops sent to Wyoming,—Arrogant and disgraceful conduct of magistrates and soldiers,—Appeal of the people to Congress,—Terrible Inundation,—Sufferings of the people,—Rapacity of the soldiers,—Sympathy of the public excited in their oehalf,—Banditti,—Renewal of the Civil War,—The State troops besieged,—Siege raised,—Commissioners again sent to Wyoming,—Ineffectual negotiations,—Movement of troops against the valley,—Colonel Armstrong appointed to the command,—Repulse of Major Moore,—The people siezed, disarmed, and imprisoned by treachery,—Armstrong plunders the fields,—Resistance of the people,—His troops defeated,—The people re-take their arms,—Armstrong returns to Philadelphia,—Another expedition,—Sympathy for the people,—Interposition of the Council of Censors,—Gloomy situation of affairs in the valley,—Armstrong makes a final retreat,—Better state of feeling,—Mediation of Colonel Pickering,—Compromise Law,—Opposed by John Franklin and some of the people,—Affray,—Franklin's arrest and imprisonment for treason,—Insurrection,—Flight of Colonel Pickering,—His return and extraordinary captivity,—Release,—Final adjustment of the controversy,—Conclusion.

Unfortunately for Wyoming, its troubles ceased not with the war of the Revolution. That contest was in fact ended by the fall of Yorktown, and the surrender of Cornwallis, in October, 1781, though not by official acknowledgment until the treaty of 1783. There was, however, a conventional cessation of active hostilities; and with the disappearance of danger from the Indians on the frontier, Connecticut again poured her hundreds of emigrants into the beautiful vale which nature had destined as the paradise of the Susquehanna. But in regard to the proprietorship of the lands, although the government of Pennsylvania had changed hands, no change had been wrought in favor of the Connecticut claimants; and the swarms of Yankees now alighting in the valley were looked upon with an evil eye. The government of the Proprietaries had been abolished at the commencement of the revolution. The principal heirs to the grant of William Penn already resided in England, and the others, John and Richard Penn, had also retired thither. Both Richard and John had administered the colonial government. The administration of Richard, who was superseded by John in 1763, had been very popular, especially with the merchants. John Penn was at the head of the Proprietaries' government at the breaking out of the rebellion, and his feelings and sympathies were for a season supposed to be in unison with those of the colonists, until after the adoption of the address to the crown, by the Congress of 1775, when Governor Penn attempted to persuade the colonial legislature to adopt a separate address, of a more conciliatory character. But the Assembly was not disposed to separate Pennsylvania from the united action of the colonies. The differences between the Governor and his refractory legislature increased, until the latter, with the people of Pennsylvania, thoroughly espoused the cause of the revolution, and the government of the Proprietaries expired on the 26th of September, 1776. About the year 1778, the legislature of the State enacted a law stripping the heirs of William Penn of all the vacant lands within its territory, leaving them only a few tracts of unsettled lands, called Manors, which had been actually located and surveyed. As an acknowledgement of the merits and claims of the family of Penn, however, the sum of one hundred and thirty thousand pounds sterling was voted them as an indemnification, in addition to the Manors. But there was at the same time due those heirs about five hundred thousand pounds, for lands they had sold the inhabitants, and for quit-rents.* It has been held that the State might have considered the proprietary claims as a royalty, to which an independent government might lawfully succeed.† Still no such claim was preferred; and the pretext for what has been considered by some an act of violence against the just rights of those heirs, was, that so large a property in the hands of a few individuals endangered the liberties of the people.‡

Having thus made itself the successor to the Proprietaries, the State of Pennsylvania was not slow in the interposition of its claim to the terri-

* Pickering's Letter to his son. The amount of Land thus seized was about six millions of acres, according to Mr. Pickering.

† Encyclopædia Americana. Art. Pennsylvania.

‡ Pickering's Letter.

tory of Wyoming, and the entire domain of the Susquehanna and Delaware companies. The articles of confederation having made provision for the adjustment of difficulties arising between states, and Connecticut insisting upon the jurisdiction it had so long exercised over the Wyoming settlements, Pennsylvania now applied to Congress for the appointment of a commission to hear the parties, and determine the question. Commissioners were accordingly appointed, who met at Trenton, in the State of New-Jersey, late in the Autumn of 1782.* After a session of five weeks, the commissioners, on the 30th of December, came to the unanimous decision that Connecticut had no right to the land in controversy, and that the jurisdiction and prëemption of all the lands within her chartered limits belonged to Pennsylvania.

The people of Wyoming viewed the proceedings of the commission of Congress with comparative indifference—considering, or affecting to consider, that the question at issue before it was one of *jurisdiction* only. Their allegiance might as

* The State of Connecticut appointed Colonel Dyer, Doctor Johnson, and Jesse Root, as agents to attend the Board of Commissioners on her behalf; and Messrs. Bradford, Reed, Wilson, and Sergeant, were appointed on the part of Pennsylvania. The Colonel Dyer here named, had been concerned in the Susquehanna Company from the first, and had been its agent in London. He was a lawyer in Windham, and was the same gentleman who has been immortalized in the celebrated tradition of the invasion of Windham by the frogs. One of the Elderkins, also named in the same tradition, was for a time an early resident of Wyoming.

well be rendered to Pennnsylvania as to Connecticut, so that they were left in the undisturbed enjoyment of their farms; and even the explicit phraseology of the decree of the commission, declaring that Connecticut had "no right to the *land* in controversy," gave them little concern, supposing, as they subsequently contended, that it meant no more than the fact that the State of Connecticut had conveyed all her right to the *soil*, to the Susquehanna Company, from which latter their title was derived. They therefore, under this mental construction, acquiesced at once in the decision, and by a formal memorial to the General Assembly, signified their willingness to conform to the laws and obey the constituted authorities of Pennsylvania.*

Far different, however, was the construction of that decree by the Pennsylvanians. They contended not only for the jurisdiction, but for the soil, and the General Assembly took immediate measures preparatory to a sweeping ejectment of the settlers. The decree from Trenton having been received, the General Assembly passed a resolution, on the 20th of February, declaring the people then settled in Wyoming, on yielding obedience to the laws, to be entitled to protection, and the benefits of civil government, in common with

* Chapman.

other citizens of the State. On the 25th of the same month, three Commissioners were appointed, who were to act as magistrates, in Wyoming, inquire into the state of the country, and recommend proper measures for adoption toward the settlers.* These Commissioners were directed to repair to Wyoming in April; meantime, in the month of March, under the transparent pretext of affording protection to the settlement, the Council ordered two companies of rangers to be raised and stationed there, under the command of Captains Thomas Robinson and Philip Shrawder. These companies arrived on the 21st and 24th of March, and taking possession of Fort Wyoming, changed its name to Fort Dickinson, in honor of the President of the Council of State.†

It was very natural that this military demonstration, the object of which, the war being over, could not be misconceived, would create great uneasiness; which feeling, when the Commissioners came to report, was at once aroused to the verge of insurrection. They reported that a reasonable compensation in land should be made to the families of those who had fallen in arms against the common enemy, and to such other set-

* These Commissioners were William Montgomery, Moses M'Lean, and John Montgomery.

† Under the first State Constitution of Pennsylvania, there was no Governor or Senate.

tlers holding under proper Connecticut titles, as were actual residents of Wyoming at the date of the Trenton decree; conditioned that they should relinquish all claim to the soil then in their possession, and make a full and entire surrender of their tenures. In other words, they were to relinquish all their present lands and improvements, purchased by unheard-of sufferings, and consecrated by the blood of their kindred; in lieu of which they were to receive an indefinite compensation, at the option of their enemies, in the wild lands of some region unknown. Conditions like these they were in no temper to brook, more especially as the arrogant conduct of the troops stationed there had already exasperated them almost to a point beyond which endurance ceases to be a virtue. The summer of that year, (1782,) was therefore passed in a state of high excitement,—the troops deporting themselves in a spirit of tyrannical domination, and committing many outrages, disgraceful to the character of civilized men.

In the month of September, Captain Robinson's company was relieved by another detachment of State troops, under Captain Christie, the command of the station at the same time being conferred upon a militia Major named James Moore. Two special Justices of the Peace were likewise appointed for the district, the names of whom were Patterson and West, with directions to repair to the disputed territory, with Major Moore, and by the aid and protection of the military, form a tribunal for the adjudication of all questions arising under the civil law. The immediate object of constituting this tribunal, the authority of which was to be sustained by the bayonet, very soon become apparent. It was none other than to dispossess the Connecticut settlers of their plantations: *per fas aut nefas*, and award them to such claimants as might present themselves under the Pennsylvania title. They began their judicial labors in the most arbitrary and oppressive manner, and the military executed their decrees in a spirit of cruelty and vindictiveness, which would have reflected discredit upon the hordes led into that afflicted region four years before by Gi-en-gwah-toh himself. The people were not only subjected to insult, but their crops were destroyed in the fields, their cattle were seized and driven away, and in some instances their houses were destroyed by fire, and the females rendered the victims of armed licentiousness.* The real object of this rigorous treatment was not only to strip the people of their possessions, but by wearying them of their "promised land," drive them from the valley.†

Considering the indomitable and fiery spirit characterizing the Connecticut emigrants during

* Chapman. † Pickering's Letter.

the severe trials they had encountered in preceding years, it is a subject of surprise that these oppressive acts were submitted to, even for a single week; and it can only be accounted for upon the supposition, that, wearied by the harrassing contentions of years, they were now earnestly seeking repose. Instead, therefore, of an immediate appeal to arms, they now sought redress by an appeal to the Legislature of Pennsylvania for protection. Their first memorial, which ought to have been acted upon in December, seeming to be unheeded, the people next spread their case before Congress, and prayed for the intervention of that body, by the appointment of a commission, under the ninth Article of the Confederation, to hear and determine the question as to the right of soil. The memorial was favorably received, and it was ordered on the 23d of January, 1784, that Congress, or a committee of the States, should hear the parties on the fourth Monday of the then ensuing month of June. But greatly to the disappointment of the people, neither Congress nor a committee of the states was in session at the time designated, " and the controversy came to no determination."

Meantime, however, the inhabitants had been doomed to suffer from a calamity of a different character, inflicted by an arm more powerful than that of man. The winter of 1783—'84, was one of uncommon severity. The weather was so intensely cold that the ice upon the surface of the river formed to an unusual thickness, and the snow fell to an extraordinary depth. Protected from the gradual action of the sun by the dense forests overspreading almost the entire country, the snow lay upon the mountains, and was piled up in the ravines, in immense masses, when suddenly a warm rain set in on the 13th of March, which continued falling until the 15th. A rapid dissolution of the snow caused a corresponding swelling of the streams tributary to the Susquehanna, and a premature breaking up of the ice was the consequence. The first breaking was at the successive rapids, from each of which the ice was borne along in masses over the still sections of the river yet sleeping beneath its frozen chains, until arrested by trees, or some other intervening obstacles, against which it lodged. By this process several dams were formed in the valley, especially at the lower end, where it is almost cut off by the approximating points of the mountains upon either side. These dams caused the waters to flow back and accumulate, until the entire valley was overflowed, and the inhabitants compelled to flee to the little hills rising in the valley,* and

* One of these elevations which impart an agreeable variety to the aspect of the valley, juts out sharply almost into the river, not far above the intersection of Mill Creek. It was the site of one of the Yankee defences against Ogden, heretofore mentioned. From its crest, the landscape is as beautiful as fancy can paint. Upon the summit of this hill sleep the re-

to the mountains, for their lives, leaving their cattle and flocks, their provisions, and the greater part of their household goods to the mercy of the flood. Some of them had more than once been compelled to look back upon the valley from the same mountains, when blazing like a sea of fire. Equally appalling, and if possible more dreary, was the spectacle, now that the valley resembled a hyperborean lake, the ice of which had been broken into floating masses by a tempest. The waters continued to accumulate for many hours, upraising houses, barns, and fences upon their bosom, until at length a large dam in the mountain-gorge above the valley gave way, causing at once a mighty increase, and a tremendous rush of the flood, which, as it hurried impetuously down, swept every thing before it. The fetters of the more tranquil sections of the river gave way at the same time, the ice heaving up in ponderous masses, and making the valley to echo with their thunder as they broke. It was a scene of terrific grandeur, to behold the maddened floods rolling onward in their irresistible strength, and bearing

mains of the Rev. Mr. Johnstone, the first clergyman of Wyoming. He was a good scholar and a man of talents—greatly beloved by the flock over which he watched for many years. He was, however, an eccentric man, entertaining some peculiar views in theology. He believed in the second coming and personal reign of Christ upon earth; and insisted upon being buried here, facing the east, so that he could see the glorious pageant of the Messiah in his second descent.

upon their bosom the wrecks of houses and barns, with stacks of hay, and huge trunks of trees, and broken fragments of timber, with piles of ice and drowned cattle, all mingled in destructive confusion together, and hurrying forward as though anxious to escape such a region of desolation for the more tranquil repose of the ocean. But it was a heart-rending spectacle to the poor settlers, thus again to look upon the entire destruction of their earthly goods, with the certainty that when the flood should abate, they could only return to wander in destitution amidst the "wreck of matter," while even the sunny face of hope had become almost as dark as despair. As the waters subsided, huge piles of ice were deposited upon the plain of Wilkesbarré, so thick that the fervid heat of almost the whole summer was required for its dissolution.*

Disheartened, but not broken, the people returned as soon as the floods would permit, and with the opening spring commenced once more the labor of repairing their dilapidated fortunes,—with which the never-ending still-beginning labors of the fabled Sisyphus were but as child's play in comparison, and, judging from the past, scarcely less promising for the future. The destruction of their cattle and provisions had been

* Chapman.

so general, that gloomy apprehensions of a famine pressed upon their minds, and there must have been great suffering but for the assistance received from abroad. And what little of food had been preserved, or was furnished to them, was snatched almost from their mouths by the soldiers, sent thither to guard and torment them, and who now became more ungovernable and rapacious than before. Such an accumulation of calamities was well calculated to awaken the sympathies of the people wherever the story was rehearsed, and those sympathies, generally, were not appealed to in vain. Mr. Dickinson, the President of the Council of State, spontaneously invited the attention of that body to the subject, and recommended the adoption of measures for the immediate relief of the sufferers ; but the General Assembly looked coldly upon a people whose coming into the state had been without leave, and whose presence had caused them so much trouble. The efforts of the President were therefore not seconded by those holding the keys of the treasury.

The sufferers, however, sustained by the all-conquering spirit of their race, recommenced their labors with their wonted energy ; and but for the conduct of he soldiery, the valley might again have become the home of peace, smiling once more in beauty. But the magistrates sent thither for that purpose revived their oppressive measures, and countenanced the outrages of the soldiers, until the people, chafed beyond longer endurance, determined upon forcible resistance to their mandates. Enraged at this resolution, the magistrates proceeded against the settlers as though they were insurgents. On the 12th of May the soldiers of the garrison were sent to disarm the people, and in the progress of the work "one hundred and fifty families were turned out of their newly constructed dwellings, many of which were burnt, and all ages and sexes reduced once more to a state of destitution. After being plundered of their lttle remaining property, they were driven from the valley, and compelled to proceed on foot through the wilderness by the way of the Lackawaxen river to the Delaware—a distance of eighty miles. During this journey the unhappy fugitives suffered all the miseries which human nature appears capable of enduring. Old men, whose sons had been slain in battle, widows, with their infant children, and children without parents to protect them, were here companions in exile and sorrow, and wandering in a wilderness where famine and ravenous beasts daily reduced the number of the sufferers. One shocking instance of suffering is related by a survivor of this scene of death: it is the case of a mother, whose infant having died, she was driven to the dreadful alternative of roasting the body by piecemeal for the daily subsistence of her remaining children!"*

It must not be supposed that atrocities like these would be sanctioned by the government of any civilized community. The General Assembly, in refusing a vote of supplies for the sufferers by the flood, were believed to have been acting under the influence of the Pennsylvania claimants to the lands of Wyoming; and the instigations of these avaricious men, beyond doubt, had prompted Justices Patterson and West, and the soldiers under them, to the course of wrong and outrage that had been pursued. When, however, the naked facts came to be known to the government, great indignation was produced. A commission was despatched to Wyoming, to inquire into the state of the settlement, and their report was such as to cause the discharge of the troops, with the exception of a small guard left at Fort Dickinson. A proclamation was likewise issued, inviting the people who had been driven away, to return to their homes, with a promise of protection on a due submission to the laws. To a considerable extent this proclamation produced the desired effect, and the people returned.

But the valley was not yet destined to become a place of quiet. The discharged soldiers had be-

* Chapman.

come partisans of the Pennsylvania land claimants. Many of them were, moreover, dissolute; and after being disbanded, they hung around the settlements, living like banditti upon plunder. By the middle of July, so many of them had rejoined the guard in Fort Dickinson, that the garrison was becoming formidable, and the inhabitants, for self-protection, repaired and garrisoned Fort Forty. On the 20th of July, a party of the people in that fort, having occasion to visit their fields of grain five miles below, were fired upon by a detachment of thirty of Justice Patterson's men, from Fort Dickinson, commanded by a man named William Brink, and two of the people, Chester Pierce and Elisha Garret, young men of promise, were killed. The loss of these distinguished young men was deeply lamented, and the inhabitants determined that their death should be avenged. Three days afterward, the garrison of Fort Forty marched upon Wilkesbarré in the night, for the purpose of making prisoners of Patterson and his men, who were in the habit of lodging without the fort, when not apprehensive of danger; but having been apprized of the intention of the people, they had disposed themselves again for the night within the fort, and made preparations for defence. Not being prepared to invest the fortress immediately, the people took possession of the flouring mill, which had been occupied by Patterson and his retainers, and having laid in a store of provisions for themselves at Fort Forty, they retired thither for the purpose of counsel and preparation for ulterior measures.

Three days afterward the fort was invested by the people. The garrison consisted of about sixty men, provided with four pieces of ordnance, and one hundred and sixty muskets. For the cannon there was no ammunition ; but having a good supply for their small arms, and having despatched an express to Philadelphia for assistance, they determined to hold out until the arrival of reinforcements. The leader of the besiegers in this insurrection — if such it might be properly called — was John Franklin, a native of Connecticut — an influential and resolute man — prime agent of the Susquehanna Company, and a colonel by popular election.* On the 27th of July, it having been determined to attempt carrying the fort by storm, Franklin, "in the name and on the behalf of the injured and incensed inhabitants holding their lands under the Connecticut claim," sent a formal summons to the garrison to surrender, not the fortress only, but likewise the possessions and other property of the besiegers, which had been taken from them "in a hostile and unconstitutional manner." It was added that if the summons should be com-

* Letter of Colonel Pickering.

plied with, they "should be treated with humanity and commiseration — otherwise, the consequences would prove fatal and bloody to every person found in the garrison." Two hours were allowed them for an answer. But before these two hours had elapsed, information was received from below, that the magistrates of the county of Northumberland, (to which Wyoming had been attached,) at the head of a body of troops, were marching to the succor of the garrison; whereupon the siege was immediately raised, and the assailants returned to Fort Forty, resolving to remain there until the magistrates should arrive.

The belligerent proceedings of the inhabitants in this emergency can the more readily be justified, when it is considered that the party in the fort, at the head of which was Justice Patterson, was now making war upon them in behalf of the Pennsylvania claimants, on their own account. Under these circumstances, the people had a right, not only to protect themselves, but to repel force by force. That such was the fact appears from the official proceedings of the Council of the State. On hearing of the affair of the 20th, in which two of the inhabitants had been wantonly murdered, the Council forthwith appointed a commission with instructions to proceed to Wyoming, and restore peace by disarming both parties. And it happened to be the approach of the commissioners under this resolution, that caused the raising of the siege of Fort Dickinson. They arrived on the 29th, and on the following day a conference was held between both parties, but without any reconciliation being effected. The commissioners* next made a demand, under the authority of the State, for the mutual surrender of the arms of the parties, and also of a suitable number of persons as hostages, for the preservation of the peace.

But neither persuasion nor demand produced the slightest effect upon either party. The truth was, both had heard that after the arrival of the express in Philadelphia, announcing the beleaguerment of the fort by the people, the Council of State had directed the Lieutenant of the county of Northampton to call forth a body of three hundred infantry, with a squadron of dragoons, to march for the subjugation of the people of Wyoming. A simultaneous order was also given to the Sheriff of Northumberland to proceed with the power of his county, to the aid of the Lieutenant of Northampton. On the same day, viz: the 29th of July, the Honorable John Boyd and Colonel John Armstrong were appointed commissioners for concerting and executing such measures as they should judge necessary for establishing the peace and good

* Chapman is the authority for these details. The commissioners were Thomas Hewitt, David Mead, and Robert Martin.

order of the disaffected district. Under these circumstances, neither party would listen to the proposition for disarming. The Pennamites * counted upon adequate military support, while the Yankees were not disposed to surrender their arms, at a moment when a larger military force than any they had yet encountered was marching for their subjugation.

Colonel Armstrong proceeded to Easton on the 1st of August, where his forces were already collecting. On the 3d he advanced to the eastern verge of the Pokono mountain. He had, however, previously detached Colonel Moore, with a party of volunteers, to a station called Locust Hill, about midway of the mountains, which the Major was directed to hold for the purpose of keeping the passage clear. Hearing of this advance of Moore, the people of Wyoming sent forward a company under the command of Captain Swift, to meet and repel him. This enterprise was executed with fidelity. Swift took the party of Moore by surprise early in the morning of the 2d of August, and after a brisk attack upon the log-house in which they were sheltered, Moore retreated with the loss of one man killed, and several wounded. Swift thereupon returned to Wy-

* *Pennamites* was the name given the Pennsylvanians by the Connecticut settlers, who in turn were designated as Yankees,—Intruders,—Insurgents, &c. Those civil broils are still called the *Pennamite wars* in Wyoming.

oming, where Colonel Armstrong soon appeared at the head, all told, of about four hundred men, including Patterson's troops, and a few milita-men from Northumberland.

The armed forces of the people were so strongly entrenched in Fort Forty, that Armstrong dared not hazard an attack. He therefore had recourse to stratagem. A plausible manifesto was issued, declaring that he had come merely for the dispensation of justice, and the pacification of the valley. His object was the protection of the peaceable inhabitants, to which end it was necessary that both parties should be disarmed. For a time his professions were distrusted by the people; but ultimately the earnestness and apparent sincerity of his protestations overcame their scruples, and numbers of them repaired to Fort Dickinson, to comply with his terms, and also to make reclamation of the property of which they had been plundered. But they had ample cause to lament their credulity, being arrested by scores, pinioned with strong cords, and marched off in pairs, strongly guarded, to the prisons of Easton and Sunbury. Forty-two were sent to the latter prison, ten of whom, however, escaped on the morning after their arrival. In both prisons they were treated with inhumanity; but the imprisonment at Easton was of short duration. On the morning of September 17th, as the jailor was conveying their breakfast to them, he was knocked down by a young man named Inman, and the whole body made their escape.

On the departure of the prisoners, Armstrong had discharged the principal part of his forces, and made preparations with the residue to gather the crops planted to his hands by those whom he had dispossessed. But his army had been prematurely disbanded. With the return of the self-liberated prisoners, the residue of the inhabitants took arms, and being strengthened by a body of emigrants from Vermont, Fort Forty was again occupied, and dispositions promptly made to protect what remained unharvested of their crops. On the 20th of September, a party of Armstrong's men, engaged in harvesting grain that did not belong to them, were attacked and driven into Fort Dickinson. A strong detachment was immediately despatched in pursuit of the "*Insurgents*," as Armstrong now called the people in arms; but the latter took refuge in a log-house, which they defended with such spirit as to repulse their assailants, who bore away, as their only trophies, two wounded men.

The people were suffering greatly by reason of the surrender of their fire arms; and hearing that Colonel Armstrong had sent to Philadelphia for reinforcements, they resolved to make an effort for the recovery of those arms, before any more troops should arrive. Having ascertained the particular block-house in which the arms were deposited, they made an attack on the night of the 25th, but were repulsed. On the following day Colonel Armstrong proceeded to Philadelphia; and on the next, the block-house was carried by the people under John Franklin, two of the Pennamite magistrates, Reed and Henderson, mortally wounded, and the arms recovered. A full statement of the transaction was forwarded to the government by Franklin, acting for the people, in which it was declared that they had not been prompted by any disposition to disregard the laws, but only to be avenged upon Patterson and Armstrong for their treachery.*

Another military expedition against the "insurgents" was immediately determined upon by the Council, to consist of two companies of fifty men each. The command was again entrusted to Colonel Armstrong, who was simultaneously promoted to the office of Adjutant General of the State. The President, Mr. Dickinson, made a strong remonstrance against this proceeding, in writing; but the Council was resolutely bent upon perseverence.† The people of the state, however,

* Chapman.

† Pennsylvania, at that time, had no officer bearing the title of governor. Under its first independent state constitution, the government of the commonwealth was vested in a House of Representatives, a President, and a Council. There was also another branch of the government instituted by

were by this time becoming weary of the contest. Nor was this all: they were beginning to look upon the settlers of Wyoming as the persecuted party, and their sympathies were kindling in their favor. With all his efforts, therefore, the new Adjutant General was enabled to raise only forty men, at the head of whom he reappeared in the valley on the 16th of October. Fort Forty was immediately garrisoned by seventy men, under Mr. Franklin. These Armstrong did not feel strong enough to attack, and he called loudly upon the counties of Northampton, Berks, and Bucks, for assistance; but in vain. Neither the Council, nor the leaders of the Pennsylvania claimants, could induce a single recruit more to engage in a service now becoming not unpopular merely, but odious.

Meantime the period for the septennial meeting of the Council of Censors had arrived, and the feelings of that body had become warmly enlisted in regard to the Wyoming proceedings. Having cognizance of the case, the Council called upon the General Assembly for the papers and documents connected with the controversy. The Assembly disregarded the call, and a mandamus was

that constitution, called a Board of Censors, chosen by the people, and directed to meet once in seven years, to inquire whether the constitution had in the meantime been violated; whether the legislative and executive branches had performed their duties faithfully; whether the laws had been duly and equally executed, &c. &c. They could also try impeachments, and recommend the repeal of unwholesome laws, &c.

issued, which was received and treated with perfect contempt. Finding their authority thus contemned and utterly disregarded, the Council openly espoused the cause of the Connecticut settlers, and passed a public censure upon the government of the state, couched in strong language, for its conduct toward those people — not indeed sanctioning the claim of the latter to the soil, but condemning all the military and pretended civil proceedings that had been adopted against them — especially for the reason, that, after becoming subjects of Pennsylvania, the settlers had not been left to prosecute their claims in the proper course, without the intervention of the legislature.

The stand thus taken by the Censors strengthened the hands of the colonists, and also those of their friends in other parts of the state. The declaration of the Censors also furnished a reasonable excuse to the people to disobey alike the orders of the Council of State, and of Colonel Armstrong. Not another recruit, therefore, could be obtained; and Armstromg found himself shut up in a blockhouse with a force too weak for offensive action, or even to forage for supplies. But the people themselves, even had they not been annoyed by the presence of the soldiery, were in a deplorable condition. All their movable possessions had been swept away by the flood in March, and the labors of the spring and summer had been subjected to such incessant interruptions, while a large portion of their corps had been taken to glut the rapacity of their enemies, that they looked forward to the approaching winter with gloomy forebodings. They again petitioned Congress, and likewise made an affecting appeal for the friendly interposition of the Legislature of Connecticut. In this latter appeal they stated "that their numbers were reduced to about two thousand souls, most of whom were women and children, driven, in many cases, from their proper habitations, and living in huts of bark in the woods, without provisions for the approaching winter, while the Pennsylvania troops and land-claimants were in possession of their houses and farms, and wasting and destroying their cattle and subsistence." The legislature of Connecticut, acknowledging their want of jurisdiction, could only express their sympathy, and promise the exertion of their friendly offices in behalf of the memorialists, both with Congress and the government of Pennsylvania. Happily, however, the settlers were speedily relieved from the presence of the military, and that by no father effort of their own. As winter approached, finding that he could obtain neither recruits nor supplies, Colonel Armstrong discharged his troops, and returned to Philadelphia.*

* Colonel Armstrong, author of the celebrated Newburgh Letters, so fraught with danger on the disbanding of the army at the close of the war

But although this was the last military demonstration of Pennsylvania against Wyoming, the controversy was not yet ended. The people, it is true, were left to the quiet pursuit of their labors during the two succeeding years; still, the question of their land titles was unadjusted, and they knew not how soon farther attempts might be made to dispossess them. There was indeed a kindlier feeling arising mutually between the parties; but every effort of the people to obtain a tribunal before which their title question should be submitted for a final decision, during these two years, was nevertheless unavailing. The population, however, continued to increase rapidly, not only in their own valley, but also above, below and around it; and in the autumn of 1786, the legislature, on the petition of the people of Wyoming, and the region north of it, to whom it was a great inconvenience to attend the court sixty and a hundred miles distant, at Sunbury, formed their territory into a new county, named "Luzerne," in honor of the Chevalier De La Luzerne, who had just at that period returned to France from his embassy to the United States. Indeed the indications, upon both sides, rendered it obvious that a compromise was desired by each.

of the revolution, and afterward distinguished in the political and literary history of the country. He was the son of General John Armstrong of Pennsylvania, distinguished in the earlier Indian wars, and sometimes called "the hero of Kittinaing." The subject of the present note died early in the year 1843, at his seat in Dutchess County, N. Y.

It happened at about the same period that Colonel Timothy Pickering, of Massachusetts, but at that time a resident of Pennsylvania, made a journey through Wyoming, to visit a tract of land in which he was interested, in and about the Great Bend of the Susquehanna, near the New-York line. While in Wyoming, Colonel Pickering embraced every opportunity to learn the feelings of the people in regard to the protracted dispute, and to ascertain the terms upon which their peaceable submission to Pennsylvania might be effected. Being convinced that the settlers were entirely satisfied with the constitution of the state, and were willing to submit to its government, provided they could be quieted in the possession of their farms, on his return to Philadelphia he reported the result of his inquiries and convictions to several distinguished gentlemen, among whom were Doctor Rush, and Mr. Wilson, an eminent lawyer, and afterward a judge of the Supreme Court of the United States. The idea was then suggested to the minds of the Pennsylvanians, that being a New England man, of high character, the services of Colonel Pickering might be of great importance in effecting an arrangement between the parties. The subject was proposed to Mr. Pickering by Dr. Rush, with the proffer of an appointment to the five principal county offices, if he would remove to Wyoming with a view of exerting himself to put an end to the inveterate and disastrous controversy. After taking time for consideration, the proposition was accepted upon the basis already indicated,—viz: that he might assure the Connecticut settlers that the Pennsylvania legislature would pass a law quieting them in their possessions. With this understanding. Colonel Pickering took the offices, and clothed with the necessary power by the legislature, to hold elections and organize the county, proceeded to Wyoming in January, 1787. After spending a full month in visiting the people, the Colonel succeeded in persuading them to apply to the legislature for a compromise law, upon the principle heretofore suggested. His object, however, had well nigh been defeated, at one of the preliminary meetings, by a suggestion from Major John Jenkins,—known to the reader in a former chapter as Lieutenant Jenkins,—who rose and remarked that they had too often experienced the bad faith of Pennsylvania, to place confidence in any new measure of its legislature; and that if they were to enact a quieting law, they would repeal it as soon as the Connecticut settlers submitted and were completely saddled with the laws of the state. Colonel Pickering, not anticipating any such act of Punic faith, repelled the suggestion with great earnestness, and at length succeeded in procuring the application. The proposition of the memorial was, that in case the commonwealth would grant them the seventeen townships which had been laid out, and in which settlements had been commenced previous to the decree of Trenton, they would on their part relinquish all their claims to any other lands within the limits of the Susquehanna purchase.* The towns were represented to be as nearly square as circumstances would permit, and to be about five miles on a side, and severally divided into lots of three hundred acres each. Some of these lots were set apart as glebes, some for schools, and others for various town purposes, &c.

Colonel Pickering proceeded to Philadelphia with the memorial, and aided, by his advice and counsel, the passage of the law. The case was environed with difficulties, not the least of which was the fact that many of the best lands, occupied by the Connecticut claimants, had likewise been granted by the Government of Pennsylvania to its own citizens. It was of course necessary that these claims should be quieted likewise. But as the state had three years before extinguished the Indian title to several millions of acres of land, there was no lack of means for making new grants to those who might suffer in the arrangement

* Chapman. These townships were, Salem, Newport, Hanover, Wilkes-barré, Pittston, Westmoreland, Putnam, Braintree, Springfield, Claverack, Ulster, Exeter, Kingston, Plymouth, Bedford, Huntington, and Providence.

with the Connecticut settlers. Be that as it might, the difficulties were surmounted; a law, which it was supposed would answer every purpose intended, was passed; under which commissioners were appointed to examine the claims on both sides;* those of the Connecticut settlers to ascertain who were entitled to hold by the terms of the law; those of the Pennsylvanians, to ascertain the quality, and appraise the value of each tract.

The commissioners met in Wyoming in May, and made their arrangements preliminary to a formal examination and adjustment of such claims as might be presented to them at another session, to be held in August and September. The law gave general satisfaction to the people within the seventeen townships embraced in its provisions; and the commissioners entered upon their labors, at the time appointed, with a fair prospect of completing the work within a reasonable time. But fresh difficulties arose in another quarter. The Connecticut settlements had been extended, in several directions, considerably beyond the limits of the towns designated, and the people of those settlements were greatly dissatisfied because they were not included in the arrangement. It is believed, moreover, that pending the negotiations for the compromise, the Susquehanna Company had

* The commissioners were Timothy Pickering, William Montgomery, and Stephen Balliott.

been exerting themselves to pour as many settlers into those unincluded districts as possible. Colonel Pickering asserts positively, that "they invited and encouraged emigrations from the states eastward of Pennsylvania, of all men destitute of property, who could be tempted by the gratuitous offer of lands, on the single condition that they should enter upon them *armed,* 'to man their rights,' according to the cant phrase of the day. By this arrangement the Company hoped to pour in such a mass of young and able-bodied men as would appear formidable to the Pennsylvania government, to subdue and expel whom would require a considerable military force, to be raised and maintained at a heavy expense of treasure, and perhaps of blood;" to avoid which evils they hoped that Pennsylvania would ultimately be brought to their own terms. John Franklin had exerted himself, beyond doubt, for that object; and he now became the leader of a new party, determined to defeat the execution of the law. He was a man of activity, shrewdness, and great energy and influence; and by visiting the people of the settlements, he soon stirred up a commotion that compelled the commissioners to flee from the country for safety. Evidence of his practices having been communicated to Chief Justice M'Kean, his warrant was issued for the arrest of Franklin on a charge of treason. It was not judged advisable to direct the sheriff of

Luzerne, who had just been elected, and whose residence was among the turbulent men under the influence of Franklin, to serve the writ, and it was therefore directed to four gentlemen of known fortitude, two of whom had served in the army of the revolution. Franklin was at the time absent on an incendiary mission, thirty-five miles farther down the valley. On his return, every necessary preparation having been made for his safe conduct to Philadelphia, he was arrested. He resisted the special officers, however, to the utmost, and would unquestionably have effected his escape, or been rescued, — for the people were already assembling with that design, — had it not been for the exertions and the courage of Colonel Pickering. Observing the commotion from the window, he rushed out with a pair of loaded pistols, and caused Franklin to be secured by cords, and bound upon the horse prepared for his journey. He was then conducted off, and taken in safety to Philadelphia, and thrown into prison.

Colonel Pickering always avowed that he should not have interfered in the case but for the conviction that the welfare of the people and the public peace depended upon securing the person of that daring man. Deeply, however, did he incur the resentment of Franklin's partizans. Their leader had scarcely disappeared in the direction of Philadelphia, before symptoms were discovered that vengeance was to be wreaked upon the head of Colonel Pickering, and he was admonished by his friendly neighbors that it would be wise for him to leave his domicil for a short period, until their passions had time to cool. He listened to the admonition, just in time to secrete himself in a neighboring wood before "the Philistines were upon him." Returning to his family in the evening, some of his neighbors assembled in arms for his protection; but before he had finished his supper, tidings came that Franklin's men were embodying in arms on the opposite side of the river, and were even then preparing to cross over and attack him. Taking a loaded pistol with him, and a few small biscuits, the Colonel retired to a neighboring field, and was soon apprised by the yells of the insurgents that he had not effected his escape a moment too soon. The noise subsiding, he correctly judged that the neighbors who had armed for his defence, and had fastened the house, had been compelled to surrender. Such proved to be the fact, and the insurgents made a thorough search of the house in the hope of finding the object of their vengeance. Having been joined by Mr. Evan Griffith, Secretary of the Commissioners, and an inmate of Colonel Pickering's house, the two retired to the mountains, where they passed the night. Through a German friend occupying one of his farms, the Colonel was enabled on the following day to communicate with his family. Ascertaining in this way that it would be unsafe for him to return, and that the search for him was yet continued, Colonel Pickering determined to make his way to Philadelphia, and from the distance watch the course of events. It was near the middle of October. He was without provisions, and thinly clad; but no time was to be lost, and he was compelled to direct his course through the deep forests and over the mountains heretofore described. There was, indeed, an indifferent road leading in the proper direction; but by attempting to travel upon this, he had well nigh fallen into the hands of a party of insurgents who were on the watch to intercept his flight. Yet, after a severe journey, the Colonel arrived in safety at Philadelphia, about a month after the convention that formed the Constitution of the United States had adjourned.

Franklin had arrived there before him, and was in jail. Deprived of his counsel and leadership, his insurgent partizans, reflecting upon the rashness of their conduct, and also upon its illegality, began to relent, and sent a petition to the Council, acknowledging their offence, and praying for a pardon. This was readily granted, and conveyed to them by Colonel Dennison, member of the Council from Luzerne. Colonel Pickering now supposed of course that he could join his family in safety;

but having arrived within twenty-five miles of Wyoming, a messenger whom he had despatched in advance, to ascertain the popular feeling, met him with a message from his friends that it would yet be unsafe for him to come into the valley. Upon the receipt of these advices, he returned to Philadelphia, where he remained until January. Meantime a state convention had been called to deliberate upon the draft of a constitution submitted to the people of the United States by the national convention on the 17th of September,—to which state convention Colonel Pickering was chosen a delegate by the people of that very county from which he was kept in banishment! What a striking illustration does this fact present, of the inconsistencies into which the people may be hurried by passion and caprice! They would select Colonel Pickering, of all others, to sit in judgment upon an instrument, which, if adopted, was to become the grand regulating machine of their political and religious principles,—the charter of their liberty, and that of their posterity, in all time to come,—while they would not trust the same individual to decide for them in the matter of a contested title to a few hundred dollars worth of land!

Having attended to his duties in the convention, Colonel Pickering presented himself among his constituents in January, 1788. Franklin yet remained in prison. Next to his confinement, the out-and-out opponents of the compromise law deemed the presence of Colonel Pickering within the disputed territory, as working the greatest detriment to their schemes. There were various indications, therefore, for several weeks, that a conspiracy was on foot to drive him from the county. Indeed it was menacingly intimated to him by Major Jenkins, in the month of April, that such was the fact. But the Colonel was neither disposed to relinquish the cause of pacification in which he had engaged, nor to abandon his farms and improvements. He therefore pursued his occupations as usual, until the night of the 26th of June, when he was awakened from his sleep by a violent opening of the door of his apartment.—"Who is there?" he demanded. "Get up," was the answer. "Don't strike," said Colonel Pickering; "I have an infant on my arm." Then rolling the child from his arm, the Colonel arose and dressed, while Mrs. Pickering slipped out of bed on the other side, and throwing on a few clothes groped her way to the kitchen for a light, on returning with which they saw the room filled with men armed with guns and hatchets, with blackened faces, and handkerchiefs tied around their heads. Their first act was to pinion the Colonel by tying his arms across his back with a strong cord,—long enough for one of the party to hold in order to prevent an escape,—having in the course of their proceedings admonished Mrs. Pickering that they would tomahawk her if she made any noise. Having thus secured his person, they advised him to take a blanket, or a thick outer garment with him, as he would be a long time in a situation to need it. Mrs. Pickering thereupon handed the Colonel his surtout, and they departed with their captive. It appeared that there were fifteen of the ruffians. Not a word more than was necessary was spoken, and their march in the darkness and stillness of the night was along the valley north to Pittstown, ten miles, where they halted at a tavern for a few minutes. After refreshing themselves with whiskey,—not omitting to offer some to their captive, which was declined,—they pursued their journey, while it was yet dark as Erebus. They had not proceeded far from the tavern, before one of the ruffians marching by the Colonel's side broke silence by saying:—

"Now, if you will only write two or three lines to the Executive Council, they will discharge Colonel Franklin, and we will release you."

The object of the abduction was at once disclosed. But the ruffians had mistaken their man. The instant reply of the Colonel was,—

"The Executive Council better understand their

duty than to discharge a traitor to procure the release of an innocent man."

"Damn him!" exclaimed one of the party, marching as a guard in the rear, whose wrath had been excited by the application of the epithet "traitor" to Franklin, "why don't you tomahawk him?"

Their march was then continued in the same sullen silence as before. Bad as they were, however, these misguided men were not altogether destitute of civility, or kind feelings. On their arrival at the Lackawannock river, finding the water so low that the canoe grounded in crossing it, one of the party waded to the shore, and divesting himself of his pack, returned and carried the Colonel over on his back.

In the course of the morning they crossed to the west side of the Susquehanna, by a ferry, and pursued their journey thirty miles from Wilkesbarré, to a log-house, near the river, at which they halted, and cooked some victuals, of which they all made a hearty meal—it being the first food they had tasted since the night before. Seeing a bed in the room, Colonel Pickering lay down to rest, and found himself unpinioned when he arose. While he was on the bed, and, as the party supposed, asleep, they were overtaken by a man from Joseph's Plains, two miles from Wilkesbarré, who informed them that the militia had turned out, and were in pursuit. The insurgents immediately disturbed the repose of their prisoner, and retired back from the river about a quarter of a mile, encamping behind a hill in the woods. Here they remained during the night, encountering a severe thunder-storm. In the morning, finding all quiet at the river, they returned to the house, where they obtained breakfast. At about ten o'clock, a man was descried on the opposite side of the river, leading his horse, at which one of the party exclaimed — "There goes Major Jenkins, now,— a d—d stinking son of a ——!" It was obvious from this remark, that Jenkins had been prompting the outrage, but with more cunning than boldness, had avoided any direct participation in its execution. He was indeed at that time leaving Wyoming for the state of New-York, where he employed himself as a land surveyor until tranquility had been restored.

Preparations were now making to cross to the eastern side of the Susquehanna; and as the blacking began by this time to disappear from the faces of the captors, Colonel Pickering discerned among the party two sons of a near neighbor, named Dudley — Gideon and Jacob. These were the only persons of the gang whom he knew. Before entering the canoe, one of them attempted to manacle the prisoner with a pair of handcuffs, against which he remonstrated; and at the interposition of a man named Earl, who also had two sons of the party, the Colonel was spared that inconvenience and degradation. Having crossed the river, after an hour's march, the leader of the party despatched all but four of his men upon separate duty. With these four to guard the prisoner, the leader struck off directly into the woods. The Colonel's apprehensions were somewhat excited by this movement—more so from the circumstance that he had heard the leader described as a bold, bad man. But his apprehensions of personal injury were groundless. They had not travelled more than an hour before a fawn was started, "and as he bounded along, this leader, who was an expert hunter, shot him, and in five minutes he had his skin off, and the carcass slung upon his back." At the distance of three or four miles from the river, on arriving at a brook that came dancing across their course, they halted, struck a fire, and began to cook some of their venison. "The hunter who had killed it,—their leader,—took the first cut. They sharpened small sticks at both ends, running one into a slice of the fawn, and setting the other into the ground, the top of the stick being so near the fire as to broil the flesh," Being hungry, the Colonel borrowed one of their knives and began cooking for himself. He observed that the hunter was tending his steak with great nicety,—sprinkling it with salt,—and as soon as it was done, with a very good grace, he presented it to their captive.

They erected a booth with branches of trees, and remained at this place about a week—most of the time upon short allowance of food, and that of a coarse quality. In the course of their conversations, they had informed the Colonel that they were to be supported by a body of four hundred men. He assured them that they were deceiving themselves, and that they would be sorry for what they were doing, since, so far from being supported, they would be abandoned to their fate. From this station they removed to another, in a narrow sequestered valley, not more than two or three miles from the river. Here they produced a chain five or six feet long, having at one end a fetter for the anckle. They said they were reluctant to put the chain upon him, but Colonel Franklin had been put in irons, and "their great men required it." The chain was then made fast to the prisoner's leg, and the other end fastened to a tree by a staple. Escape was now impossible. Another booth was erected, and when they lay down for the night, one of the guards wound the chain around one of his own legs. But the Colonel had no design of attempting an escape. Satisfied that they did not intend to take his life, he determined in his own mind to await the course of events with as much patience as he could command.

They had been at this place but two or three days, when, one morning, before his guards were awake, the Colonel heard a brisk firing, as of musketry, in the direction of the river. But of this circumstance he said nothing to his keepers, not doubting, in his own mind, that it was a skirmish between the insurgents and the militia, sent after them, and for his rescue. Such proved to be the fact. After breakfast one of his keepers went down to a house in their interest by the river, but returned in haste, to inform his comrades that "the boys," as they called their associates, had met the militia, and that Captain Ross, who commanded the latter, was mortally wounded.* They were now at Black Walnut Bottom, forty-four miles above Wilkesbarré. During the whole time, the guards of Colonel Pickering were in communication with their comrades in the vi-

* Happily this statement was erroneous. The Captain Ross here spoken of, is the late General Ross of Wilkesbarré. "A company of about fifteen men under Captain William Ross pursued the rioters, but as they had concealed themselves in the woods, among the mountains of Mahoopeny, the place of their retreat was not easily ascertained, particularly as their movements were only in the night; for during the day they lay concealed to guard their prisoner, who was kept bound to a tree. About the dawn of the day, Captain Ross's company fell in with a company of the rioters, near the mouth of Meshoppen Creek, and a skirmish ensued in which Captain Ross was wounded. Colonel Myers and Captain Schotts also proceeded with a portion of the militia, in pursuit of the rioters. A sword was afterward presented to Captain Ross, by the Supreme Executive Council, for his gallantry in this affair."—*Chapman.*

cinity; and after this affair with Captain Ross, they were evidently becoming more uneasy every hour. They changed their stations several times, and again crossed to the west side of the river, under cover of the night. On the 15th of July, Gideon Dudley, who seemed to have become the leader of the party, visited the station where Colonel Pickering was kept, and attempted to renew the negotiation for his influence in behalf of Franklin. But the Colonel positively refused to purchase his own liberty in that manner. He was then asked by Dudley if he would intercede for *their* pardon, in the event of his release. He told them he would answer no questions until they knocked off his chain. It was instantly taken off. The Colonel then said to them, that in the belief that they had been deluded and deceived,—that they had been acting in obedience to the orders of those whom they called their "great men,"—he would exert his influence for their pardon, if they would give him their names; adding, that he entertained no doubt of being able to obtain it. The demand of names was not readily assented to, causing the delay of a day in the negotiation. On the 16th they removed to the house of a man named Kilburne, father of two of the party. The Colonel, who had been nineteen days without a razor for his beard, or a change of clothes, was here provided with shaving ap-

32

paratus and a clean shirt and stockings, and then informed that he was at liberty. A comfortable dinner was next prepared, after which "the boys" importunately renewed their application in behalf of Franklin. This request was again peremptorily refused. In regard to themselves,—thirty-two of the party being then present,—the Colonel again proffered his influence in their behalf, on condition that the names of their "great men" should be given up. But after a side consultation they rejected the terms, declaring that the severest punishment in the world to come ought to be meted to any one of their number who should betray them.

Their last request to Colonel Pickering was, that he would write a petition for them to the Executive Council, and be the bearer of it himself to Wilkesbarré, whence he might forward it for them to Philadelphia. To this request he assented; and forthwith took his departure for his own home where he arrived on the following day without farther molestation.

The sequel to this singular outrage upon Colonel Pickering is briefly told. Without waiting for the result of their petition to the Council, most of the actual perpetrators of the outrage fled northward, taking refuge in the State of New-York. On their way thither they encountered a detachment of militia, under the command of Captain

Roswell Franklin, who had been sent out in pursuit of them, and with whom they exchanged several shots. By one of them Joseph Dudley was badly wounded. The others escaped. Dudley was conveyed to Wilkesbarré, a distance of sixty or seventy miles, in a canoe. The physician who was sent for had no medicine, and the wants of the wounded man were supplied from the medicine chest of Colonel Pickering, which had been made up by Dr. Rush. He survived but a few days, and Mrs. Pickering furnished a winding sheet for his burial.

At the Oyer and Terminer held in Wilkesbarré the succeeding autumn, several of the rioters were tried and convicted. "They were fined and imprisoned, in different sums, and for different lengths of time, according to the aggravation of their offence. But they had no money wherewith to pay their fines, and the jail at Wilkesbarré was so insufficient, that they all made their escape, excepting Stephen Jenkins, brother of Major John Jenkins." Although concerned in the plot, he was not in arms with the insurgents; and when the others escaped, he preferred to remain and trust to the clemency of the government. The consequence was that he soon afterward received a pardon.

Captain Roswell Franklin, whose name has just been mentioned, is pronounced by Colonel Pickering to have been a worthy man, but he came to a melancholy end. "Wearied with the disorders and uncertain state of things at Wyoming, he removed with his family into the State of New-York, and sat down upon a piece of land to which he had no title. Others had done the same. The country was new and without inhabitants. They cleared land, and raised crops, to subsist their families and stock. In two or three years, after all their crops for the season were harvested, their hay and grain in stack, and they anticipated passing the approaching winter comfortably, Governor George Clinton sent orders to the sheriff of the nearest county to raise the militia and drive off the untitled occupants. These orders were as severely as promptly executed, and the barns and crops all burnt. Reduced thus to despair, Captain Franklin shot himself."* John Franklin, so

* Pickering's Letter to his Son. There is reason, however, to question the accuracy of this statement as to the suicide of Roswell Franklin, as will be seen by the following obituary notice, copied from a newspaper published at Auburn, (N. Y.) in the Spring of 1843:—"DIED, on the 28th ult., at his late residence near Aurora, Maj. ROSWELL FRANKLIN, in the 75th year of his age. The deceased was a native of Connecticut — his father emigrated to the valley of Wyoming, Pennsylvania, — both were engaged in the battle with the Indians and English at that place, which was so disastrous to the States. The mother and one sister were butchered before their eyes, another sister was taken prisoner by the Indians and retained among them eleven years at Niagara. The deceased was also taken prisoner and retained among them about three years near Mount Morris, Livingston county. In the spring of 1787, the deceased emigrated with his father to the banks of Cayuga Lake, where the now beautiful village of Aurora stands. With boughs and barks they formed a shelter, and in the Autumn of that year, the first 'log cabin' ever erected in Cayuga

often mentioned, and whose arrest and imprisonment for his treasonable practices was the cause of the abduction of Colonel Pickering, was indicted, and remained in prison for a considerable period. He was ultimately liberated on bail; and after all opposition to the government in Luzerne county had ceased, he was fully discharged. His popularity with the people remained, and he was afterward, for several years, a member of the Pennsylvania Legislature. Meeting with Colonel Pickering in subsequent years, they interchanged the ordinary civilities that pass between gentlemen.*

The prediction of Major John Jenkins to Colonel Pickering, at the time when the latter gentleman undertook the pacification of the valley, that even should the General Assembly pass the desired compromise act, they would repeal it at their

county by civilized man, was raised by them, (only twelve feet square.) A gentleman of Aurora has in his possession, a portion of the sill of this Cabin, also a portion of the Oak stump which stood near the door, dug out and used for pounding corn. The deceased was a most exemplary man.—For more than forty years he was a deacon in the Presbyterian churches of Aurora and Genoa." The place where Captain Roswell Franklin settled, therefore, was not upon the disputed territory referred to by Colonel Pickering, nor do the circumstances narrated agree with the facts indicated in this obituary of the Son.

* In closing this narrative of the captivity of Colonel Pickering in Wyoming, it is proper to say that the facts have been drawn immediately from the letter to his son, cited occasionally in the notes to some of the preceding chapters. For a copy of this letter, which was first read by the author about ten years ago, he is indebted to William M'Ilhenny, Esq., Librarian of the Philadelphia Athenæum, who found it in Hazard's Pennsylvania Register, where it was published in the spring of 1831.

own pleasure,* was verified, sooner, perhaps, than the prophet himself anticipated. But the turbulent settlers had themselves to thank for this violation of the public faith, if a violation of faith it could be called which was superinduced by the bad conduct of many of those for whose chief benefit the law had been originally designed. The law was suspended in the year succeeding the transactions detailed in the present chapter, and was afterward entirely repealed. "Thus the question of title was again thrown into its former position, and during the succeeding ten years continued to retard the settlement of the country, and to create continual contention and distrust between the respective claimants. But the situation of the inhabitants was very different from what it had been in former stages of the controversy. They were represented in the General Assembly by one of their own number, and were the executors of the laws within their own district. Pennsylvania had adopted a new constitution, and was governed by a more liberal policy. Petitions were again presented to the legislature for the passage of another law, upon the principles of the one which had been repealed, and, in April, 1799, an act was passed in conformity to the prayer of the petition, so far as it regarded the seventeen townships contemplated by the original law."*

* Chapman.

The difficulties connected with the settlement of that portion of the Susquehanna Company's claim not included by the act, were continued two or three years longer, during which the Company exerted itself as before, in sending forward clouds of adventurous spirits to plant themselves upon the disputed territory; nor did they desist until the Legislature of Pennsylvania had provided against farther intrusions by a bill of severe pains and penalties. Ultimately the claims were all quieted, and the Pennsylvania titles fairly established.

The population of that portion of Pennsylvania, is chiefly from New-England; and for the last thirty-five years the valley of Wyoming has been as remarkable for its tranquillity, as for the fifty preceding years it had been for its turbulence. It is indeed a lovely spot, which, had Milton seen it before the composition of his immortal Epic, might well have suggested some portions of his gorgeous description of Paradise. The lofty and verdant mountains which shut the valley from the rest of the world, correspond well with the great poet's

"——————enclosure green,
* * * * * * * * *
Of a steep wilderness; whose hairy sides
With thicket overgrown, grotesque and wild,
Access denied; while overhead up grew
Insuperable height of loftiest shade,
Cedar, and pine, and fir, and branching palm,
A sylvan scene; and as the ranks ascend,
Shade above shade, a woody theatre
Of stateliest view."

Wyoming is larger, by far, than the Thessalian vale which the poets of old so often sang, though not less beautiful. If its mountain-barriers are not honored by the classic names of Ossa and Olympus, they are much more lofty. Instead of the Peneus, a mightier river rolls its volume through its verdant meadows; and if the gods of the Greek Mythology were wont to honor TEMPE with their presence, in times of old, they would prove their good taste, and their love of the romantic and beautiful, in these modern days, by taking an occasional stroll among the cool shades and flowery paths of WYOMING.

NOTES

TO GERTRUDE OF WYOMING.

PART I.

STANZA 3, 1. 6.

From merry mock-bird's song.

The mocking-bird is of the form, but larger, than the thrush; and the colors are a mixture of black, white, and gray. What is said of the nightingale by its greatest admirers, is what may with more propriety apply to this bird, who, in a natural state, sings with very superior taste. Towards evening I have heard one begin softly, reserving its breath to swell certain notes, which, by this means, had a most astonishing effect. A gentleman in London had one of these birds for six years. During the space of a minute he was heard to imitate the woodlark, chaffinch, blackbird, thrush, and sparrow. In this country (America) I have frequently known the mocking-birds so engaged in this mimicry, that it was with much difficulty I could ever obtain an opportunity of hearing their own natural note. Some go so far as to say, that they have neither peculiar notes, nor favorite imitations. This may be denied. Their few natural notes resemble those of the (European) nightingale. Their song, however, has a greater compass and volume than the nightingale, and they have the faculty of varying all intermediate notes in a manner which is truly delightful.—*Ashe's Travels in America*, vol. ii. p. 73.

STANZA 5, 1. 9.

And distant isles that hear the loud Corbrechtan roar.

The Corybrechtan, or Corbrechtan, is a whirlpool on the western coast of Scotland, near the island of Jura, which is heard at a prodigious distance. Its name signifies the whirlpool of the Prince of Denmark ; and there is a tradition that a Danish Prince once undertook, for a wager, to cast anchor in it. He is said to have used wollen instead of hempen ropes, for greater strength, but perished in the attempt. On the shores of Argyleshire, I have often listened with great delight to the sound of this vortex, at the distance of many leagues. When the weather is calm, and the adjacent sea scarcely heard on these picturesque shores, its sound, which is like the sound of innumerable chariots, create a magnificent and fine effect.

STANZA 13, l. 4.

Of buskin'd limb and swarthy lineament.

In the Indian tribes there is a great similarity in their color, stature, &c. They are all, except the Snake Indians, tall in stature, straight, and robust. It is very seldom they are deformed, which has given rise to the supposition that they put to death their deformed children. Their skin is of a copper color; their eyes large, bright, black, and sparkling, indicative of a subtle and discerning mind; their hair is of the same color, and prone to be long, seldom or never curled. Their teeth are large and white; I never observed any decayed among them, which makes their breath as sweet as the air they inhale. — *Travels through America by Capts. Lewis and Clarke, in* 1824—5—6.

STANZA 14, l. 6.

Peace be to thee! my words this belt approve.

The Indians of North America accompany every formal address to strangers, with whom they form or recognise a treaty of amity, with a present of a string or belt of Wampum. Wampum (says Cadwallader Colden) is made of the large whelk shell, Buccinum, and shaped liked long beads; it is the current money of the Indians.—*History of the Five Indian Nations, p.* 34.—*New-York edition.*

STANZA 14, l. 7.

The paths of peace my steps have hither led.

In relating an interview of Mohawk Indians with the Governor of New-York, Colden quotes the following passage as a specimen of their metaphorical manner: "Where shall I seek the chair of peace? Where shall I find it but upon our path? and whither doth our path lead us but unto this house?"

STANZA 15, l 2.

Our wampum league thy brethren did embrace.

When they solicit the alliance, offensive or defensive, of a whole nation, they send an embassy with a large belt of wampum and a bloody hatchet, inviting them to come and drink the blood of their enemies. The wampum made use of on these and other occasions, before their acquaintance with the Europeans, was nothing but small shells which they picked up by the sea-coasts, and on the banks of the lakes; and now it is nothing but a kind of cylindrical beads, made of shells, white and black, which are esteemed among them as silver and gold are among us. The black they call the most valuable, and both together are their greatest riches and ornaments; these among them answering all the end that money does with us. They have the art of stringing, twisting, and interweaving them into their belts, collars, blankets, and moccasins, &c., in ten thousand different sizes, forms, and figures, so as to be ornaments for every part of dress, and expressive to them of all their important transactions. They dye the wampum of various colors and shades, and mix and dispose them with great ingenuity and order, and so as to be significant among themselves of almost every thing they please; so that by these their words are kept, and their thoughts communicated to one another, as ours are by writing. The belts that pass from one nation to another in all treaties, declarations, and important transactions, are very carefully preserved in the cabins of their chiefs, and serve not only as a kind of record or history, but as a public treasure.—*Major Rogers's Account of North America.*

STANZA 17, l. 5.

As when the evil Manitou.

It is certain that the Indians acknowledge one Supreme Being, or Giver of Life, who presides over all things; that is, the Great Spirit; and they look up to him as the source of good, from whence no evil can proceed. They also believe in a bad Spirit, to whom they ascribe great power; and suppose that through his power all the evils which befall mankind are afflicted. To him, therefore, they pray in their distresses, begging that he would either avert their troubles, or moderate them when they are no longer unavoidable.

They hold also that there are good Spirits of a lower degree, who have their particular departments, in which they are constantly contributing to the happiness of mortals. These they suppose to preside over all the extraordinary productions of Nature, such as those lakes, rivers, and mountains, that are of uncommon magnitude; and likewise the beasts, birds, fishes, and even vegetables or stones, that exceed the rest of their species in size or singularity.—*Clarke's Travels among the Indians.*

The Supreme Spirit of good is called by the Indians Kitchi Manitou; and the Spirit of evil, Matchi Manitou.

STANZA 19, l. 2.

Fever-balm and sweet sagamite.

The fever-balm is a medicine used by these tribes; it is a decoction of a bush called the Fever Tree. Sagamite is a kind of soup administered to their sick.

STANZA 20, l. 1.

And I, the eagle of my tribe, have rush'd with this lorn dove.

The testimony of all travellers among the American Indians who mention their hieroglyphics, authorizes me in putting this figurative language in the mouth of Outalissi. The dove is among them, as elsewhere, an emblem of meekness; and the eagle, that of a bold, noble, and liberal mind. When the Indians speak of a warrior who soars above the multitude in person and endowments, they say, "he is like the eagle, who destroys his enemies, and gives protection and abundance to the weak of his own tribe."

STANZA 23, l. 2

Far differently, the mute Onieda took, etc.

They are extremely circumspect and deliberate in every word and action; nothing hurries them into any intemperate wrath, but that inveteracy to their enemies, which is rooted in every Indian's breast. In all other instances they are cool and deliberate, taking care to suppress the emotions of the heart. If an Indian has discovered that a friend of his is in danger of being cut off by a lurking enemy, he does not tell him of his danger in direct terms, as though he were in fear, but he first coolly asks him which way he is going that day, and having his answer, with the same indifference tells him that he has been informed that a noxious beast lies on the route he is going. This hint proves sufficient, and his friend avoids the danger with as much caution as though every design and motion of his enemy had been pointed out to him.

If an Indian has been engaged for several days in the chase, and by accident continued long without food, when he arrives at the hut of a friend where he knows his wants will be immediately supplied, he takes care not to show the least symptoms of impatience, or betray the extreme hunger that he is tortured with; but on being invited in, sits contentedly down and smokes his pipe with as much composure as if his appetite was cloyed, and he was perfectly at ease. He does the same if among strangers. This custom is strictly adhered to by every tribe, as they esteem it as a proof of fortitude, and think the reverse would entitle them to the appellation of old women.

If you tell an Indian that his children have greatly signalized themselves against an enemy, have taken many scalps, and brought home many prisoners, he does not appear to feel any strong emotions of pleasure on the occasion; his answer generally is — they have "done well," and he makes but very little inquiry about the matter; on the contrary, if you inform him that his children are slain or taken prisoners, he makes no complaints: he only replies, "It is unfortunate: — and for some time asks no questions about how it happened.—*Lewis and Clarke's Travels.*

STANZA 23, l. 3.

His calumet of peace, &c.

Nor is the calumet of less importance or less revered than the wampum, in many transactions relative both to peace and war. The bowl of this pipe is made of a kind of soft red stone, which is easily wrought and hollowed out; the stem is of cane, alder, or some kind of light wood, painted with different colors, and decorated with the heads, tails, and feathers of the most beautiful birds. The use of the calumet is to smoke either tobacco, or some bark, leaf, or herb, which they often use instead of it, when they enter into an alliance, or any serious occasion, or solemn engagements; this being among them the most sacred oath that can be taken, the violation of which is esteemed most infamous, and deserving of severe punishment from Heaven. When they treat of war, the whole pipe and all its ornaments are red; sometimes it is only red on one side, and by the disposition of the feathers, &c., one acquainted with their customs will know at first sight what the nation who presents it intends or desires. Smoking the calumet is also a religious ceremony on some occasions, and in all treaties is considered as a witness between the parties, or rather as an instrument by which they invoke the sun and moon to witness their sincerity, and to be, as it were, a guarantee of the treaty between them. This custom of the Indians, though to appearance somewhat ridiculous, is not without its reasons; for as they find that smoking tends to disperse the vapors of the brain, to raise the spirits, and to qualify them for thinking and judging properly, they introduced it into their councils, where, after their resolves, the pipe was considered as a seal of their decrees, and as a pledge of their performance thereof, it was sent to those they were consulting, in alliance or treaty with; so that smoking among them at the same pipe, is equivalent to our drinking together, and out of the same cup. —*Major Rogers's Account of North America*, 1766.

The lighted calumet is also used among them for a purpose still more interesting than the expression of social friendship. The austere manners of the Indians forbid any appearance of gallantry between the sexes in day time; but at night the young lover goes a calumeting, as his courtship is called. As these people live in a state of equality, and without fear of internal violence or theft in their own tribes, they leave their doors open by night as well as by day. The lover takes advantage of this liberty, lights his calumet, enters the cabin of his mistress, and gently presents it to her. If she extinguishes it, she admits his addresses; but if she suffer it to burn unnoticed, he retires with a disappointed and throbbing heart.—*Ashe's Travels.*

STANZA 23, l. 6.

Train'd from his tree-rock'd cradle to his bier.

An Indian child, as soon as he is born, is swathed with clothes, or skins; and being laid upon his back, is bound down on a piece of thick board, spread over with soft moss. The board is somewhat larger and broader than the child, and bent pieces of wood, like pieces of hoops, are placed over its face to protect it, so that if the machine were suffered to fall, the child probably would not be injured. When the women have any business to transact at home, they hang the board on a tree, if there be one at hand, and set them a-swinging from side to side, like a pendulum, in order to exercise the children.—*Weld*, vol. ii. p. 246.

STANZA 23, l. 7.

The fierce extremes of good and ill to brook
Impassive——

Of the active as well as passive fortitude of the Indian character, the following is an instance related by Adair, in his Travels :—

A party of the Seneca Indians came to war against the Katahba, bitter enemies to each other. In the woods the former discovered a sprightly warrior belonging to the latter, hunting in their usual light dress: on his perceiving them, he sprang off for a hollow rock four or five miles distant, as they intercepted him from running homeward. He was so extremely swift and skilful with the gun, as to kill seven of them in the running fight, before they were able to surround and take him. They carried him to their country in sad triumph; but though he had filled them with uncommon grief and shame for the loss of so many of their kindred, yet the love of martial virtue induced them to treat him during their long journey, with a great deal more civility than if he had acted the part of a coward. The women and children, when they met him at their several towns, beat him and whipped him in as severe a manner as the occasion required, according to their law of justice, and at last he was condemned to die by the fiery torture. It might reasonably be imagined that what he had for some time gone through, by being fed with a scanty hand, a tedious march, lying at night on the bare ground, exposed to the changes of the weather, with his arms and legs extended in a pair of rough stocks, and suffering such punishment on his entering into their hostile towns, as a prelude to those sharp torments for which he was destined, would have so impaired his health and affected his imagination, as to have sent him to his long sleep, out of the way of any more sufferings. — Probably this would have been the case with the major part of white people under similar circumstances; but I never knew this with any of the Indians; and this cool-headed, brave warrior, did not deviate from their rough lessons of martial virtue, but he acted his part so well as to surprise and sorely vex his numerous enemies :—for when they were taking him, unpinioned, in their wild parade, to the place of torture, which lay near to a river, he suddenly dashed down those who stood in his way, sprang off, and plunged into the waters, swimming underneath like an otter, only rising to take breath, till he reached the opposite shore. He now ascended the steep bank, but though he had good reason to be in a hurry, as many of the enemy were in the water, and others running very like bloodhounds, in pursuit of him, and the bullets flying around him from the time he took to the river, yet his heart did not allow him to leave them abruptly, without taking leave in a formal manner, in return for the extraordinary favors they had done, and intended to do him. After slapping a part of his body, in defiance to them, (continues the author,) he put up the shrill warhoop, as his last salute, till some more convenient opportunity offered, and darted off in the manner of a beast broke loose from its torturing enemies. He continued his speed, so as to run by about midnight of the same day as far as his eager pursuers were two days in reaching. There he rested till he happily discovered five of those Indians who had pursued him :—he lay hid a little way off their camp, till they were sound asleep. Every circumstance of his situation occurred to him, and inspired him with heroism. He was naked, torn, and hungry, and his enraged enemies were come up with him ; but there was now every thing to relieve his wants, and a fair opportunity to save his life, and get great honor and sweet revenge, by cutting them off. Resolution, a convenient spot, and sudden surprise, would effect the main object of all his wishes and hopes. He accordingly creeped, took one of their tomahawks, and killed them all on the spot,—clothed himself, took a choice gun, and as much ammunition and provisions as he could well carry in a running march. He set off afresh with a light heart, and did not sleep for several successive nights, only when he reclined as usual, a little before day, with his back to a tree. As it were by instinct, when he found he was free from the pursuing enemy, he made directly to the very place where he had killed seven of his enemies, and was taken by them for the fiery torture. He digged them up, burned their bodies to ashes, and went home in triumph. Other pursuing enemies came, on the evening of the second day, to the camp of their dead people, when the sight gave them a greater shock than they had ever known before. In their chilled war-council they concluded, that as he had done such surprising things in his defence before he was captivated, and since that in his naked condition, and now was well-armed, if they continued the pursuit he would spoil them all, for surely he was an enemy wizard, and therefore they returned home.—*Adair's General Observations on the American Indians*, p. 394.

It is surprising, says the same author, to see the long continued speed of the Indians. Though some of us have often run the swiftest of them out of sight for about the distance of twelve miles, yet afterward, without any seeming toil, they would stretch on, leave us out of sight, and outwind any horse.—*Ibid.* p. 318.

If an Indian were driven out into the extensive woods, with only a knife and a tomahawk, or a small hatchet, it is not to be doubted but he would fatten even where a wolf would starve. He would soon collect fire by rubbing two dry pieces of wood together, make a bark hut, earthen vessels, and a bow and arrows: then kill wild game, fish, fresh-water tortoises, gather a plentiful variety of vegetables, and live in affluence,—*Ibid.* p. 410.

STANZA 24, l. 7.

Moc sins is a sort of Indian buskins.

STANZA 25, l. 1.

Sleep, wearied one! and in the dreaming land
Shouldst thou to-morrow with thy mother meet.

There is nothing (says Charlevoix) in which these barbarians carry their superstitions further, than in what regards dreams: but they vary greatly in their manner of explaining themselves on this point. Sometimes it is the reasonable soul which ranges abroad, while the sensitive continues to animate the body. Sometimes it is the familiar genius who gives salutary counsel with respect to what is going to happen. Sometimes it is a visit made by the soul of the object of which he dreams. But in whatever manner the dream is conceived it is always looked upon as a thing sacred, and as the most ordinary way in which the gods make known their will to men. Filled with this idea, they cannot conceive how we should pay no regard to them. For the most part they look upon them either as a desire of the soul, inspired by some genius, or an order from him, and in consequence of this principle they hold it a religious duty to obey them. An Indian having dreamt of having a finger cut off, had it really cut off as soon as he awoke, having first prepared himself for this important action by a feast. Another having dreamt of being a prisoner, and in the hands of his enemies, was much at a loss what to do. He consulted the jugglers, and by their advice caused himself to be tied to a post, and burnt in several parts of the body.—*Charlevoix, Journal of a Voyage to North America.*

STANZA 26, l 5.

The crocodile, the condor of the rock—

The alligator, or American crocodile, when full grown, (says Bertram,) is a very large and terrible creature, and of prodigious strength, activity, and swiftness in the water. I have seen them twenty feet in length, and some are supposed to be twenty-two or twenty-three feet in length. Their body is as large as that of a horse, their shape usually resembles that of a lizard, which is flat, or cuneiform, being compressed on each side, and gradually diminishing from the abdomen to the extremity, which, with the whole body, is covered with horny plates of squamæ, impenetrable when on the body of the live animal, even to a rifle-ball, except about their head, and just behind their fore-legs or arms, where, it is said, they are only vulnerable. The head of a full grown one is about three feet, and the mouth opens nearly the same length. Their eyes are small in proportion, and seem sunk in the head, by means of the prominency of the brows; the nostrils are large, inflated, and prominent on the top, so that the head on the water resembles at a distance, a great chunk of wood floating about: only the upper jaw moves, which they raise almost perpendicular, so as to form a right angle with the lower one. In the forepart of the upper jaw, on each side, just under the nostrils, are two very large, thick, strong teeth, or tusks, not very sharp, but rather the shape of a cone; these are as white as the finest polished ivory, and are not covered by any skin or lips, but always in sight, which gives the creature a frightful appearance; in the lower jaw are holes opposite to these teeth to receive them; when they clap their jaws together, it causes a surprising noise, like that which is made by forcing a heavy plank with violence upon the ground, and may be heard at a great distance. But what is yet more surprising to a stranger, is the incredibly loud and terrifying roar which they are capable of making, especially in breeding-time. It most resembles very heavy distant thunder, not only shaking the air and waters, but causing the earth to tremble; and when hundreds are roaring at the same time, you can scarcely be persuaded but that the whole globe is violently and dangerously agitated. An old champion, who is, perhaps, absolute sovereign of a little lake or lagoon, (when fifty less than himself are obliged to content themselves with swelling and roaring in little coves round about,) darts forth from the reedy coverts, all at once, on the surface of the waters in a right line, at first seemingly as rapid as lightning, but gradually more slowly, until he arrives at the centre of the lake, where he stops. He now swells himself by drawing in wind and water through his mouth, which causes a loud sonorous rattling in the throat for near a minute; but it is immediately forced out again through his mouth and nostrils with a loud noise, brandishing his tail in the air, and the vapor running from his nostrils like smoke. At other times, when swoln to an extent ready to burst, his head and tail lifted up, he spins or twirls round on the surface of the water. He acts his part like an Indian chief, when rehearsing his feats of war.—*Bertram's Travels in North America.*

STANZA 27, l. 4.

Then forth uprose that lone wayfaring man.

They discover an amazing sagacity, and acquire, with the greatest readiness, anything that depends upon the attention of the mind. By experience, and an acute observation, they attain many perfections to which Americans are strangers. For instance, they will cross a forest or a plain, which is two hundred miles in breadth, so as to reach, with great exactness, the point at which they intend to arrive, keeping, during the whole of that space, in a direct line, without any material deviations; and this they will do with the same ease, let the weather be fair or cloudy. With equal acuteness they will point to that part of the heavens the sun is in, though it be intercepted by clouds or fogs. Besides this, they are able to pursue, with incredible facility, the traces of man or beast, either on leaves or grass; and on this account it is with great difficulty they escape discovery. They are indebted for these talents, not only to nature, but to an extraordinary command of the intellectual qualities, which can only be acquired by an unremitted attention, and by long experience. They are, in general, very happy in a retentive memory. They can recapitulate every particular that has been treated of in council, and remember the exact time when they were held. Their belts of wampum preserve the substance of the treaties they have concluded with the neighboring tribes for ages back, to which they will appeal and refer with as much perspicuity and readiness as Europeans can to their written records.

The Indians are totally unskilled in geography, as well as all the other sciences, and yet they draw on their birch-bark very exact charts or maps of the countries they are acquainted with. The latitude and longitude only are wanting to make them tolerably complete.

Their sole knowledge in astronomy consists in being able to point out the polar star, by which they regulate their course when they travel in the night.

They reckon the distance of places, not by miles or leagues, but by a day's journey which, according to the best calculation I could make, appears to be about twenty English miles. These they also divide into halves and quarters, and will demonstrate them in their maps with great exactness by the hieroglyphics just mentioned, when they regulate in council their war parties or their most distant hunting excursions.—*Lewis and Clarke's Travels.*

Some of the French missionaries have supposed that the Indians are guided by instinct, and have pretended that Indian children can find their way through a forest as easily as a person of maturer years; but this is a most absurd notion. It is unquestionably by a close attention to the growth of the trees, and position of the sun, that they find their way. On the northern side of a tree there is generally the most moss; and the bark on that side, in general, differs from that on the opposite one. The branches towards the south are, for the most part, more luxuriant than those on the other sides of trees and several other distinctions also subsist between the northern and southern sides, conspicuous to Indians, being taught from their infancy to attend to them, which a common observer would, perhaps, never notice. Being accustomed from their infancy likewise to pay great attention to the position of the sun, they learn to make the most accurate allowance for its apparent motion from one part of the heavens to another; and in every part of the day they will point to the part of the heavens where it is, although the sky be obscured by clouds or mists.

An instance of their dexterity in finding their way through an unknown country came under my observation when I was at Staunton, situated behind the Blue Mountains, Virginia. A number of the Creek nation had arrived at that town on their way to Philadelphia, whither they were going upon some affairs of importance, and had stopped there for the night. In the morning, some circumstance or other which could not be learned, induced one half of the Indians to set off without their companions, who did not follow until some hours afterward. When these last were ready to pursue their journey, several of the towns-people mounted their horses to escort them part of the way. They proceeded along the high road some miles, but, all at once, hastily turning aside into the woods, though there was no path, the Indians advanced confidently forward. The people who accompanied them, surprised at this movement, informed them that they were quitting the road to Philadelphia, and expressed their fear lest they should miss their companions who had gone on before. They answered that they knew better, that the way through the woods was the shortest to Philadelphia, and that they knew very well that their companions had entered the wood at the very place where they did. Curiosity led some of the horsemen to go on; and to their astonishment, for there was apparently no track, they overtook the other Indians in the thickest part of the wood. But what appeared most singular was, that the route which they took was found, on examining a map, to be as direct for Philadelphia as if they had taken the bearings by a mariner's compass. From others of their nation who had been at Philadelphia at a former period, they had probably learned the exact direction of that city from their villages, and had never lost sight of it, although they had already travelled three hundred miles through the woods, and had upwards of four hundred miles more to go before they could reach the place of their destination.—Of the exactness with which they can find out a strange place to which they have been once directed by their own people, a striking example is furnished, I think, by Mr. Jefferson, in his account of the Indian graves in Virginia. These graves are nothing more than large mounds of earth in the woods, which on being opened, are found to contain skeletons in an erect posture: the Indian mode of sepulture has been too often described to remain unknown to you. But to come to my story. A party of Indians that were passing on to some of the seaports on the Atlantic, just as the Creeks, above mentioned, were going to Philadelphia, were observed, all on a sudden, to quit the straight road by which they were proceeding, and without asking any questions, to strike through the woods, in a direct line, to one of these graves, which lay at the distance of some miles from the road. Now very near a century must have passed over since the part of the Virginia in which this grave was situated, had been inhabited by Indians, and these Indian travellers, who were to visit it by themselves, had unquestionably never been in that part of the country before; they must have found their way to it simply from the description of its situation, that had been handed down to them by tradition.—*Weld's Travels in North Amerioa*, vol. ii.

NOTES

TO GERTRUDE OF WYOMING.

PART III.

STANZA 16, l. 4.

The Mammoth comes.

THAT I am justified in making the Indian chief allude to the mammoth as an emblem of terror and destruction, will be seen by the authority quoted below. Speaking of the mammoth or big buffalo, Mr. Jefferson states, that a tradition is preserved among the Indians of that animal still existing in the northern parts of America.

"A delegation of warriors from the Delaware tribe having visited the governor of Virginia during the revolution, on matters of business, the governor asked them some questions relative to their country, and among others, what they knew or had heard of the animal whose bones were found at the Saltlicks, on the Ohio. Their chief speaker immediately put himself into an attitude of oratory, and with a pomp suited to what he conceived the elevation of his subject, informed him, that it was a tradition handed down from their fathers, that in ancient times a herd of these tremendous animals came to the Big-bone-licks, and began a universal destruction of the bear, deer, elk, buffalo, and other animals which had been created for the use of the Indians. That the Great Man above looking down and seeing this, was so enraged, that he seized his lightning, descended on the earth, seated himself on a neighboring mountain on a rock, of which his seat and the prints of his feet are still to be seen, and hurled his bolts among them, till the whole were slaughtered, except the big bull, who, presenting his forehead to the shafts, shook them off as they fell, but missing one, at length it wounded him in the side, whereon, springing round, he bounded over the Ohio, over the Wabash, the Illinois, and finally over the great lakes, where he is living at this day."—*Jefferson's Notes on Virginia.*

STANZA 17, l. 1.

Scorning to wield the hatchet for his bribe,
'Gainst Brant himself I went to battle forth.

I took the character of Brant in the poem of Gertrude, from the common Histories of England, all of which represented him as a bloody and bad man, (even among savages,) and chief agent in the horrible desolation of Wyoming. Some years after this poem appeared, the son of Brant, a most interesting and intelligent youth, came over to England, and I formed an acquaintance with him, on which I still look back with pleasure. He appealed to my sense of honor and justice, on his own part and on that of his sister, to retract the unfair aspersions which unconscious of its unfairness, I had cast on his father's memory.

He then referred me to documents which completely satisfied me that the common accounts of Brant's cruelties at Wyoming, which I had found in books of Travels, and in Adolphus's and similar Histories of England were gross errors, and that, in point of fact, Brant was not even present at that scene of desolation,

It is, unhappily, to Britons and Anglo-Americans that we must refer the chief blame in this horrible business. I published a letter expressing this belief in the *New Monthly Magazine*, in the year 1822, to which I must refer the reader—if he has any curiosity on the subject—for an antidote to my fanciful description of Brant. Among other expressions to young Brant, I made use of the following words: "Had I learnt all this of your father when I was writing my poem, he should not have figured in it as the hero of mischief." It was but bare justice to say thus much of a Mohawk Indian, who spoke English fluently, and was thought capable of having written a history of the Six Nations. I ascertained also that he often strove to mitigate the cruelty of Indian warfare. The name of Brant, therefore, remains in my poem a pure and declared character of fiction.

STANZA 17, l. 8 and 9.

To whom nor relative nor blood remains,
No, not a kindred drop that runs in human veins.

Every one who recollects the specimen of Indian eloquence given in the speech of Logan, a Mingo chief, to the Governor of Virginia, will perceive that I have attempted to paraphrase its concluding and most striking expressions :—"There runs not a drop of my blood in the veins of any living creature." The similar salutation of the fictitious personage in my story, and the real Indian orator, makes it surely allowable to borrow such an expression ; and if it appears, as it cannot but appear, to less advantage than in the original, I beg the reader to reflect how difficult it is to transpose such exquisitely simple words without sacrificing a portion of their effect.

In the spring of 1774, a robbery and murder were committed on an inhabitant of the frontiers of Virginia, by two Indians of the Shawanee tribe. The neighboring whites, according to their custom, undertook to punish this outrage in a summary manner. Colonel Cresap, a man infamous for the many murders he had committed on those much injured people, collected a party and proceeded down the Kanaway in quest of vengeance; unfortunately, a canoe with women and children, with one man only, was seen coming from the opposite shore, unarmed, and unsuspecting an attack from the whites. Cresap and his party concealed themselves on the bank of the river, and the moment the canoe reached the shore, singled out their objects, and at one fire killed every person in it. This happened to be the family of Logan, who had long been distinguished as a friend to the whites. This unworthy return provoked his vengeance; he accordingly signalized himself in the war which ensued. In the autumn of the same year a decisive battle was fought at the mouth of the great Kanaway, in which the collected forces of the Shawanese, Mingoes, and Delawares, were defeated by a detachment of the Virginia militia. The Indians sued for peace. Logan, however, disdained to be seen among the supplicants; but lest the sincerity of a treaty should be disturbed, from which so distinguished a chief abstracted himself, he sent by a messenger the following speech to be delivered to Lord Dunmore :—

" I appeal to any white man if he ever entered Logan's cabin hungry, and he gave him not to eat; if he ever came cold and naked, and he clothed him not. During the course of the last long and bloody war, Logan remained idle in his cabin, an advocate for peace. Such was my love for the whites, that my countrymen pointed as they passed, and said, Logan is the friend of white men. I have even thought to have lived with you, but for the injuries of one man. Colonel Cresap, the last spring, in cold blood, murdered all the relations of Logan, even my women and children.

" There runs not a drop of my blood in the veins of any living creature : —this called on me for revenge. I have fought for it. I have killed many. I have fully glutted my vengeance. For my country, I rejoice at the beams of peace :—but do not harbor a thought that mine is the joy of fear. Logan never felt fear. He will not turn on his heel to save his life. Who is there to mourn for Logan? not one !"—*Jefferson's Notes on Virginia.*

COPY OF THE DEED OF PURCHASE,

REFERRED TO IN THE FOREGOING WORK.

To all People to whom these Presents shall come, Greeting; Know ye that we Ka-hick-to-ton, Abraham Pieters, Willem Tharigjoris (Brant Cauwignoge) (Henderick Pieters Tejanoge) (Canageogaije Set I-ta-va-rie) (Johans So-ge-howane) (Johani Canadegaie) (Nikes Carigiagtadie) (Conaggnause) (Johanes Signagerat) Cores-tago Senosses A-gwe-iota.—

Being Chief Sachems and Heads of the five Nations of Indians called the Irequois and the Native Proprietors of a large Tract of Land on, about, and adjacent to the River Susquehannah, between the forty-first and forty-third Degrees of North Latitude, and being within the Limits and Bounds of the Charter and Grant of his late Majesty King Charles the Second to the Colony of Connecticut—and———

Whereas a large Number of the leige and good Subjects of his Royal Majesty George 2nd of Great Britain, &c., King, inhabitants of his Said Majesty's English Colony of Connecticut, &c., to the Number of about Six Hundred have applyed to us for the Purchase of said above mentioned Tract of Land, for a Plantation to settle upon.

Thereupon Whereas a constant and cordial Friendship from the time of our Progenitors and Predecessors to this Day hath always been subsisting between us and our Brethren the English Subjects of this Said Majesty King George, and of his Royal Predecessors, Kings and Queens of Great Britain, and the Continuation of which we heartily desire. And Whereas, the Enabling and Incouraging our Said English Brethren to Plant and Settle in a nearer Neighbourhood to us than heretofore, may greatly contribute to our safety and Defense against the unjust Encroachments and Insults of French and Indians in Alliance with them, and to the Benefitt and Increase of our Trade, and also may be very conducive to our obtaining a more full and clear Knowledge of the true God and the Christian Religon and thereby Fix and Establish a more firm Solid and lasting Friendship with his said Majesties English Subjects.

Now Thereupon for and in Consideration of the Sum of Two Thousand Pounds of Current Money of the Province of New York to us, to our full satisfaction, before the Ensealing hereof Contented and Paid, the Receipt whereof to full content we do hereby Acknowledge, and thereupon do Give, Grant, Bargain, Sell, Convey And Confirm———

——*UNTO*——

Hez. Huntington, Esq.
Roger Wolcott, Jr. Esq.
Col. Elisha Williams
Phineas Lyman, Esq.
Daniel Edwards, Esq.
Col. Samuel Talcott
George Wyllys, Esq.
Thos. Wells, Esq.
Eliphalet Dyer, Esq.
Jabez Fitch, Esq.
John Smith, Esq.
Ezekiel Pierce, Esq.
Thos. Saymore
Wm. Pitkin, Jun. Esq.
Eleazar Fitch, Esq.
John Fitch
Samuel Grey, Esq.
Jedediah Elderkin
John Abbe
William Andrews
Moses Barnett
John Backus
Noah Briggs
Caleb Bates
Jonathan Baker
Nehemiah Barker
Ezra Belding
Wm. Buck
Jehial Barnam
Gideon Bingham
Robert Crery, Jun.
Benjaman Crery
Christopher Crery
Abijah Crery
Giles Chirchel
Barnet Dixon
David Downing
John Dixon
John Dorrance
James Dixon
Nathaniel Daniels
Samuel Dorrance
Richard Downer
Josiah Dean, Jun.
Asa Douglass
Gideon Demoring
Jos. Eaton
Josh. Elderkin
Edward Ewings
Elias Frink
Elijah Frances
John Gaston
John Grosvenor
Eben. Grosvenor
Stephen Gardner
Stephen Gardner, Jun.
Jonathan Gardner
David Griswold
Elijah Griswold
Robert Hunter
John Hunter
Henry Hewett
John Howard
Sarah Huntington
Stephen Hardon
John Hough
Josiah Horsford
Daniel Horsford
John Judd
Wm. Jackson
John Jenkes
Joseph Kyle
Archibald Casson
Samuel Casson
Adam Kason
Jeremiah Kenny
Moses Kenny
Gideon Kenny
Nathan Kenny
John Kenny
Spencer Kenny
John Kagwin
Hugh Kennady, Jun.
Thomas Kennady, Jun.
Seth Kent
James Kasson
John Leavins
Ebenezer Larnard
Stephen Lee
Isaac Lee
Edward Mott
James Montgomery
John Montgomery
Gaun Miller
Samuel McFarland
John Montgomery, Jun.
Joseph Moffitt
Manassah Minor
Thomas Mansfield
John Maning, Jun.
Josiah Orcutt
Wm. Parkes
Mathew Patrick
Jacob Patrick
Joseph Phillips
Benj. Pierce, Jun.
Robert Parkes
Nathan Parkes
Jeremiah Ross
Stephen Rodes
Obediah Rodes
Noah Stantly
John Stantly
Tim. Stantly
Thomas Snell
Lemuel Smith
John Stephens
Isaac Shepard
Jesse Spaldwen
Thomas Stewart
John Streater
Nehemiah Stephens
Andrew Stephens
Benj. Stephens
Solomon Stoddard
Ebenezer Smith, Jun.
Eben Smith
Uriah Stephens
Joseph Smith, Jun.

Samuel Silsby
Simon Tubbs
Jos. Taylor
Philip Turner
Lemuel Taylor
Judah Wright
Eliphalet Whittlesey
Jos. Watden
David Waters
Isaac Warner
Wm. Williams
John Wiley, Jun.
Thos. Wiley
Hugh Wiley
James Wiley
Eben. Wright
Isaac Woodwarth
Wm. Whiting
Wm. Churchill
Josiah Curtice
Nathan Booth
Ichabod Welles
Phineas Judd
Stephen Skinner
Wm. Fitch
James Bradford
Matthew Patrick, Jun.
Nathaniel Wales, Jun.
Nathaniel Hovey
Prince Tracy
Noah Gilbert
Daniel Knowlton
William Huston
Moses Fish
John Johnson, Jun.
Wm. Chandler, Esq.
Nathaniel Warner
Gershom Durrance
Thomas Pierce
Samuel Chandler, Esq.
Nathaniel Berry
Nathaniel Wales, Esq.
Zebediah Farrum
Daniel Stoughton
Jonas Shephard
Matthew Tolcutt

Joseph Church
Ezekiel Williams
John Humphry, Esq.
Roger Hooker
Alexander Walcott
Samuel Talcott
Thos. Hosmore, Esq.
Jonathan Hale, Esq.
Abner Moseley
Peletiah Mills
Daniel Goodwin
Jonathan Humphry
Jonathan Pettibone
Andrew Robe
David Phelpes
Hezekiah Humphry
Hezekiah Phelpes
John Veites
Joseph Welles
Timothy Seymore
Russell Woodbridge
Wm. Stantly
Samuel Welles
John Wait
Benjamin Caldwell
Alexander Gaston
Rowland Burton
Alexander Phelpes
Niles Colman
David Barker
Benj. Pumroy
John Fitch, Jun.
Joseph Warren
Seth Dean
Samuel Hunten
Noah Webster
Thomas Howard
Zebulon Warterman
Eben. Leach
Penuel Bowen
Israel Dimock
Abiel Abbott
Thomas Stedman
James Stedman
Eben. Griffin
Thomas Stephens

Thomas Stephens, Jun.
Benj. Lee
Stephen Fuller
Paul Holt
Benj. Collings
James Wilson
James Douglass
John Campbell
Hugh Wyley, Jun.
Benj. Parke
Bartholemew Arthur
Thos. Jones
Joseph Taylor
John Read
Wm. Swetland
Peter Swetland
Jonathan Harriss
Elisha Scovil
Eben. Williams
Abel Griswold
Stephen Jenkins
David Deway
Gershom Breed
John Newton
John Grant
Ephraim Gardner
Gershom Hinkley
Joshua Ransome
Miles Gordon
Isaac Tracey
James Hide
Asa Waterman
John Baldwen
Elijah Backus
Phinehas Holden
Christopher Palmer
Thomas Anderson
Allen Willey
John Rothbone
Daniel Ely
David Dodge, Jun.
Eben. Watson
Sam. Stoughton
Sam. Welles, Jun.
Isaac Sheldon
Eben. Beacher

Oliver Wolcott
Elijah Sheldon
Eben. Marsh, Esq.
Sam. Cockrin
Benj. Green
Ephraim Andrews
Daniel Turner
George Palmer
Capt. Uriah Stephens
Samuel Orton
Jacob Hensdel
Thos. Williams
Zebulon Stephens
Thos. Watson
Jos. Bird, Esq.
John Holmes
John Dean
Increase Mosely, Esq.
John Hutchinson, Esq.
Eben. Fletcher
Joshua Whitney
Sam. Slaughter
Robert Hannis
Noah Stephens
David Whitney, Esq.
Jedediah Stephens
Jonathan Smith
Thos. Parmely
Oliver Sanford
Azeriah Orton
Josiah Everit
Francis Everit
Josiah Everit
Timothy Rose
Timothy Everit
Silas Storey
Hezekiah Hooker
Jedediah Richards
Peter Granson
Richard Reat
Eben. Gransan
Daniel Berry
John Franklin
Robert Walker
Edward Spaldwen
Josiah Cleavland

Samuel Lee
Elier Andrews
William Phellows
Seth Norton
Levi Watson
Eliphalet Ensign
Lemuel Orten
Eleizer Gooden
Daniel Wilcoxs
Sam. Gooden
Turbal Whitney
James Bird
Thomas Bird
John Miner
Joseph Allen
James Dunham
Robert Wincott
Thos. Stephens
Joshua Rothbone
Jonathan Rothbone
Elijah Dean
John Read
Edward Waldow
Jacob Rothbone
Isaac Gallop
Jonathan Wealder
Daniel Rothbone
Daniel Miner
Valentine Rothbone
Auger Judson
Zachariah Clark
Peter Curtice
James Levingworth
Jedediah Mills
Sam. Defouest
Elisha Mills
Francis Hawley
Edmund Lewis, Jun.
Daniel Hide
Josiah Lewis, Jun.
John Laboree
Ephraim Judson
John French
Jabez Sommers
Josiah Robingson
Nathaniel Baker

Joseph Arnold
Benj. Thompson
Daniel Morriss
John Andrews
Benj. Rhamsey, Jun.
Josiah Wakeman
Daniel Sherwood
Cornelius Hull
Stephen Wakeman, Jun.
Thomas Couch
Josiah Beardsely
Ephraim Bennet
Matthew Curtice
Jonathan Booth
Caleb Baldwen
Jonathan Willard
Doctor Moffitt
Thomas Stantly
Joshua Wylls
Joseph Hubbart
Isaac Sayer
Samuel Flag
Daniel Lothrop
John Elderkin
Stephen Beckwith
Jeremiah Clements
Samuel Gore
Benjamin Gale
William Whitney
Barsillai Handel
Isaac Lawrance
Joseph Palmeter
Malachi Butler
Joseph Toleate
John Spencer, Jun.
Elijah Hide
Nathaniel Cushman
Caleb Hide
Obediah Newcomb
Joseph Bingham, Jun.
John Strong
Noah Dewey
Joseph Skiff
Jonathan Hale
Jabez Dean
Joseph Weight

Obediah Gore	Jacob Kimball	Silas Wells
Abel Clarke	Thomas Boles	John Wells
Seth Smith	Elisha Tracy	Samuel Barns
John Birchard, 3d.	Joseph Tracy, Jun.	Constant Catlin
Joseph Dennison, Esq.	Isaac Saben	John Hanford
Samuel Tracy	William Lothrop	Jedediah Norton
Ephraim Bill	Daniel Rockwell	Elisha Hale
Herbart Pride	Benedick Arnold	Jacob Drake
Thomas Welles	Nathaniel Parkes	Ashael Drake
Thos. Fish	George Danniss	Barnabas Hatch
Thomas Branch, Jun.	Rachel Milner	Josiah Cowls
Benjamin Wentworth	John Edgerton	John Webster
Simon Huntington	Samuel Walworth	John Cooke
Isaac Tracy, Jun.	Christopher Storke	Reubin Swift
John Wood	Thomas Walworth	Isaac Mosley
Oliver Spicer	Stephen Billings	Jonathan Landon
Benjamin Giles	Jonathan Stricklin	John Patterson
Thomas Giles	John Bliss	Nathan Pason
Jonathan Gennings	Samuel Hunn	Oliver Badcock
Simon Backus	Seth Alden	Solomon Grant
Ebenezer Grover, Jun.	John Burchard	Benjamin Newcomb
Joseph Billings, Jun.	Robert Boyington	Joseph Lippit
Robert Kenady	Macock Ward	Samuel How
John Williams	Jacob Drake, Jun.	Walter Hewit
Daniel Lathan	Ashbel Woodbridge	Henry Stephens
John Choate	Eleizer Talcott	

All of ye aforesaid Colony of Connecticut in New England:

AND TO

Jabez Bowen, Esq.	Samuel Dorrance	Jonathan Moray
Jonathan Randale, Esq.	Michael Dorrance	Charles Harris
Rob. Randale, Esq.	Elnathan Walker	William Sheldon
Jonathan Nicolls	Amos Stafford, Jun.	Eliakam Walker
Robert Hazzard	Simeon Draper	Richard Charnton
Benjamin Bowen	Thomas Mattison	Beriah Brown
Francis Colgrove	Daniel Lawrence	John Reynolds
Martin Howard	Amos Stafford	John Reynolds, Jun.
Philip Wilkinson	Samuel Drown	Jonathan Reynolds
Daniel Ayrault	John Bucklin	Benjamin Sheffield
George Dorrance	Thomas Burt	Jonathan Hamilton

Of the Colony of Rhode Island, in New England, aforesaid:

AND TO

Daniel Shoemaker	John Adkins, Esq.	Daniel Henshaw
Benjamin Shoemaker	Samuel Depew, Esq.	Aaron Depew
Joseph Skinner	John Panather, Esq.	Solomon Gennings
Abram Fencumps, Esq.		

All of the Government of Pennsylvania:

AND TO

Timothy Woodbridge	David King	John Wing, Jun.
John Wing		

Of the Province of ye Massachusetts Bay;

AND TO

Hendrick Burghert, Jun.	Jacob Boseboom	Jonathan Buck
Aaron Sheldon	Kiliaen De Kidder	Baltazar Lydius
Joseph Woodbridge	John Henry Lydius, Esq.	John Rosa
Benjamin Ashby	Jeremiah Hogeboom	

Of the Province of New York:

Being in all five Hundred and Thirty-four in Number—

To each and every of the Persons before and above mentioned and Named, Two Twelve Hundred and Twenty four parts of the Large Tract or Parcel of Land as hereafter Described and Bounded.

And we do also for and upon the Consideration Afore Said, give, grant, Bargain, Sell, Convey and Confirm,

—*UNTO*—

[HERE BEGINS HALF SHARES.]

Eliphalet Newel	Gideon Baldwin	Gideon Lawrence
Jacob Dana	Abel Barnes	Jesse Stephens
John Webb	Hezekiah Orton	Alexander Hinman
Oliver Parish	John Wough	Nathaniel Crandell
Paul Hebard	Thomas Lylly	Joshua Birch
Hezekiah Huntington	Samuel Norton	Eli Colton
Eben Bebbens	Hezekiah Hooker	Daniel Alden
Abram Snow	Thomas Fellows	Nathaniel Loomis
Eleazar Dones	James Hannas	Oliver Crery
Joseph Spaulding	Joseph Fellows	Aaron Crery
Curtis Spaulding	Henry Bass	George Crery
Thomas Brown	Benjamin Follit	William Crery
John Eddy	Simeon Dean	Eben Cheney
Judah Hay	John Steel	John Cogswell
Joseph Alexander	Elisha Steel	John Cone
John Campbell, 3d.	Samuel Church	John Coleburt
James Campbell, Jun.	Eben Lewis	Abraham Harden
Jacob Simons	Caleb Wheeler	Jonathan Sanger
Jeduthan Simons	Jehial Bryant	Thomas Steel
Benjamin Parks	Cotton Fletcher	Thomas Warner
Henry Arnold	John Fellows	Zachariah Bicknale
John Wells	Samuel Ford	John Royce
Jacob Sisco	Job Marsh	Samuel Douglass
Hezekiah Demmon	John Pirkens	Joshua Dunlap
Samuel Douglass	Thomas Porter	Alexander Stewart
James Morriss	Andrew Bacon	Benajah Bill
Samuel Jackson	Thomas Day	Elias Frink, Jun.
Samuel Gordon	David Bredwell	Joseph Hazen

Samuel Webb, Jun.	Jacob Simons, 3d.	Elisha Cornish
Seth Wright	Zebulon Hebard	Isaac Pettebone
John Larabe	Joshua Read	Timothy Moses
Nathaniel Hide	Gideon Hebard	Oliver Humphrey
Ephraim Dean	Joseph Badcock	Jacob Case
Phinehas Lewis	Samuel Bennit	Abel Pettebone
John Strong	David Palmer	William Manly, Jun.
Hezekiah May	Benajah Parks	Giles Pettibone
Thomas Wells	Josiah Parks	Abram Pettibone
Josiah Griswold	Gideon Haskell	John Barker
James Lockwood	Jacob Geers	John Spencer
Elisha Williams, Jun.	Benjamin Geers	Samuel Hulbert
Ezekiel Porter	John Read, Jun.	Gideon Burr
Samuel May	Elnathan Street	Richard Cook
Joseph Webb	Constant Caston	Seth Loomiss
Thomas Belding, Jun.	William Manly	Joseph Case
Samuel Curtice	Caleb Moses	Jona. Levingsworth
John Hart	Mark Levingsworth	Thomas Humphries
Wm. Wadsworth	John Levingsworth	Moses Bellamy
Peter Judson	Ezra Stiles	Aaron Bellamy
Nehemiah Lewis	Jonathan Fitch	John Hagens
Lott Norton	Nathaniel Barns	Ephraim Robingson
David Bigilo, Jun.	James Case	John Andrews
John Young	Daniel Bale	Miles Riggs

All being of the Colony of Connecticut aforesaid, to the number of one Hundred and Thirty-Six Persons ; To each one of the last mentioned persons to the aforesaid number of one Hundred and Thirty-Six ; The one Twelve Hundred and Twenty-fourth part of the same Large Tract or Parcel of Land aforesaid, of all which afore Named Persons the sum aforesaid was Received, which Said given and granted Tract of Land is Butted, Bounded and Described, as Followeth, (Viz.)

Beginning from the one and fourtyeth Degree of North Latitude at ten miles Distance East of Susqueannah River, and from thence with a northwardly line Ten miles East of the River To the 42d or beginning of the forty Third Degree North Latitude, and so to extend West, Two Degrees of Longitude, one hundred and Twenty miles South, to the Beginning of the forty-Second Degree, and from thence East to the afore mentioned Bound, which is ten Miles East of Susquehannah River, together with all and every, the Mines, Minerals or Ore of what kind soever, standing, growing, being found or to be found upon any Part, or Parcel thereof, and all other the Hereditaments and Appurtenances to the Said Parcel or Tract belonging or in any way appertaining, and the Reversion and Reversions, Remainder and Remainders, &c.

To have and to hold all the above Granted and Bargained Premises with all the Appurtenances thereof,

Unto all the above and afore Named Persons, in Manner and Proportion aforesaid, and to their Heirs and Assigns, and to their only proper use, benefit and behoof forever, as a free, Clear and Absolute Estate of Inheritance, in fee simple, free of all incumbrances whatsoever.

And We the Afore Said, Cahik-to-ton, Abram Pieters, Willem Tarigjoris, (Brant) Cauwignoge, &c., &c., &c. Sachems and Chiefs as aforesaid, do Hereby covenant to and with all the afore Named grantees, and each and every of them, that at and until the Ensealing and Delivering hereof, we are the True, sole, and Lawful owners of the above granted Premisses, and have good Right, Power, and authority to Bargain and Sell the Same in Manner and Form as above Writen; and Furthermore, we the above Named Cahik-to-ton, Abram Pieters, Willem Tharigjoris, (Brant) Cauwignoge, Sachems and Chiefs as afore said, do by these Presents for us, our Heirs and Successors, Covenant and promise to and with all and every of the afore Named Persons, Grantees in this Deed, all the above Granted and Bargained Premisses and Appurtenances thereof, unto all and every of the afore Named Persons, Grantees in this Deed, and to their and every of their Heirs and Assigns, in Manner and Proportion afore said, forever to Warrant, Secure, and Defend—in Witness whereof we have each of us Set our Marks, And Affixed our Seals, This Eleventh Day of July, in the Twenty-Eighth Year of the Reign of Our Sovereign Lord George ye Second of Great Britain, &c. King, Anno Domini one Thousand Seven Hundred and fifty-Four.

Signed Sealed and Delivered in Presence of

EPH. WILLIAMS, Jr.
JOSEPH KELLOGG.

his
KAHIK-TO-TON, [Racoon.] *Chief of ye Senekas.* (Seal.)
mark.

his
ABRAHAM [Letter A.] PIETERS, (Seal.)
mark. *Sachem of Canajoharic of ye Tribe of ye Bear.*

his
WILLEM [Turtle.] THARIGJORIS, [Seal.]
mark. *Sachem of Canajoharie.*

his
BRANT [Wolf.] CAUWIGNOGE, [Seal.]
mark. *Sachem Mohoks.*

Signed Sealed and Delivered in Presence of

JAMES SHARPE,
MARTIN LYNDE,

his [Beaver.] mark. CANAGEGAIE. [Seal.]
One of the Sachems of Onondage.

SET his [Ξ] mark. I-TA-VA-RIE. [Seal.] *of ye Mohoks ye Turtle.*

JOHANIS his [Letter C.] mark. SOGEHOWANE, [Seal.] *Do. Do.*

SENOSIEN his [Turtle.] mark. [Seal.] *Onider.*

JOHANIS his [X] mark. CANA-DEGAIR, [Seal.] *Bear, Do.*

NIKES his [Letter N.] mark. CARIGIAGTA-TIE, [Seal] *Wolf Canajoharie.*

Signed Sealed and Delivered in presence of

SYBRANT VAN SCHACK, Jun.
JOHANNIS J. WENDEL,

CONAGGJESE his [Turtle.] mark. [Seal.]

JOHANS his [Bear.] mark. TEGNAGERAT, [Seal.]

OKWEIOLA, his [Turtle.] mark. [Seal.]

} ONOIEDES.

his
[Weazle.] CANSTAGO. [Seal.]
mark.

Hartford ss: 20th January, 1755.

I, John Ledyard, one of his majesties Justices of the Peace for said County, have Examined and Compared the foregoing Deed with the originall and find it to be a true Copy thereof.

JOHN LEDYARD.

[EXTRACTS FROM THE DIARY OF SIR WILLIAM JOHNSON, RESPECTING THE AFFAIRS BETWEEN THE INDIANS AND THE CONNECTICUT PURCHASERS OF THE WYOMING LANDS.]

Johnson Hall, Wednesday, February 9th, 1763.

Onaharissa with two other Onondagas arrived here and acquainted Sir William, that the Sachems of their Nation would wait on him in a few days, on authority of a message delivered them from Sir William, lately, by some Senecas who had been at his House, which as delivered to them, was very alarming, and gave them all the greatest uneasiness.

4 Strings of Wampum.

Wednesday, March 23d, 1763.

Had a meeting with ye Mohawks and several Senecas from Schenectady, at Fort Johnson, when ye Mohawks made claim to ye Lands from ye Flatts of Schenectady, to a place called Ga-ga-wariuni, alledging it never was sold by their Forefathers, but lent by them for a Forage for their Cattle.

* * * * * * * * *

* * * * * * * * *

While they were in Council, Col. Eliphalet Dyer and Mr. Woodbridge, of Stockbridge, arrived at Fort Johnson, in order to know whether the Six Nations were coming down to a Meeting proposed to be held at Albany ye 22d. Inst., with them and the New England People, who were now come to Albany for ye purpose and had with them between three and four hundred pounds as a present to give ye Six Nations in case they would consent to their (ye New England Peoples) settling, and enjoying the Land of and about Skahandowana* on the Susquahana; also six Bullocks and three bar-

* One of the Indian names of Wyoming. W. L. S.

rels of Pork. This invitation was sent last autumn in writing, by one John Smith, who was with a number of his Country People at Skahandowana, and delivered to Thomas King of Oyhquago, who I told them, had not I thought delivered it to the Six Nations. As I heard them say nothing about it when a few days ago assembled at my House. The before mentioned gentlemen then made me an offer to be a Partner in ye Land, and to send up the money to me, also the Bullocks and Pork, &c., that I might call ye Six Nations and give it them provided they agreed to their proposal, all which I refused with ye slight it deserved, and gave them my opinion on the whole affair, and also told them the unhappy consequences that would in all probability follow, should they (as they often hinted) form a settlement in them parts. After many fruitless efforts to prevail on me to join and assist them, they returned to Albany.

The Mohawks who were yet present being desirous to know their business, were told it in part, and seemed very uneasy about it, giving it as their opinion, that if the New Englanders persisted in their design of settling said Lands, it would be of very bad consequences.

Johnson Hall, Friday, March 25th, 1763.

Several of ye Mohawks came to acquaint me they had appointed proper persons to attend the Chenussio Meeting, and to know whether I would have them wait for ye General's answer to, or opinion of, what passed at ye late Meeting with ye Six Nations. Then Abraham their Chief spoke as follows:

Brother, We could not rest these two days past, since we heard that our Brethren of Connecticut were so intent upon settling a number of their People at *Skahandowana*, and being fully sensible of ye fatal consequences that must attend a proceeding of ye nature, we in a full meeting of all our People resolved to come to you, and beg you would with this belt of Wampum and a letter from yourself acquaint our Brother the Governor of Connecticut that there is to be a Council of all ye Six Nations in a short time at *Chenussio*, where that affair [among other matters] will be thoroughly considered, and therefore desire they may not move from New-England before they are made acquainted with the result thereof. Gave a Belt.

To which Sir William replied:

Brethren, I approve of your appointment, and as I understand that some of your People are going to Canajoharie to morrow, I would advise them to enquire of the Canajoharees what time they intend setting off for ye Meeting, and should it be found necessary to set off before I receive ye General's answer and opinion of what passed at ye late Meeting. I will in that case forward it by a chosen Messenger, so that the Chenussio people may be acquainted therewith, and act accordingly.

Brethren, I think your proposal of sending a Message to ye Governor of Connecticut to stop the People of his government going to *Wioming* or

Skahandowana until the result of the approaching Meeting of ye Six Nations at *Chenussio* is known thereon, is a friendly and prudent step, wherefore shall comply with your request, and hope the Governor may agree thereto.

Then the Meeting broke up.

[The following letter from Governor Fitch, together with the proceedings of a council held with a Deputation of Chiefs sent from the Six Nations to Hartford, to remonstrate against the settlement of Wyoming by the people of Connecticut, I have discovered among the manuscripts of Sir William Johnson :—]

GOVERNOR FITCH TO SIR WILLIAM JOHNSON.

Hartford, 30*th*, *May*, 1763.

SIR,

I have the Honour of your Letter by Lt. Johnson, acquainting me with the Delegation of the Confederate Nations of Indians. Five of them with the interpreter arrived here under Mr. Johnson's Conduct last Thursday, and on Saturday they were admitted to make their Speech and Deliver the Message they said they were charged with in the presence of the Council and Assembly. And this Day in like manner I made a Speech to them with which as the Interpreter informed, they were well satisfied.—I should have inclosed Copies of them but the Time is short and Lt. Johnson will have them, to which I beg leave to refer you——

Soon after receiving your Letter with the Speech and Belt some time ago, I received Orders from theSecretary of State signifying it as his Majesty's Pleasure I should use both Authority and Influence to prevent the prosecution of the Settlement of the Lands on the Susquehannah, &c., till the matter could be laid before the King, and in Consequence of those Orders (which I acquainted the principal Gentleman of the Company with) they have agreed to stop all proceedings towards a Settlement and acquiesce in the King's Order. I therefore conclude there will now remain no uneasiness among the Indians.

I am Sir with great regard your most obedient
and most humble Servant——
THOS. FITCH

SIR WILLIAM JOHNSON, *Baronet*, *&c.*

A CONFERENCE WITH DEPUTIES OF THE SIX NATIONS OF INDIANS.

In the Council Chamber at Hartford, in the Colony of Connecticut, on the 28th Day of May, 1763.

Present

The Governor, Council, and Assembly of said Colony.

Togwerote Mohock

Sagagenguaraghta, (Speaker) Toghuasquantha	Onondagas	Deputies of the Six Nations
Soheres Oghsegwaròna	Cayugas	

G. Johnson, Esq., D. Agent, Attending with William Printup, Interpreter, sent by Sir Wm. Johnson, Agent for Indian Affairs.

The Deputies after being taken by the Hand, and bid Welcome into the Government, seated themselves, Sagagenguaraghta, arose and delivered a Speech, which from the Interpreter was taken as followeth, viz :

BRETHREN,

We were sent by the Chiefs of the six Nations, and it has pleased God that we are arived safe at this place to see you.

BRETHREN,

We are Deputies from all the Chiefs, and they understand that you are not quite sound within, and we give this to clear your eyes that you may see, and open your ears that you may hear, and cleanse your hearts that you may entertain cordially what we shall speak to you.

A Belt of Wampum.

BRETHREN,

We have no Writings of it, but we have a Tradition that God, the Maker of all things hath given to the Six Nations our large Country to dwell and subsist in, and made them a strong People, and our Nations have of Old appointed a Fire Place at Onondauga, and by that means united together and so became a strong and Powerfull Confederacy, and afterwards they saw at Albany a white People and found means to enter into a Conference with them and made a Silver Chain, a strong Chain of Friendship, which they and We have from Time to Time brightened and kept clean, and at this first Interview liked you so well, that we gave you room for you to settle upon our land, and you have since become very numerous and prosperous, for which we are glad and Rejoice.

AND BROTHERS,

We have been very helpfull and assisted one another against our Enemies, and by the Help of God we have gained the superiority over them.

AND BROTHERS,

You'll excuse us, we have no Records of former Proceedings, but hint at such things as were done formerly by our Forefathers and have nothing further to offer on this Head.

Now we are come to another Head.

BROTHERS,

We have heard very grievous News this Winter, that you were about to come with Three hundred families to settle on our Lands which was very astonishing to Us, and that you designed to build Forts and strong Places, on our Lands, and for that Reason our Sachems considered upon it and have sent us down to this Place. By that Means, Brothers, we are here to acquaint you with what news we hear, that you have a Design to settle on the Susquahannah River and Claim the Land to the West Seas.

We have heretofore given away Land to the white People but of the sale of this Land the Six Nations know Nothing that they have ever given it away or sold it to any, and what Little we have left, we intend to keep for ourselves: we know not of any such Sale, and if any such thing has been asked, it must have been done by particular persons in a separate manner, and not in any General Meeting or Council of the Six Nations as has been the usual Manner of their giving or selling their Lands.

BROTHERS,

Our custom is not to keep anything secret. We have heard that one Lydius, at Albany has endeavored to purchase some Lands at Susquahanna, and it is not the manner of the Six Nations to keep anything in Reserve, he was up among the Six Nations to obtain a Sale, but could not obtain it, but we have heard that he has since got a Deed from the Indians, which he obtained from them singly, or one by one, and that from stragglers and such as we know nothing of.

We have often sold Lands to the white People, but then it was done with consent of the whole in some General meeting; and this is the Land which we have reserved for ourselves as we have but little left, and we are surprised at such a measure being taken to obtain a Deed without our General knowledge or consent.

We have been told that Lydias has reported that he paid a great deal of money for this Land, which we know nothing of; and this is our hunting Land which we depend upon for our support and are not willing by any means to part with it.

[Then the Speaker presented a broad Belt which he held in his hands.]

BROTHERS,

We would have you take this matter into your serious Consideration. We here present you the Emblem of the Six Castles belonging to our Nations, and through it is the Road or Path through which we come to strengthen and confirm our covenant Chain, and consider whether settling on those Lands in such a manner, may not unhappily tend to break this covenant Chain.

BROTHERS,

Seriously take it into your consideration, and think how you would like it, to have your lands taken from you in an unfair and injurious manner. You are a praying People, better acquainted with Books and Learning than we, and must needs know better what is right than to think it well to have your Lands as we may say stolen from you. Surely you could not like to be treated in such a manner, to have your Land taken from you that you depended upon for your support.

BROTHERS,

Take it seriously into your Consideration how strong our Union used to be formerly, when we were as it were united under one head, and were one Body, and Blood, and happily united in our Affections.

BROTHERS,

As I have told You before, that we have been sent here by our Chiefs to let you know that we have heard about your Design of entering upon our Land, and we deliver in this Belt to show the minds of the confederate Nations, that you do not incroach on these Lands which we have reserved and design to keep for ourselves and our children to the latest posterity, and will not part with them; they are such as we set by and will not sell.

BROTHERS,

If you proceed to incroach on our Lands We shall not be Easy, but will return Home to our own places and apply ourselves to the the King our Father to obtain Justice, and I myself will go, and on my going out of the house will return home, and leave you to consider on it;—and now I have said all I have to say.

Then the Governor directed the Interpreter to tell them that he was able to give them a satisfactory Answer, and desired they would stay till the Beginning of the Week at which Time they should have an Answer.

To which they answered, that their Chiefs directed them to make no Delay, but as soon as they had made their Speech they were to return, but at the Governor's Desire they would stay for an Answer. They then withdrew.

Att the Councill Chamber in Hartford, May 30th, A. D. 1763.

Present as above,

viz: The Governor made answer to the Foregoing Speech in the words following.

BRETHREN,

We heartily welcome You to this Place, and are glad to see You safe arrived, and that You are sent by Your Chiefs to brighten the Covenant Chain made by our Fore-Fathers.

You tell us Your Chiefs think we are not all sound within, and give a Belt to Clear our Eyes to see, open our Ears to hear, and make our Hearts clean that we may cordially receive what You speak to us.

BRETHREN:

We are sorry your Chiefs think we are not sound within; we assure You our Eyes are clear, our Ears are open, and we cordially receive You as Friends and kindly receive your message.

BRETHREN,

We rejoice with You that God has prospered the arms of the Great King George our Common Father, so that Your and our Enemies are subdued, and now we hope we shall live in Peace and Friendship as long as the Sun and Moon shall endure.

We come now to Your Message.

BRETHREN,

You tell us the news You have heard, that we were about to come with 300 Families to settle an the Susquehannah River, which was very astonishing to You, and that we designed to build Forts on Your Land.

BRETHREN:

We assure and tell You this Government has not given any Orders for any such Settlement; We are no Ways concerned in that matter, only as Friends to You have endeavoured to prevent the People from going to settle those Lands.

We have indeed been told that a Number of particular Persons, some living in Connecticut, some in the Massachusetts, some in New-York, and some in other Governments were about to settle on these Lands, but we advised them not to proceed in their attempts. And Lately I received Orders from the King our Common Father commanding me to use my Authority and Influence to prevent those People from attempting to settle on those Lands till the matter should be laid before the King.

In Obedience to his Majesty's Commands I acquainted the Chief men among them with the King's Orders and advised them to lay aside the Prosecution of that Settlement for the Present.

AND BRETHREN,

I have now the Satisfaction to acquaint You that I am Well informed those people have had a meeting and have in Testimony, as well of his Majesty's fatherly Care as of their ready Submission to, and acquiescence in, his Orders, unanimously agreed that no person whatever of their Company shall enter upon,or make any Settlement on any of those Lands until his Majesty our common Father's pleasure be known in that matter.

BRETHREN:

Seeing we are Your Friends, and agreable to the King's Orders have taken so much Care to prevent those Settlements which are so grevious to You, and have now given You accounts that the attempts are Stopt, we think You will be fully satisfied and inform our Brothers, your Chiefs and your Nations of this, and Rest easy and quiet.

We assure You of our cordial Friendship and wish You a safe Journey Home, and desire You to present our kind Compliments to the Sachems of the Six Nations. Farewell.

To which the Deputy's of the Six Nations Replyed as follows, viz;

Brethren, we have heard with attention what you have Said and are well pleased with the Same, and we hope you will Endeavour to prevent any more people from making purchases of us: and as to those Lands, we have Talked about, we Do not at present Design to part with them, but if ever we Do, it Shall be to those purchasers of your people before any others If they Desire it; We are to Receive no presents on this Occasion, but as to your offer to Discharge our Expenses while in this town we Gratefully Accept and Acknowledge the Same and heartily bid you Farewell.

A true Copy examined By

GEORGE WYLLYS, SEC'Y.

INDEX.

*

www.ingramcontent.com/pod-product-compliance
Lightning Source LLC
LaVergne TN
LVHW021149110826
845150LV00005B/1173

* 9 7 8 1 4 2 5 5 4 7 4 3 1 *